Volo's Guíde to Waterdeep

A Toast to Waterdeep

Here's to the City of Splendors
Deep water where the edge of the sea
Meets rivers of gold; all the coins ever made
Flow past—gods, throw some to me!

(A traditional toast, sung in the taverns of Waterdeep)

Credits

Design: Ed Greenwood
Editing: Julia Martin
Cover Art: Robh Ruppel
Interior Art: Valerie Valusek
Cartography: Joel Meyer and
Dennis Kauth
Typesetting: Angelika Lokotz
Production:

9379

ISBN 1-56076-335-3

TSR, Inc.
POB 756
Lake Geneva
WI 53147
USA

TSR Ltd.
120 Church End
Cherry Hinton
Cambridge CB1 3LB
United Kingdom

Contents

Preface

The engaging rogue Volo has done a better job on this tome, know ye, than on his misguided volume on magic (*Volo's Guide to All Things Magical*). It were best he should leave dabbling in Art to those who know better.

Naetheless, he missed a lot of Waterdeep that even an occasional visitor such as myself can spot. Much, no doubt, passed unseen beneath his very nose. He's got some things quite wrong, too—but ye'll discover what when ye meet them, even if that's (ahem) just a might late.

My colleague, Ed of the Greenwood, has prevailed upon me to include some small items of import to gamers. Reluctantly, I have done so, adding probable details—trust not in their veracity, I warn ye!—of various Waterdhavians at the back of this tome (including the impetuous Volo himself). All the rest, errors and all, I've left. I must warn ye. Khelben and his lady Laeral laughed to tears on several occasions while reading this work—and as I can find little amusing in it, I can only conclude they found hilarious errors!

May the gods smile upon ye, traveler, broader than they do upon Volo.

Elminster of Shadowdale

P.S. FR1 *Waterdeep and the North* remains the definitive guide to features of Waterdeep, augmented by the *City System* and *Ruins of Undermountain* boxed sets, the *Knight of the Living Dead* gamebook, and the module FRE3 *Waterdeep*. Those desiring to explore alleys Volo mentions would do well to consult where the alleys meet with the sewers, on page 28 of *Waterdeep and the North*, if they wish to avoid (or find, I suppose) danger.

One note more: For the safety of Waterdeep, I've refrained from passing on details of the abodes or persons of Durnan, Khelben "Blackstaff" Arunsun, Laeral, Mirt, Piergeiron, and certain others—and cut out much or all of what Volo had to say about them, too. If you'd know such folk, meet them yourselves—and learn what they'll grant ye. Enjoy thy read...

Volo's Ratings System

Daggers (Alleyways, Courtyards,etc.)	Pipes (Inns)	Tankards (Taverns)	Coins (Prices)
Worst			Lowest
Better			Average
Best			Highest

4

A Word from Volo

his guidebook is the result of extensive, often hazardous explorations of the City of Splendors, most colorful city of the Sword Coast. It is the dream of many folk across Faerun to someday visit this fabled, bustling market-place and grandest of abodes. This tome attempts to steer visitors to sights and folk they want to see—or avoid.

No one traveler can go every-where and see all in Waterdeep, and with passing time, some things I have written will change.

With a few exceptions, I couldn't enter the villas and walled homes of the nobles without invitation, so they do not appear herein (and for obvious reasons, I dare not write of my few covert glimpses of their splendors—ladies, I'll not forget).

If you visit a guildhall in Waterdeep and are not a mem-ber, you are typically shown (as I was) into a small number of meeting rooms, and are not free to wander. Watching, attentive guards deter prying, and the result is a boring visit unless you have business with the guild. Guild members would not look favorably on my giving away secrets, either, and so I avoid describing guild buildings. For the same reason, temples, shrines, and other places restricted to those of one faith aren't explored in these pages.

My forays into the City of the Dead, the sewers, and various City fortresses were also severely limited, and their coverage here reflects that. I believe only a longtime citizen of Waterdeep—which I'm not—should attempt a guide to the pleasant parkland that houses the city's legions of dead.

Anyone drawing near any gate of the city can see Mount Water-deep—and that's as close as most of us are ever going to get. Every-one goes to gawk at Castle Water-deep and at Piergeiron's Palace (again, seeing little indeed of their inside, except by invitation of the Lords), so I've largely left those out, too.

A traveler could spend a lifetime in Waterdeep and not fully sample its every nuance, pleasure, back alley, or experi-ence. There must be many noteworthy places I've missed. Those omissions aside, I think you'll agree this is the best guide-book to Waterdeep available. I urge you all to remember with favor the name of:

Volo

(Volothamp Geddarm)

Castle Ward

ome to most of Waterdeep's administrative buildings and buildings of state, this first ward of the city is the heart of power in Waterdeep today. It's also the area most folk who'll tell you of Waterdeep talk about. Much has been written about it,[1] so in these pages, I'll treat it more lightly than any other ward of Waterdeep. Any fool can see the mountain and the castle from far off. You don't need my words to find them!

Although it looks large on a map, much of it is taken up by Mount Waterdeep, the rugged height that protects much of the city from the full fury of the winter storms (which blow from west-northwest). The mountain is honeycombed with caverns and passages where the city guard maintains its armories, the city's granary, and its flying griffon steeds. These caverns are linked to Castle Waterdeep, from which the ward takes its name, and various clifftop eyries (landing and springing-aloft areas for the griffons)—and, it is rumored, to both Piergeiron's Palace and the many levels of Undermountain, the vast dungeon or subterranean city beneath Waterdeep.

City watch and guard patrols are heavy in this ward. The city guard deliberately puts on a show of force in this district.[2]

Landmarks

The most prominent landmarks of Castle Ward are the mountain and the castle. The next most important is the many-spired Palace of Waterdeep, popularly known these days as Piergeiron's Palace, after the First, and only

---

[1] FR1 *Waterdeep and the North* describes features of Mount Waterdeep (page 22), Castle Ward (page 23), and all city features at some length. The *City System* boxed set includes detailed maps of the main aboveground structure of Castle Waterdeep, as well as detailed street maps of the city, and a selection of building floor plans. Module FRE3 *Waterdeep* contains notes on the Yawning Portal inn and a partial map of Blackstaff Tower.

The *Ruins of Undermountain* boxed set describes the uppermost levels of vast Undermountain, including its surface connections and the infamous subterranean smuggling port known as Skullport. The novel *Elfshadow* gives the reader a taste of Waterdhavian social life, and a glimpse of many features of the city—including some ancient *gates* linking it with far places.

[2] City watch patrols are detailed on page 17 of FR1 *Waterdeep and the North*. In this ward, four-sword detachments pass a given point about every 8 minutes and look into a tavern or inn dining room about every 20 minutes.

As detailed on pages 15–16 and 23 of the *City System* set booklet, the city guard also patrols Castle Ward, in six-man detachments. Typical patrol details are as given therein, on page 23. Reinforcements will be a dozen LG hm F3s to F6s clad in chain mail and armed with maces, long swords, daggers, slings, and a polearm appropriate to the situation.

Guard patrols pass a given street location about every 15 minutes, but appear in 1d4 minutes when a city watch patrol blows a warning horn in this ward.

publicly known, Lord of Waterdeep. His court is held there, and he entertains visiting embassies and envoys there on an almost daily basis. Accompanying one of them is probably the best way to get a look inside. The palace has four gates. From the north, these are Horn Gate, Sally Gate, Main Gate, and Guard Gate. You'll be challenged if you try to use any way in but the Main Gate.

So pass through it. The entry hall beyond is impressive enough—an echoing room all of polished marble, empty except for benches along the walls carved into the likenesses of seated lions, and the massive pillars that hold the upper floors of the palace up.

For me, though, the most impressive thing in the palace was the scale model of the entire city—building by building—set on a huge stone table in the office of the city clerks. To find it, turn right and go through the archway at the end of the entry hall. The large, grand stairs leading out of the hall in the other direction are the way to Piergeiron's court and audience chambers.

The palace stands with its back hard against a cliff face of Mount Waterdeep. To the north and south are barracks. A small tower set into a mountain cleft to the north guards an entrance to the tunnels of Mount Waterdeep.

Known, imaginatively enough, as the Mountain Tower, it is strictly off limits to the public.

There is a large open courtyard in front of the palace. To even get to the Main Gate, you must pass a lone tower in the midst of this open space: Ahghairon's Tower.

This slim stone tower has been totally enclosed above, around, and beneath in a series of potent, invisible magical barriers since the death of the famous wizard, many years ago.[3] Don't approach too closely—on the north side, a skeletal figure still stands facing the tower with arms raised, about 10 feet away from its side. It is all that remains of a wizard who tried to get into the tower in order, no doubt, to seize Ahghairon's magic for himself. He *dispelled* the outermost barrier, a *forcecage*, but was trapped between it and the *prismatic sphere* within when the *forcecage* reformed behind him.

The man's name has been forgotten with the passage of years, and his robes and flesh have both rotted away, but the magic of the tower holds the bones in position. Until Piergeiron forbade it some years ago, it was a favorite game of local children to rearrange the wizard's bones. They can be dislodged with a stick, but they always drift slowly back into the same position, floating upright,

[3] For details of the defenses of Ahghairon's Tower, see page 22 of *Waterdeep and the North*.

with arms outspread.

If you travel north along the northern tongue of Mount Waterdeep from the palace, and turn west at its end, you will come to the sea at the end of Julthoon Street, which is the northernmost boundary of the ward. The land here falls away swiftly, so you are higher than the city wall and can readily look over it, far out to sea. Here, in war, great engines have been set up to hurl rocks and fire at ships approaching the shore. In peacetime, these are all hidden away inside Mount Waterdeep and, rumor has it, in storage on the ethereal plane[4]—along with six companions of the silent sentinel who'll be standing looking out to sea with you: the Walking Statue of Waterdeep.

This 90-foot-tall stone golem was created by Khelben "Blackstaff" Arunsun, the Archmage of Waterdeep. One of seven identical constructs, it is intended to fill and defend any gap in Waterdeep's walls created by a besieging foe. Of gray granite, it looks like a regal human with an impassive face—and it spends the years here, enduring the birds, as it stares endlessly out to sea, awaiting a call to service that

Waterdhavians hope will never come.[5] It is sometimes used as a guiding beacon for expected ships during very rough storms. Wizards of the Watchful Order cast light spells upon it, and Piergeiron moves it to a desired signaling location.

The cliff that you and the Walking Statue are standing on top of is known as the Gull Leap for the seabirds that nest here, and for its use by misguidedly depressed people and stampeding cattle before the city wall was built. If you stay close to the wall and turn south, going along the western side of the tongue of Mount Waterdeep, you'll be in a little hidden corner of Waterdeep that even many folk in the city have never seen, and know about only vaguely. A street called the Cliffride runs to four luxurious villas that stand here amid trees and terraced gardens in a little ledge walled in by Mount Waterdeep.

These grand stone houses were built long ago by various noble families in this exclusive and readily defensible enclave. They soon fell out of favor. Lashed by the full fury of the sea storms, they are damp all year round and a nightmare of slick

---

[4] Rumor, Elminster tells us, has it correctly. The ethereal plane also holds many extra sections of city wall that can appear in position along the eastern boundary of the city if Waterdeep is threatened.

[5] Location #44 on the color map. The Walking Statue is AC1, MV 4, has 18 HD and 140 hp, attacks once per round at THAC0 3, doing 6d10 damage with its mighty fists (against buildings 3 points of structural damage per round if the AD&D® 1st Edition rules governing siege damage are used), and is harmed by spells as a normal stone golem is (see Vol. 1 of the *Monstrous Compendium*). To damage the Walking Statue, you must strike it with a +3 or better magical weapon. It is a minor crime of the Second Plaint (see *Waterdeep and the North*, pages 18–19) to deface the Statue by marking it.

ice everywhere outside and deathly chill inside during winter. They can be rented from their owners for 25 gp/month and up (50 gp/month during the summer), and are residences large enough to house up to 40 people each. As one proceeds south, they are: Fair Winds, on the sea side of the road; Marble-hearth, on the land side; Storm-watch, on the sea side; and, tucked into the end of the land, overhung by a frowning cliff, Heroes' Rest. Heroes' Rest was nicknamed Cold Comfort by the Company of Crazed Venturers, who spent a winter here. The name has stuck in the city, and few now remember the proper name. If you're wealthy enough and don't mind fighting off the thieves who'll inevitably come to investigate anyone rich enough to stay here, these can be pleasant places indeed for a visitor to Waterdeep to stay for a month or more during a warm summer. Otherwise, be glad your bones sleep somewhere more dry.

The largest landmark of the built-up area of Castle Ward is also the largest open space in the city: the Market. The Market is encircled by Traders' Way on the north and Bazaar Street on the south. It is a huge marketplace often crammed with a maze of stalls and camped vendors. You can easily spend days and nights—except in winter—lost in the myriad shopping opportuni-

ties here. The place never closes for mere darkness. But be aware: Many thieves spend days and nights there, too.

It has been said many times that you can buy *anything* in Waterdeep, from ancient spells to floating cloud castles. Well, if you can't find it elsewhere in the city, come here.

The formal boundaries of Castle Ward are drawn by the water of the harbor and the coast up to Julthoon Street, and run along the south side of Julthoon Street to Shield Street, where they turn south to Traders' Way, run east to enclose the Market, and then turn south along the High Road all the way to Snail Street. Castle Ward takes in the west side of Snail Street down to Shesstra's Street, where it turns west to Gut Alley, runs north on it to Belnimbra's Street, and thence to Lackpurse Lane. Dock Ward is to the east and south of Lackpurse Lane, and Castle Ward on its north and west as it runs to the harbor.

Folk in love with power but not yet rich enough to rise above the pursuit of it are said around the city to dwell in that part of Castle Ward north of the broad avenue of Waterdeep Way. More southerly parts of the ward are dominated by the barracks and warehouses attached to the castle and by the Bell Tower (used to

signal fires, attacks, and calls for assembly at the palace[6]), or are largely indistinguishable from the neighboring Dock Ward and the Trades Ward. Castle Ward's dockside is, however, far more heavily patrolled than Dock Ward, and hence safer for goods and visitors.

There's also an interesting feature in a warehouse located in the docks here at the foot of Coin Alley on its east side. In the warehouse's cellar is a shaft opening into a tidal wash under the building—a basin fitted with iron gratings. When the tide is in, fish often swim in. The gratings prevent some from swimming back out. At low tide, the warehouse owner can go down and fish in his own pond for fish to sell or for a meal.

The most famous feature of Castle Ward's docks, however, is Mirt's Mansion. This fortress-home nestles on the slopes of Mount Waterdeep amid stands of trees. It can be reached from Coin Alley or Tarnished Silver Alley, both of which run to it, or from its own dock, the aptly named Smugglers' Dock.

Mirt the Moneylender is widely believed to be a Lord of Waterdeep. When in the city, this gruff ex-mercenary opens his house (before highsun only) for supplicants needing to borrow money. Although he seems a very

---

[6] Location #9 on the color map. Map 3 of the *City System* boxed set gives a typical barracks floor plan and one for the palace stables.

patient, even kindly sort when it comes to the repayment of loans, it doesn't seem that way to talk to him—and anyone thinking of paying an unauthorized visit to his home is warned that it bristles with more human, monstrous, and magical guards than I've ever seen in one place before.[7]

The ward is also home to perhaps the most luxurious inn in Waterdeep, the Jade Jug, and to a large and splendid temple dedicated to Lathander. Consisting of eight linked towers standing in their own walled, tree-cloaked compound, the Spires of the Morning rise to greet the morning sun in the angle between Julthoon Street and Calamastyr Lane. Traders' Way runs right to the temple gates.[8]

Between the temple and the Palace, along the eastern face of Mount Waterdeep, another splendid tower rises, surrounded by its own wall. This is Blackstaff Tower, home of the Archmage of Waterdeep, Khelben "Blackstaff" Arunsun, his lady Laeral, and their apprentices.[9] Laeral is a mage of power herself, who was once leader of the adventuring company known as the Nine, and sister to Alustriel, High Lady of Silverymoon; The Simbul, Witch Queen of Aglarond; Storm Silverhand, the Bard of Shadowdale, and others.

The ward is also home to many guildhalls: the House of Gems, of the Jewellers' Guild;[10] the Map House, headquarters of the Surveyors', Map & Chart-Makers' Guild;[11] Fellowship Hall, of the Fellowship of Innkeepers;[12] the Master Bakers' Hall, of the Bakers' Guild;[13] Guildhall of the Order, of the Solemn Order of Recognized Furriers & Woolmen;[14] the Pewterers' and Casters' Guildhall;[15] the House of the Fine Carvers, of the Guild of Fine Carvers;[16] and the Market Hall, of the Council of Farmer-Grocers.[17] The most spectacular of these headquarters is the Tower of the

---

[7] Location #1 on the color map. Elminster refuses to furnish any details of Mirt or his mansion—which should confirm to most of you, as it did to Ed, that Mirt *must* be a Lord of Waterdeep. Partial mansion floor plans appear on Map 2 of the *City System* boxed set.

[8] Location #43 on the color map. Partial floor plan maps of the temple appear on Map 4 of the *City System* boxed set.

[9] Location #32 on the color map. Partial maps of the tower appear in FR3 *Waterdeep*, and it also features in the novels *Elfshadow* and *Waterdeep*. Elminster refused to pass on any details of Khelben, Laeral, or the tower. Pages 52 and 58 of FR5 *The Savage Frontier* mention Laeral's fate prior to Khelben's rescuing her and the beginning of their relationship.

[10] Location #11 on the color map.

[11] Location #15 on the color map. Its floor plan appears on Map 3 of the *City System* boxed set.

[12] Location #16 on the color map.

[13] Location #22 on the color map.

[14] Location #34 on the color map.

[15] Location #37 on the color map.

[16] Location #39 on the color map.

[17] Location #42 on the color map.

Places of Interest in Castle Ward

Homes

House of Loene

The walled home of the beautiful adventuress Loene resembles a miniature castle. Towers and turrets are everywhere, largely because Loene loves round rooms and curving stairs.

By night, or when expecting unwelcome visitors, Loene activates the magic of the ornate, 20-foot-high iron fence surrounding her house. Any who touch it suffer miniature lightnings.[19]

Loene's home fronts on Waterdeep Way and backs onto Gem Street. During her remodeling of the mansion she purchased on this site, she tore down its extensive, warehouse-like rear and had a lawn, a garden, and a mature elm tree magically transplanted here—an interesting project that kept the mage Nain Keenwhistler busy for quite some time.

Loene's luxurious home is said to be furnished with beautiful things and to contain hidden

Order, seat of the Watchful Order of Magists & Protectors,[18] which rises on the Street of Bells, and is visited by many desiring to arrange a guild fireguard on their property or to purchase the casting of a spell.

Several shopkeepers in the ward are also the heads or spokesmen for their guilds. If you like the taste of power and authority, Castle Ward is the place to go.

---

[18] Location #30 on the color map. Page 44 of *Waterdeep and the North* gives spellcasting prices charged by this guild, and explains something of their services (see also page 32). All of the guilds are covered in the FR1 *Waterdeep and the North* sourcebook.

[19] Loene (pronounced *LOW-enn*) is detailed on page 53 of *Waterdeep and the North*, and also features in the novel *Elfshadow*. Her fence deals 2d4 points of electrical damage per contact or per round of continual contact, and has a special *spellguard* upon it. When *dispel magic* or *disintegrate* spells are cast on it, they are absorbed, their energy transformed instantly into *chain lightning* that strikes first at the source of the magic, and deals d6 of damage per level of the caster of the original attacking spell.

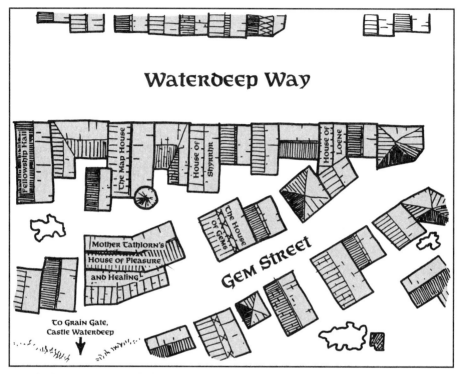

Waterdeep Way

The Map House

House of Shyrrhr

House of Loene

Fellowship Hall

The House of Gems

Gem Street

Mother Cathiorn's House of Pleasure and Healing

To Grain Gate, Castle Waterdeep

magic items acquired during her adventures, but it is open only to her friends. It has other magical defenses, I'm told, that make it a veritable fortress.

House of Shyrrhr

This Lady of the Court is good friends with Piergeiron, whom she aids by chaperoning visiting diplomats and learning all she can from them to pass on to the First Lord of Waterdeep. Her small but luxurious house on Waterdeep Way is simply but cozily furnished, with carpets, lounge cushions, three bedrooms with round canopied beds, a round bathing pool, and a formal dining room where she can entertain.[20]

Shops

Aurora's Whole Realms Shop Catalogue Counter

Throughout this guide, I mention the outlets of this popular Realms-wide retail chain in each ward of the city because most

---

[20] The house of Shyrrhr (pronounced *SHEER-hur)* is #14 on the color map. It contains little but a grand selection of wines, a room-sized closet of fine gowns, about 20 gp, and—on many nights—Piergeiron, who has slipped through a secret tunnel connecting the pantry of Shyrrhr's house with the palace. They like to relax and talk together, and trust each other absolutely. Piergeiron pays Shyrrhr's few expenses in return for her spying and hospitality services to the city.

city-bred travelers live near one, or at least are familiar with Aurora's catalogue. This makes for minimal delay and uncertainty when emergency purchases must be made, and results in goods of known quality.

The Castle Ward Aurora's outlet is the first shopfront west of the Jade Jug, on the north side of Waterdeep Way. It provides home delivery for patrons by means of a coach and a six-man team within Castle Ward only. It also has four guards who work in shifts of two and two, a calmly cultured, middle-aged lady counter clerk, Cathal Sunspear, and a service-mage, Xanatrar Hillhorn. Xanatrar is known for his excellent singing at parties and whenever he wants to impress a good-looking lady.

Balthorr's Rare and Wondrous Treasures

This shop stands on the east side of the Street of the Sword, south of Selduth Street. The wealthy shopper can buy a wide selection of curios here, especially coins from all over Toril, gems, and regalia. The proprietor is an expert on the currency, uniforms and badges used by most realms and military units of Faerun, and can make up colorful stories about the history of particular items on the spot. I've heard that he'll buy things without asking questions as to their origin— making him very handy for adventurers who want to exchange battle trophies for money.

Proprietor: Balthorr "the Bold" Olaskos, a hearty, loud-voiced, bubbling fellow with a ready smile and firm handshake, is the proprietor.[21]

The Golden Key

This shop, on the east side of Warriors' Way, north of Waterdeep Way,[22] sells locks and fastenings of all sorts *except* large, vault-like doors, door bars, and strongchests. The proprietor makes custom locks to order, and guarantees that he's never sold a key that will open the lock you buy from him to anyone else. (In other words, your lock is unique.) Many of his locks require several keys turned in certain combinations to open. All products are made on the premises, except for certain door chains, which are imported from the northern

---

[21] Location #28 on the color map. Balthorr is a fence for stolen goods—at 40% of street value—especially coins, gems, and regalia (see *Waterdeep and the North* pages 31–32).

[22] Location #21 on the color map. Ansilver has at least four gargoyle guardians in his shop to prevent thefts. He also wears a magical *master key* around his neck, that he tries to keep very secret. Over the years many have seen him use it and have deduced that it opens all normal locks on contact. If it encounters mechanical or magical traps on a lock, it reveals this to the wielder without triggering them, but does not open the lock or deactivate the traps. Its precise powers are not known to any in Waterdeep except Ansilver.

Moonshaes where they have been hardened in dragon fire!

Proprietor: Ansilver the Locksmith, a white-haired, elderly, but alert man, is the proprietor. He wears thick spectacles, has a sharp-beaked nose, and has a habit of humming continually.

Halambar Lutes & Harps

This shop, found on the east side of the Street of the Sword and a good walk up from Waterdeep Way, sells all sorts of stringed musical instruments, from the lyre of Amn to the twostring of Mintarn. It is famous up and down the Sword Coast for the distinctive mellow sound of its lutes, but even Inner Sea folk have heard of the shop's prize attraction: the Harp that Sings by Itself.

This small, dark traveling harp sits on its own velvet-covered plinth, safely above the reach of inquisitive (or acquisitive!) visitors, and softly plays old airs, ballads, and lays of the North. It is said by some to have belonged to the famous bard Mintiper Moonsilver, but most dispute this. It is older than he, and was known to have been in Silverymoon when he was wandering the North. Its full powers aren't known to any alive in the Realms today, and it is a unique magic item, truly beyond price. Halambar won't let

Proprietor: Kriios Halambar, guildmaster of the Council of Musicians, Instrument-Makers, and Choristers owns and runs this shop. He is an inscrutable, heavy-lidded man of long black hair, large black-pupiled eyes, and a strong streak of snobbery.[23]

The Halls of Hilmer, Master Armorer

This shining shop has a front of armor plate—old armor from vanquished foes of Waterdeep, bolted together, polished a deep, gleaming blue, and protected from weather and theft by potent spells. Beware lightning-like arcs of energy, should you strike or wrench at a piece!. It stands on the west side of the Street of Bells north of Water-deep Way, its gleam visible up and down the street.

Inside is a showroom and fitting room, with doors into a weapons practice room for clients to practice running, turning, fighting, and climbing stairs in armor, and the huge, cluttered workshops of Hilmer and his apprentices. Plate armor hangs—or, in the form of full suits, stands everywhere. Hilmer only makes plate, but he's gener-ally acknowledged as the best, or

patrons touch it and won't sell it. (I have discovered that the plinth it sits upon is actually a covered stone golem, placed there by Khelben "Blackstaff" Arunsun to protect the harp.)

Halambar's instruments typically cost 1,000 gp each or more. He has smaller, plainer pieces made by his apprentices or secondhand pieces that go for mere hundreds of gold pieces. A place to visit, even if you're not musical.

Here's a special gift idea, for the rich only: For 600 gp, you can buy a jewel case or snuff box en-chanted to play a short melody when opened. Exquisite, but somehow I feel you'd grow tired of the same tune quickly.

---

[23] Location #26 on the color map. The distinctive sounds of Halambar lutes are largely due to his secretly soaking the wood he makes them of in Waterdhavian harbor water in his cellars. The precise powers of the Harp are left to the DM. Anyone who successfully makes off with it will be pursued by the Harpers—to whom the instrument is a treasure—as well as by agents hired by Halambar. It actually has nothing to do with Mintiper and was made long ago in lost and fallen Myth Drannor.

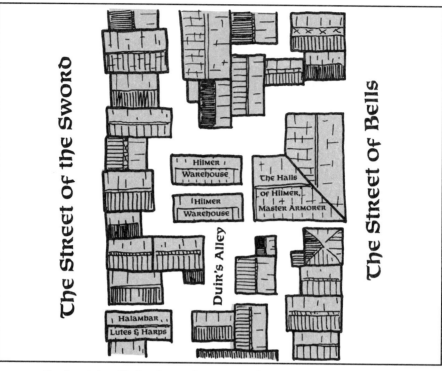

The Street of the Sword

Hilmer Warehouse

Hilmer Warehouse

The Halls of Hilmer, Master Armorer

Duir's Alley

Halambar, Lutes & Harps

The Street of Bells

among the best, in all the Sword Coast lands. His custom suits generally cost 4,000 to 6,000 gp, depending on the size of the wearer and the ornamentation. He hates chasing and over-elaborate fluting, but has done enameled armors for Calishite satraps, at 8,600 gp each.

Hilmer will sell existing armor apprentice pieces and replacement pieces, such as gauntlets, that are not custom fitted for mere hundreds of gold pieces, but he will not set his mark (a stamp of a gauntlet closing on a sword, and breaking it into three pieces) on such shelf stock. Hilmer armor is *all* custom made.

Hilmer knows at a glance if armor fits properly, and at a touch if its metal is suspect or if a wearer is using a blade or shield too heavy for him. He is a master craftsman and regularly ignores offers of estates and thousands in gold to become master armorer of this or that kingdom.

Thieves leave his shop alone. It's much easier to steal Hilmer armor from those who have bought it—because several of the suits of armor are animated metal constructs, that defend the place at all times! Others protect his nearby metals warehouses.

Proprietor: Hilmer, the proprietor, is a tall, strong, and soft-

spoken man, with shoulders as wide as most doors and hands with a grip of iron. He is a just, honest man.[24]

Olmhazan's Jewels

This glittering shop stands on the west side of the High Road, just across from the mouth of Spend-thrift Alley. Its front is fashioned of silvered and polished stone to resemble a huge faceted gem. "Olmhazan," said one noble to me at a feast, "has never been restricted by such trifles as good taste."

Inside, all the gems one can think of, except very rare or magical sorts, such as amaratha, kings' tears, and rogue stones, can be bought. A scattering of beljuril shards makes the impressive display of gems wink and sparkle continually.

Thieves are few since one was partially devoured by the guardians of the shop: two trained mimics. One masquerades as a gem display counter, and the other as part of the front door-jamb and the gigantic gem storefront.

Proprietor: Jhauntar Olm-

hazan, Gentleman Speaker for the Jewellers' Guild, owns and runs this shop. He is a sneering, superior sort, who dismisses all country folk and those who dwell around or east of the Sea of Fallen Stars as barbarians.[25]

Phalantar's Philtres & Components

This shop can be found on the east side of the Street of Bells, just north of Waterdeep Way. The odor of exotic spices wafts out onto the street whenever its circular door is opened. Inside is a strange wonderland of dried branches, firmly stoppered jars, and interesting-looking shells, skulls, baskets of bones, and labeled drawers.

Here you can buy medicines, herbs, and rare substances used in the making of perfumes, scented oils, poisons, and as material components in the casting of spells. The herbs aren't very fresh, but a wizard will find the selection here better than anywhere else I've ever seen— and the proprietor doesn't ask questions about why you want baatezu blood or deadly night-

---

[24] Location #28 on the color map. Hilmer's guardians are battle horrors, which are variant helmed horrors (detailed in FA1 *Halls of the High King*). His helmed horrors are lawful neutral and bound in loyalty to him. Rumor has it that he acquired them in the ruins of Myth Drannor in his early adventuring days.

They are INT High (14); AL LN; AC 2; MC 12, Fl 12 (A) plus *dimension door* 1/day, up to 60 yards; HD 16; THAC0 12; #AT 1 plus two 2–5 hp dmg *magic missiles* every 3 rounds; Dmg by weapon or 1d4; SD spell immunities; SZ M; ML 20; see *Halls of the High King*, page 42, for details.

[25] Location #38 on the color map. Add 15–25 gp to the base prices of all gemstones to arrive at Olmhazan's selling prices.

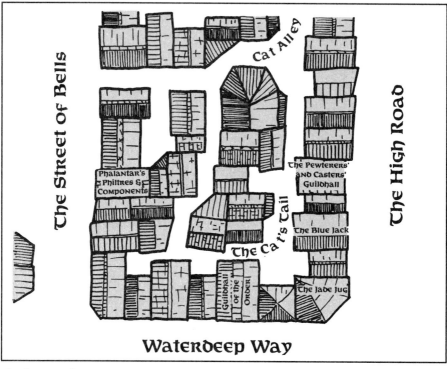

The Street of Bells

Cat Alley

Cat Alley

The High Road

Phalantar's Philtres & Components

The Pewterers' and Casters' Guildhall

The Cat's Tail

The Blue Jack

Guildhall of the Order

The Jade Jug

WaterDeep Way

shade or ask your name.

Theft is discouraged by the dust-covered, immobile stone form of a man, face eternally frozen in a look of fear, who's propped, arms spread and in a frantic running position, against a wall inside the door. "Oh yes," the proprietor purred, when I asked about him. "He tried to leave without paying, late one night when I wasn't even open. He ran afoul of a certain substance I keep handy. I haven't decided when to release him yet.

Try not to brush against him. 'Twould be a pity if he fell and shattered."

Nobles tell me this shop[26] is guarded not only with *dust of petrification*, but with traps that release various paralyzing and sleep-inducing gases. They tell me the owner will sell you scrolls and any minor magic items he has on hand, too—if you ask quietly, and aren't known to have any connections to the city watch or city guard.

Proprietor: Phalantar Orivan, a

---

[26] Location #33 on the color map. Phalantar is a fence for stolen goods at 35% of their street price (see pages 31–32 of *Waterdeep and the North*). He is very rich. He sponsors some adventuring bands in return for a share of their loot (substances he can sell in his shop, including evil or flawed magic items they don't want) and bankrolls some mercenary companies in the Sword Coast lands, too, in return for a share of their profits.

man of soft, smooth movements, who always seems to be gently smiling, is the proprietor. He is said to deal with adventurers and mages regularly, and to be fabulously rich.

Taverns

The Blue Jack

This watering hole is named for the blue leather armor worn by the proprietor in his long-ago adventuring days. The armor still hangs, in rotting tatters, above the bar. The tavern specializes in low prices and fast service. This specialization is a success; the place is always crammed. Folk go elsewhere to sit and chat or do business, but duck in here to load up on food and drink before hurrying on about their day. The Jack, as citizens call it (a short form of the name, true, but most call it that because of the many drinking jacks you can empty there), stands on the west side of the High Road, just north of its intersection with Waterdeep Way.

In such a busy place, encounters between enemies are not uncommon—but the staff can hurl drinking jacks hard and accurately from behind the bar, and six able-bodied scrappers can be mustered if the kitchens and bar are emptied by the proprietor.

Patrons are not encouraged to stay long—there are stools and stand-up elbowrests, but no booths or seats, and little food. Only cold cut platters, garlic sauce, pickles, handwheels of cheese, and hot biscuits covered with melted butter are available (1 cp per serving, each).

The drinkables are similarly limited: ale at 1 cp/jack, bitters at 2 cp, stout at 3 cp, zzar at 4 cp, and wine at 4 cp/tallglass (either Neverwinter white or red wine from Amn).

Proprietor: Immithar the Glove, a fast-moving, canny fellow, is the tavern's proprietor. He is quick with a joke or to mimic—perfectly—the speech of other folk.[27]

The Crawling Spider

This strange place has a mock underground decor done with plaster slurry and rock rubble. Glowing mosses and lichens have been placed on the walls and ceiling and are watered regularly. These, plus a few netted *glowing globes*, provide a dim light for the place. Stuffed spiders have been affixed to the ceiling or hang from threads. The waitresses, hired for their sensuous walks and love of male company, wear black bodysuits and masks to make them look like drow.

Who drinks here? Dwarves, half-orcs, and other subterra-

---

[27] Location #36 on the color map.

nean dwellers who miss home, adventurers, and—surprisingly—priests of all faiths, looking for a thrill! They form a regular clientele, and have ever since this place opened. Of all the taverns in Waterdeep, the Crawling Spider has the most dedicated patrons. They will come clear across the city to drink here, ignoring other places.

The Spider never seems to close. The visitor soon discovers that one of the cave mouths leads to the jakes and another to a cellar dance floor. Many cave mouths open off this floor and lead to tiny private caverns used for intimate personal conferences and for

planning shady business.

If visitors cause trouble, patrons will leap to take care of it. And they include many veteran adventurers among their number!

The fare differs each night, but it's always 1 sp/head, and always includes soup, a loaf of bread, meat, and fried greens. Drinks are extra. Ale is 2 cp/tankard, stout 4 cp, and zzar or wine is 5 cp/tallglass. Whiskey is 1 sp/flagon, and it's vile!

Proprietress: Welvreene Thalmit, a short, raw-voiced, and alluring woman with dark eyes, is this tavern's proprietress. She is romantic at heart who loves adventurers.[28]

---

[28] Location #23 on the color map.

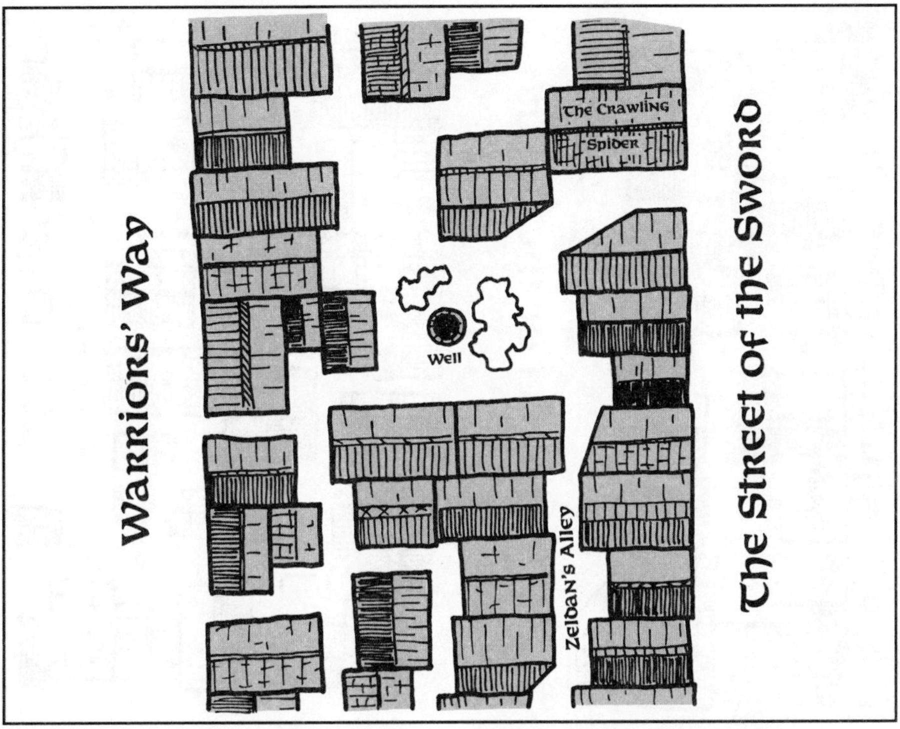
Warriors' Way
The Crawling Spider
Well
Zeldan's Alley
The Street of the Sword

The Dragon's Head Tavern

This modest place caters to older Waterdhavians: married couples, retired ex-adventurers, shopkeepers, merchants, and others who like to sit quietly and talk over their drinks.

Pipe smoke usually hangs heavy in the air in this place, and—because this place faces Ahghairon's Tower and the palace beyond—talk is often of politics, the future of Waterdeep, and of grand plans. Diplomats and visitors like to drop in here because it's safe and they're unlikely to be hailed by anyone or drawn into an argument.

The stuffed, mounted blue dragon's head for which the tavern is named was from a hatchling. It is dusty and moth-eaten with age, but still thrusts, large and menacing, well out into the taproom. One of the bartenders often hangs towels to dry from its teeth.

Tobacco (5 cp/pouch) and drinks can be bought at the bar—but aside from sausage rolls (4 cp/platter or 2 cp/ handplate) and stew (1 cp/bowl), there's little food to be had here. Drinks are 1 cp/tankard for ale, 2 cp for stout, 2 cp/tallglass for wine, and 3 cp

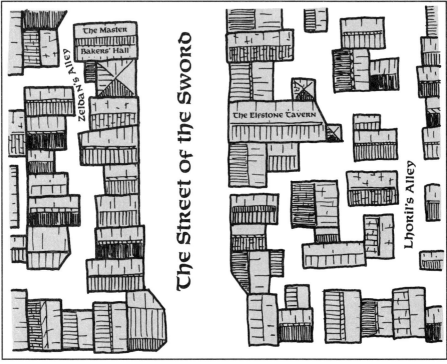

for zzar. The bar has an extensive selection of brandies, liqueurs, and rarities (such as firewine and elverquisst), which are sold by the glass. These cost from 7 sp/glass for brandy, to 9 gp/glass for elverquisst or Tashlutan amberthroat.

Proprietor: The proprietor, Vorn Laskadarr, is short, stubble-faced, and unlovely to the eye, but also quick, efficient, and kindly.[29]

The Elfstone Tavern

This old, dimly lit tavern stands on the east side of the Street of the Sword, north of Waterdeep Way. It caters to elves and half-elves, and is an earthy-smelling place, where living trees have been encouraged through elven patience and forestry skill to grow up from the cellar and through the taprooms. By day, rooftop shutters are pulled aside to let rain and sunlight in for the trees. By night, *dancing lights* spells bathe the place in soft, floating, blue motes of light.

Here elves gather to drink Evereskan clearwater (2 gp/tallglass), moonwine (4 gp/tallglass), elverquisst (14 gp/

---

[29] Location #20 on the color map. Its floor plan appears on Map 3 in the *City System* boxed set.

24

tallglass), guldathen nectar (16 gp/glass) and maerlathen blue wine (17 gp/glass), and dine on biscuits spread with roe, shrimp, spiced silverfin, crab meat, or mint jelly (all 1 gp/platter). You can also eat skewers of sizzled squirrel, rabbit, or venison done in a green sauce (2 gp each). These are so good that the gods would ask for more!

Gentle harp, pipe, flute, and choral music is performed, and service is fast, near-silent, and graceful. This is a place where dwarves and half-orcs will be driven away, some humans and halflings are tolerated in small parties, and even half-elves are just accepted—elves can be very supercilious when they choose to be. I saw even the various sorts of elves ignoring or otherwise being rude to each other. However, the mood is usually light or serene, and the owner and staff are moon elves, who welcome all. They will not allow anything to get too far out of hand.

If the elven patrons weren't such snobs, I'd give this place five full tankards. Go there to taste the food, if not to linger.

Proprietress: Yaereene Ilbae-reth is the tavern's seemingly unaging proprietress. She is a tall, charming and regal elven woman with silvery eyes, who goes about with a grinning faerie dragon perched delicately on her shoulder.[30]

The Red-Eyed Owl

This is the closest thing Water-deep has to a "local"—a comfortable, unimpressive, welcoming gathering place for the neighborhood. It is the kind of place where friends will come in and hail each other across the room, the food and drink will be pleasant, if unspectacular, and you'll be allowed to sit in peace and while an evening away over a tankard or two.

Food is a heavily spiced seafood stew (called coast chowder) or roast oxen done with a sweet-and-sour sauce and a dash of brandy to flame the outside as it's brought, blazing, to your table. Either way, it's 5 cp for a heaping platter or huge bowl (with huge slabs of fresh, warm crusty brown bread).

Drink is 1 cp/tankard for ale, 2 cp for bitters, 3 cp for stout, 4 cp/tallglass for zzar or red wine, and 5 cp for the rather sour white wine that is brought in from the proprietor's own land, and which he's inordinately fond of. It goes well with all sorts of cheese, though (especially the firmer, heartier sorts), and he sells it for carry-out at 2 sp/bottle or 1 gp for a half-anker keg.

The Owl faces west. It is a rambling old wooden building that looks as if it's about to fall

---

[30] Location #24 on the color map.

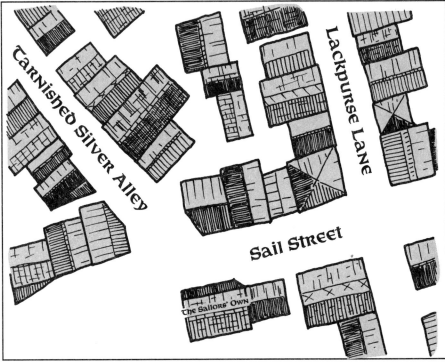

into the street. But it has looked that way for at least 40 winters, patrons assured me, and hasn't fallen down yet. It is the point of an arrowhead-shaped block bounded by Rainrun Street, the confluence of Gut Alley and Belnimbra's Street, Snail Street, and an unnamed alley.

Proprietor: Balarg "Twofists" Dathen, a bluff, bristle-bearded man with long, unkempt red hair, owns and runs the tavern. His rough voice is much used for coarse jests, and he has an unutterably deadly aim with a hurled platter or tankard when anyone tries to start trouble.[31]

The Sailors' Own

This dockside tavern stands on Sail Street, across from the mouth of Tarnished Silver Alley, with water lapping at the docks only a few strides away. The reek of fish—and rotting seaweed—hangs strongly about the whole area. Inside the tavern, the sailors seem to be trying to blot it out with the smells of their various and often exotic tobaccos.

The place is low-beamed and crowded, with weary sailors slumped on benches playing at

---

[31] Location #5 on the color map.

board games, cards, or merely getting thoroughly drunk. They are often left to sleep the night through here.

Anyone who's going to be sick is expected to make it out the dockside door first. Anyone who starts a fight will be thrown *through* that same door—luckily, it usually opens at the impact—by the proprietor, a man of prodigious strength. I saw him lift an entire table with one hand while he reached under it to snatch up a drunken sailor with the other! His aim and strength are sufficient to hurl a struggling brawler through the dockside door boots first—high enough to just clear the threshold and sail across the

quayside beyond, straight into the water. It's worth a few coppers just to see this, but you don't want to be anywhere near when such trouble starts.

This place is just what its name implies. It belongs to the sailors, and they don't really want anyone else here. If you're not one, duck into it to avoid bad weather or thugs, but otherwise steer clear.

Interestingly, sailors here don't like to eat any sort of seafood— they get little else on long voyages, I suppose. The fare here is pork, ox, or horse, either in roast portions (2 cp/platter) or stewed with onions and greens (1 cp/ bowl). Drink is ale (2 cp/tankard),

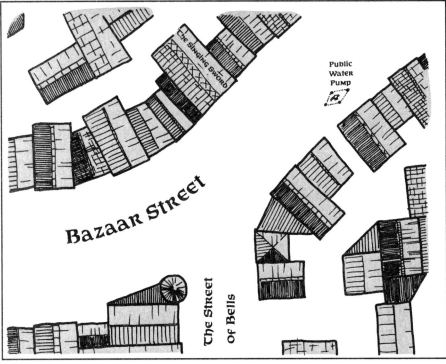

Public
Water
Pump

The Singing Sword

Bazaar Street

The Street
of Bells

stout (3 cp/tankard), zzar or brandy (4 cp/tallglass), or whiskey (1 sp/tallglass). That's the entire menu.

This tavern has an interesting sideline. The proprietor sells charts (with an emphasis on nautical usefulness) of many areas along the Sword Coast and around the known Sea of Swords for 45 gp each and up. A good or rare one will run into the hundreds of gold pieces.

Proprietor: The proprietor, Guthlakh "Hands" Imyiir, is huge, slow, and deliberate. He is also very strong and slow to smile, but not surly by any means.[32]

The Singing Sword

This busy tavern stands on the north side of Bazaar Street, at the head of the Street of Bells. Three floors of busy diners enjoy one of the largest menus in Waterdeep, including the justly famous turtle soup—served in a turtle's upside-down shell—here each day. They are entertained by the high-voiced ballads of the wondrous magical blade for which the tavern is named.

This black-bladed long sword was brought to Waterdeep long

---

[32] Location #3 on the color map.

TROLLSONG

Anonymous

In a cave there lived an old troll
His diet grisly, his manners droll.
Many a youth he caught and ate,
"Raw, with carrots—really great."

In a castle there lived a knight
His lance was long, his armor bright.
Many quests he carefully planned
But never went, his courage unmanned.

In a village there dwelt a maid
The fairest that e'er the gods made.
Poor but proud, she lived alone
Beauty naught but skin and bone.

In a deep forest berries grew
Bright and red, good but few.
Hither went the lady fair
Her savage hunger to repair.

In one sniff the troll knew
The makings of a small meat stew
Had wandered near his hidden home.
To he who waits, all meals roam.

In a huff that knight so bold
Rode out to spend grudging gold.
For his cupboard was bare, ale low—
And through the forest he did go.

In a trice, the lady found her food:
Berries ripe, and berries good.
By the handful she did eat.
(The troll approached on nimble feet.)

Full, the maiden turned to go.
Out leaped the troll, crying, "So!
My dinner's come, in cap and gown!"
And the knight, unseeing, rode him down.

"Oh, my hero!" sighed the lady,
"My life is thine—marry me!"
The knight, afraid, backed his steed—
Hooves again treading troll mead.

"Good lady," stammered the warrior bold,
"My sight is poor, my limbs are old.
Am I then thy only choice?"
"Yes," she cried, "And I rejoice!"

"Oh, dear," then said noble knight
And fainted dead away from fright.
Over backwards he did crash
His armor making troll hash.

"Oh, my lord!" cried the gentle maid.
"So noble, so modest, so gently made!"
And loving arms around him put,
Trampling troll cakes underfoot.

"What? Ho!" the dazèd knight did moan.
"I am beaten and overthrown!
By my honor, I surrender me
To my foe the victory!"

And he struggled to one knee
His conqueror bright to see—
Beheld in wonder blushing maid.
(Under both, troll tiles thinly laid.)

"I am yours! Command me, I beg!"
Quoth the knight, making a leg.
"Up then, sir!" said that lady
"My lord and husband thou shalt be!"

And up he got, armor a-clank,
(Troll blood unwitting spurs drank),
And set his lady upon his horse.
Together they rode o'er troll—of course.

And when the hooves had died away,
The troll on the ground did stay,
Feeling every little bit of pain
As his bits came together again.

But men, like trolls, never learn
Beautiful maidens sharp to spurn,
And so the song goes round again
The fallen always suffering pain.

Oh, in a cave there lived an old troll….
(Song repeats)

ago, and is thought to have been forged in ancient Netheril. It customarily stands upright, hilt uppermost, in the open central well of the tavern, encircled by the spiraling stairs to the upper floors, and is silent.

Once an hour, one of the tavern staff—usually a pretty girl in mock armor, struggling under the weight of the blade—lifts the blade and holds it high, for it will only sing when grasped and ordered. The will of the holder actually determines the song—and angry or upset holder's thoughts have been known to make the blade segue into a second song after it has begun singing.

The sword's magic has never failed yet. It seems immune to the effects of *dispel magic*—in fact, applying one when the blade is held by a living being causes it to snarl in anger and scorn! It seems to know 30 or so songs, mainly tragic ballads, love laments, or roaring warriors' songs, with a few comedy pieces thrown in. Its voice is high, clear, and almost bell-like on high notes, but somehow male—though it has been known to mimic the voices of others who sing along with it in order to better harmonize.[33]

I've included the lyrics of *Trollsong*, a comedy ballad that seemed a special favorite of the patrons, so that you can sing along if you visit the Sword and not feel out of place. Everyone in the place roars and minces their way through this one, and bellows for it to be sung at least twice through each time.

The Sword has a simple way of dealing with prices: All meals are 1 gp per platter, whatever you order. This includes a tallglass or tankard of whatever you want. Subsequent drinks are 1 sp/ tankard for any beer or 1 gp/ tallglass for zzar or any wine. The exotic drinkables (elverquisst, dragonstongue, firewine, and Fires of Mirabar whiskey) are few or missing altogether— no surprise, at these prices.

Whenever I went, I found the Sword to be a lively place, brightly lit and full of crowds of folk enjoying their meal—and their visit with friends at adjacent tables. This is obviously a popu-

---

[33] The Singing Sword is location #41 on the color map. The Singing Sword is a chaotic good, intelligent *long sword +2*, which has the extraordinary powers of *levitation* and *teleportation* (as detailed in the DUNGEON MASTER™ Guide, page 187). When wielded by a bard, it allows him or her to strike one extra attack with it per round, at an additional +2 attack bonus (so the attack roll is at +4, though the damage roll remains +2). It is immune to *dispel magic, disintegrate* and all lightning or electrical spells or magical effects, and confers this protection to its wielder and all within a 5' radius. Such effects are drawn into the sword and harmlessly absorbed to sustain and renew its own magic.

The Sword sings when it pleases. It performs for Gothmorgan because it likes him—and will use its extraordinary powers to elude anyone it doesn't want wielding it. It will only allow Gothmorgan, a good-aligned bard (or in an emergency, if Gothmorgan, his staff, or the tavern are threatened, anyone willing to wield it to defend them) to wield it. It may have other, as yet unknown, powers—and Elminster believes it is of Netherese origin.

lar place with many regulars. The food's good, too. Any visitor to Waterdeep will find this place worth a visit to hear the Singing Sword burst into song.

Proprietor: Gothmorgan Ilibuld, the proprietor, is tall, laconic, and always watchful, but ever the polite host.

The Sleepy Sylph

This popular tavern stands at the southwest corner of the intersection of Rainrun and Snail Streets, at the other end of the same small block of buildings as the Red-Eyed Owl. Its frankly risqué signboard depicts the sylph the tavern is named for.

But while the Owl is a cozy local watering hole, this place caters to visitors. Lots of colored *driftglobes* float about, and many scantily clad waitresses (wearing diaphanous robes and fairy wings of silken gauze stretched over fine wire) hurry about, dodging the strolling minstrels hired by the tavern.

Under the many-hued, drifting lights, patrons can eat almost nothing and drink as much as they can afford. Only skewered whole fowl—chicken, quail, turkey, or pheasant—are on the menu (1 gp each). Each fowl comes with a darkbread trencher and a plate of lemon slices that most patrons use to cut the grease from their fingers after eating the fowl.

Drink is 3 cp/tankard for ale, 5 cp for bitters, 7 cp for stout, 1 sp/tallglass for zzar or house red or white wine, and 2 gp to 25 gp by the bottle for more exotic things. Locals in the neighborhood no doubt come here for a single drink, to enjoy the music and to watch the waitresses—and then go to the Owl, just steps away, to eat and drink at about a third the price. (I saw more than watching going on, but turned modestly back to my glass, which was practically sobbing to have more little drinks poured into it.)

For the money, though, you get spotless white tablecloths, good food brought to you in a hurry, music, and a chance to see other rich folk dining. If you aren't rich, why are you here?

Proprietor: The owner and operator of the Sleepy Sylph is Callanter Rollingshoulder, a tall, fat man dressed in dark silken robes and a red Calishite sash, with the bushy ends of his truly magnificent mustache adorned with tiny, golden, chiming bells.[34]

Inns

The Jade Jug

On the northwest corner of the intersection of the High Road and Waterdeep Way stands what

---

[34] Location #6 on the color map.

has been called Waterdeep's plushest inn. It deserves its prime location—many noble families would envy the spotless, luxurious accommodations. Every detail, from handsoap bowls beside the piped-water baths, within easy reach of a reclining bather, to the bedside icebox filled with shrimp snacks and chilled wine, has been thought of. Guests are attended by a personal servant of their choice for the duration of their stay from those not presently engaged with another customer. Their every need is attended to: Food is brought, a coach (or, in icy winter weather, a sledge) is brought around if the guest wishes to go out in the city, and anything a guest gets dirty is instantly whisked away and replaced with a clean duplicate.

Decor is muted, not garish or in bad taste (unlike the Unicorn's Horn across the way). Quite simply, I felt like a pampered king during my one-night stay. But with rooms 12 gp to 30 gp/night and suites 25 gp to 50 gp, one night was simply all I could hope to afford!

Until you've been bathed by a cheerful, skillful, beautiful maid who wears white gloves as she soaps you, you haven't lived. If you've gold enough, go to the Jade Jug. I'll never sneer at pampering again.

Proprietress: The charming, beautiful, one-armed hostess is Amaratha Ruendarr. She notices every detail, and remembers the names of guests' pets, children, or mates from their last visit, a year or more ago![35]

The Pampered Traveler

This inn, with large, conical-roofed, many-windowed turrets at its either end, stands like an exotic castle, dark and somehow inviting, on the northeast corner of the meeting of Selduth Street and the Street of Bells. Room rates here run from 6 gp to 12 gp/night, depending on the room you choose.

The Pampered Traveler's name sets high expectations, and they are not disappointed. Servants conduct you to your large and well-furnished rooms, which are kept warm but not over-warm, and come within breaths if you ring for them. Each room has a bell pull by the door.

On the main floor is a huge smoking room with a roaring hearth full of old, soft, vast armchairs that can easily swallow up smaller visitors, a play-nursery for the children of

---

[35] Location #35 on the color map. Volo had a last-minute thought about the Jug. He recommends that merchants with gold enough to bring their mate to Waterdeep once a year for a week's shopping and sightseeing save the Jug for the last night. Have the house staff pack all your purchases for the journey and engage a coach to take you to your transportation home, while you relax and let your personal servants pamper you! Bliss!

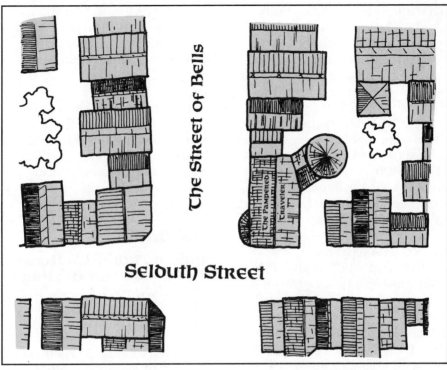

The Street of Bells

Selduth Street

guests (a rare and thoughtful feature), a gaming room, and three small, private meeting rooms for the use of guests. There is also, surprisingly, a library filled with books hand-copied by the staff and a reading table with a glass top, under which can be seen as full and complete a map of the known Realms as far west as the Moon-shaes, as far east as Thay, and as far south as the Shaar, as I've seen anywhere. (The staff spends one morning a week, each, on the task of hand-copying the books.)

The proprietor is keenly interested in exploration. Present in the library, along with a chapbook put out by the Mer-chants' League describing the exploits of the famous Dabron Sashenstar and his mapping of a trade route linking known lands to Sossal, there are even copied letters from sea captains who have reached Maztica, far away across the sea.

All of the guests are welcome to read—though I get the feeling anyone who departed with as much as a single page would be pursued by the master of the house until he separated the thief from his head! I have also heard of a man staying free at the inn for a week in exchange for gifting the proprietor with a

particular highly valued book.

When I cautiously discussed reading matter with the master, he said the only things he didn't want in his library were magical texts. They intrigued him, but they also brought potential danger into his inn and attracted the wrong sort of readers. Twice he had to break down the doors of his library and put out fires—and once run pell-mell through the streets to Blackstaff Tower to call on Khelben Arunsun himself to come and bind a summoned abishai baatezu!

Most of the staff are middle-aged, motherly, pleasant women ("Young, pretty ones bring only trouble," the master told me). They do a good job of cleaning up after messy guests as they go along and of bringing wine, hot cider, ale or stout to guests upon request. (These drinks are included in your room price).

In the morning, there's complimentary hot egg, vegetable, and beef broth soup (better than it sounds), and each evening guests are welcome to come down to the common rooms and cut themselves slices of beef, goat, venison, or pork from the sideboard platters. Mustards, pickles, horseradish, and hot southern sauces are on hand to garnish the meat. All of this is included in your room fee—but if you bring in your own guests (who are not staying at the inn) to dine with you, their fare costs you an additional 1 gp/meal per head.

All in all, a quietly luxurious place to stay. This is undoubtedly the wealthy scholar's choice of hostel.

Proprietor: The Pampered Traveler is run by Brathan Zilmer, guildmaster of the Fellowship of Innkeepers. He is a solemn, careful, darkly handsome man with an air of mystery and wariness about him.[36]

Festhalls

Mother Tathlorn's House of Pleasure and Healing
Festhall & Spa

This is the most famous house of pleasure in Waterdeep, and that's not surprising. Located on Gem Street, just off Waterdeep Way, and across from the foot of the road down from the Grain Gate of Castle Waterdeep, it's a large, five-floored building with two additional levels of dungeons below ground, in which absolutely no expense has been spared on props.

There are wardrobes full of all sorts of clothes, from silk and lace nightdresses to pirate outfits, full plate armor (made of silver-painted padding, to lessen injuries), and barbarian berserker garb. There are several rooms full of jungle plants, with heated

---

[36] Location #40 on the color map.

pools in them and carefully tended mossy banks. There are four-poster beds with trampolines and rings that can be set aflame. There are even pairs of *rings of levitation* to be used in rooms with *glowing globes* and floating mirrors. If you can think of it, someone already has, and it can be found here.

The strength of any festhall, however, lies in its staff, who must be skilled and must enjoy their work. The men and women in this festhall are experts. (Mother Tathlorn owns another festhall—she won't reveal which one—in which staff are trained on the job. They don't get to work here until they are skilled at their craft.)

Mother Tathlorn's has on staff several priests of Sune. In return for offerings to the goddess, they heal torn muscles and sprained limbs. Almost all of the rest of the staff are trained and capable masseuses—and in fact, the most popular service performed at Mother Tathlorn's is massage and bathing, especially of elderly male and female citizens of Waterdeep who are wealthy enough to afford it—either daily, or whenever they can muster coins enough.

Here in warm, cozy, private comfort, your aches and pains can be soothed away in a scented or mineral water bath or in heated steam baths, and you can drift off to contented slumber,

secure in the knowledge that your person and well-guarded belongings are safe. Or, you can visit with a friend, or even strangers, while all of you are massaged. Unlike in some other realms, in Waterdeep there's nothing embarrassing about going to a festhall. It's simply part of life for those who enjoy it.

There are two privacy floors, where staff and the many doors, hangings, dim lighting and secret passages make sure patrons don't see each other. These floors also have separate entrances via tunnels into an adjacent building to the west on Gem Street, so that patrons who demand discretion won't be seen entering or leaving. Mother Tathlorn also has six skilled bouncers—one a wizard armed with a *wand of paralyzation* and *silence* spells—for patrons who become difficult.

All of this luxury and pleasure doesn't come cheaply. Expect to spend 4 gp at the door, plus 25 gp per staff person who assists you.. Patrons who don't pay the full shot when they depart must leave collateral. Lacking collateral, they must go home with only a thin cloak and the keys to their lodgings (a practice that affords the Watch much innocent amusement—especially on snowy nights). Most regular patrons run a credit account—but also tip staff members very handsomely, often effectively doubling their fee.

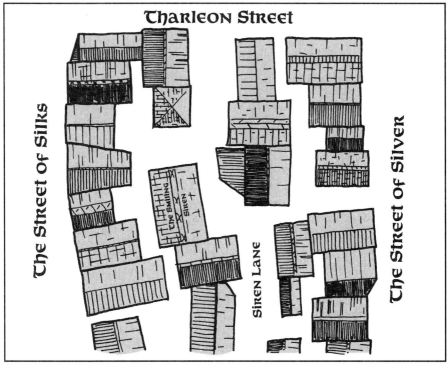

Proprietress: The festhall's prioprietress, Mother Tathlorn, is old and stout, but charming. She is skilled at massage and in reading the needs of a customer who is shy, drunk, or unfamiliar with the common tongue.[37]

The Smiling Siren Nightclub & Theater

This large, but plain-looking, stone and mudbrick building stands in the center of a block of shops and apartments, in the fork of its own access street, Siren Lane.[38] It's home to a company of popular local actors who can perform everything from rowdy comedy (their stock in trade) to high tragedy.

Nobles often hire the place for an evening for exclusive performances involving the actors and actresses saying and doing what the noble always wanted them to in a particular play, rather than

---

[37] Location #12 on the color map.

[38] Location #31 on the color map. When the haunted theater featured in the *Knight of the Living Dead* adventure gamebook closed, the traveling troupes came here instead. (See #42A in that book. The haunted theater was on the south side of Waterdeep Way, the third building west of Fellowship Hall). That theater has been closed for over five winters now, and has become known as the Hall of the Juggling Ghost. It was previously Raeral's Splendors.

the way it was written. Such private performances often involve risqué audience participation or private jokes—or even entirely new (sometimes wretched) plays, written by the noble who's hired the company.

More often, however, the Siren is home to traveling troupes of vaudeville jugglers, comedians, and nearly nude dancers or burlesque dancers. When these aren't available, the theater company performs—usually a weekly revue consisting of time-honored gag routines and sketches rewritten to include references to daily happenings and current jokes.

Admission varies from 4 cp/head to 6 gp/head, depending on who or what is performing. Famous bards are the most expensive—and fastest sellout—draws. The take is split evenly between theater and performers. The theater in all cases provides heating via warm flue pipes fed by a hearth under the stage, lighting (usually *glowing globes*) and security. Most traveling troupes charge from 2 sp to 8 sp/head (1 gp/head if burlesque dancers are involved). The weekly revue put on by the locals is always 4 cp.

Before and between performances, the place is used for drinking and dancing to live music, sometimes with show dancers on the stage. Ale is 3 cp per tankard, stout is 6 cp, and zzar or wine is sold by the bottle, at 7 sp each.

Proprietor: Perendel Wintamer, a young, earnest, mustachioed mage, runs this nightclub. He often must use his spells to clear birds out of the dark upper reaches of the building.

Alleys

Castle Ward's alleys are among the safest in the city. Since most folk of importance travel about with bodyguards or friends, thieves aren't in the habit of making strikes in this ward. The most frequent users of the alleys by day are tradesmen making deliveries. By night they are used most often by city watch or city guard patrols hurrying from this place to that.

Many of the so-called alleys in this ward have long since become proper streets, such as Coin Alley and Tarnished Silver Alley, and are not included here.

Asmagh's Alley

Running south off Selduth Street through the interior of the long city block between the Street of Silver and Warriors' Way, this long, winding alley is considered to end when it meets Palfrey Lane to the south.

It is named for a notorious apothecary who flourished (if that's the word) in Waterdeep

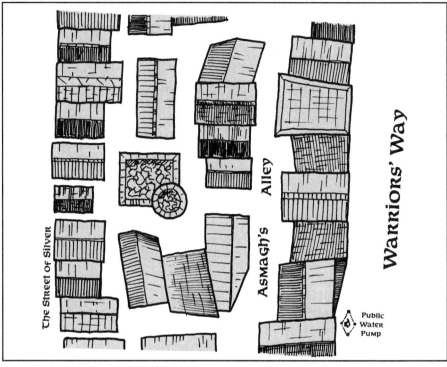

some 60 winters ago. He was a poisoner, and buried his victims by night, lifting the stones of this alley to place them underneath and carrying away the dirt left over in his cart. After he was discovered at it and slain, the Watch uncovered over 80 bodies under these flagstones, and searched diligently, to be sure they missed none. It's an old Waterdhavian joke to refer to Asmagh as "the Ambassador," because, they say, "He welcomed so many folk to the City" ("the City," to a citizen of Waterdeep, means the City of the Dead).

Today, this long way is crowded with delivery crates, barrels,

scattered garbage, and rats. Thugs sometimes mug folk here on the darker nights, trusting to the length of the alley to run down prey. Sometimes they even scatter marbles, beforehand, so their fleeing prey is sure to take a nasty fall.

Buckle Alley

This narrow passage winds east and westward across four city blocks, from the High Road in the east to the heart of the block west of the Street of Silver at its other end. It lies about a third of the way south from Selduth Street to

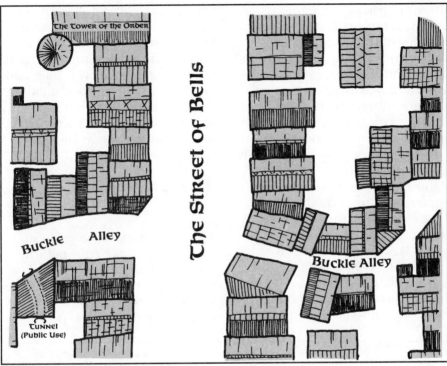

The Tower of the Order

The Street of Bells

Buckle Alley

Tunnel
(Public Use)

Buckle Alley

Waterdeep Way, and has always been a busy thoroughfare used by carters, tradesmen making deliveries, and local folk on foot.

It is named for an old saying. City guardsmen were told to buckle on their blades before they set foot in it, as it was once the heart of Thieves' Guild territory, before that organization was driven out of Waterdeep.

Of old, thieves used to sit on stools in this alley drinking, drawn swords laid naked across their laps in case the city watch showed up. Their favorite tipple was Black Grog Ale, from the pirate isles of the Sea of Fallen Stars.

That brew is still a favorite in this area today. Barrels of it are imported all the way from Immurk's Hold for the locals to buy here, or to consume at local taverns.

Cat Alley, a.k.a. Cats Alley

Winding through the interior of the city block bounded by Waterdeep Way, the High Road, Buckle Alley, and the Street of Bells, this narrow passage has many confusing twists and turns. Many a visitor to the city has become lost in its mud and dark corners. Deliveries are made here, and

there are rows of apartments and warehouses that stand in the interior of the block and can only be reached by means of this alley. Traditionally, gangs of street youths have battled for control of this many-branched passage, but in recent years, heavy city watch patrols have ended the wildest turf battles and made this a fairly safe place to walk.

Recently, however, a masked, rapier-wielding, quietly chuckling assailant has made this a dangerous place for women after dark. By his dress and manner he is wealthy and probably noble, but he has not yet been apprehended, and has cut away a lot of female garments,

frightened a lot of folk, and caused at least two deaths: one lady who couldn't escape him and was found run through, and a would-be rescuer was killed on another occasion. The chuckling masked man calmly cut the rescuer's throat, and then strolled away, leaving the lady he had trapped untouched.

The Cat's Tail

The southernmost loop of Cat Alley, this passage runs behind two guildhalls, the Blue Jack tavern, and the Jade Jug, whose stables stand across it. The influence of the money and power

vested here has caused this alley to be brightly lit by *glowing globes* by night that are firmly fixed in high wall brackets and on roof overhangs and patrolled by private guards, who are armed with warning horns,[39] clubs, and daggers. Patrons from the Jack have been known to aid these guards when they sound their horns—and as a result, the masked assailant who haunts Cat Alley keeps clear of this southern loop, and thieves are few indeed. The guards like to gossip about events in the city, and for a copper piece or two will even recommend taverns, shops, inns, certain folk, festhalls—and even fences.[40]

Duir's Alley

This alleyway enters the city block bounded by the Street of Bells, the Street of the Sword, Waterdeep Way and Selduth Street on its east side, just beside (to the north of) the Halls of Hilmer. It forks, going north and south past Hilmer's two metals warehouses to run down the west side of the interior of the block. The alleyway branching off to run down the eastern interior of the block is called Lhoril's Alley.

Today, this busy, winding

passage is often the scene of spell demonstrations and practice, as patrons or staff spill out of the rear of the Elfstone Tavern and unleash magic down the alley—sometimes to the vast surprise of someone coming along it!

More than once, visitors to Waterdeep coming to the apartments in the center of this block after dark have been astonished to find two or more elves chatting, wineglasses in hand, as they float in midair, surrounded by a glowing nimbus of blue light. The elves generally ignore such passersby—but if someone stops and is obviously listening, they have been known to drive the eavesdropper away with spells.

Elsambul's Lane

This short alleyway runs up and down the interior of the city block bounded by Bazaar Street, the Street of the Sword, Cymbril's Walk, and Warriors' Way. It is crossed, and most easily reached, by Lamp Street.

Elsambul was a priest of Mask, who lived somewhere along this alley over 70 winters ago. He held the view that thieves should not be crude snatch-and-grab thugs, but a deft, subtle brotherhood of organized companions. He began to gather a band under his

---

[39] The city watch and guard will respond to these in 1d4+1 minutes.

[40] Consider these guards as F1s with 8 hp each. They patrol in groups of five, the leader being an F2 with a short sword and 18 hp. Fences are listed on pages 31–32 of *Waterdeep and the North*.

41

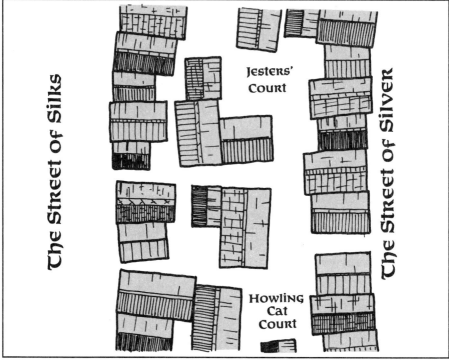

The Street of Silks

The Street of Silver

Jesters' Court

Howling Cat Court

leadership, but was betrayed by an underling. He fell fighting defiantly here, using his magic to take as many foes as possible with him—a defiant last stand that left the alley red with blood and strewn with bodies (or parts of bodies), local tavern tales attest.

Elsambul began the practice of writing cryptic messages for his gang along the walls of this lane, and this graffiti writing has been taken up by others. It is absent from almost everywhere else in Waterdeep. Today, the visitor can see some amusing, puzzling, and disgusting messages from one Waterdhavian to another (most of them unattributed).

Many of the messages hint at treasure to be won, dragons to be duped or destroyed, and great adventure. Others promise revenge or that something will not be forgotten. Adventures should find them intriguing— and perhaps even useful.

It helps to be a confident adventurer just to go into this alley. You never know just who (or what—I'm sure I saw purple tentacles under that hood!) you may find reading the messages.

Howling Cat Court

This small open space inside a city

block (west of the Street of Silver and east of the Street of Silks, and south of Selduth Street) is infamous as a clandestine meeting place for ladies of the evening and their clients, street gangs, and others. Thieves lurk here, too. The city watch comes here often, frequently in triple patrol strength—because they never know just who they'll find here. Once it was a dozen angry, heavily armed minotaurs, released from magical stasis by an evil mage!

Jesters' Court

This famous local landmark and meeting place lies north of Howling Cat Court, just south of Selduth Street in the same block. It's a large courtyard used by ladies of the evening and by minstrels (sometimes both are the same person, as with the famous Masked Minstrel). Sometimes on warm summer evenings it becomes an improvised dance court for the locals, lit by *faerie fire* or *dancing lights* conjured by a mage or apprentice.

Of old, jugglers and comics used to perform here for thrown coins (hence its name), but none are left now but a few men too old to perform. They sometimes come here of afternoons to just stand and remember.

By night, trouble in Howling Cat Court tends to spill over into here, too—and more than once warring gangs, bands of thieves, or adventuring groups have drawn steel and had it out here, until bodies were slumped on the cobbles and the shouts, screams, and clangor and skirl of blades brought both the watch and the city guard on the run. By Waterdhavian legend, it's also the place for couples in love to meet before eloping.

Lemontree Alley

Opening off Shadows Alley north of Cage Street in the first block of buildings east of Piergeiron's Palace, this tiny, three-legged passage is crowded with the lemon trees for which it is named. Brought here by a local wizard, whose spells give heat enough to keep them alive, these tropical trees are an unexpected delight. Waterdeep is much too cold for them to survive under normal conditions. Those who are tempted to take fruit from the trees, break a branch off, or just take a swing at one of them, are warned that the wizard, Narthindlar of the Nine Spells, has set a guardian monster on these trees: a bear (a monster zombie) that usually sits quietly under one of the trees. If you harm or take from a tree, it rises up and drives you away.[41]

---

[41] See Volume 1 of the *Monstrous Compendium* under "Zombie." The bear will not leave the trees, but will fight until destroyed or until offenders leave the vicinity.

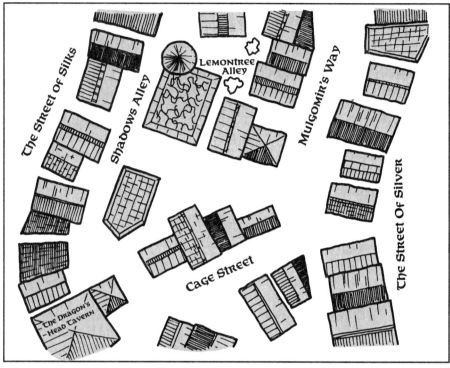

Narthindlar has provided benches under the trees, and can sometimes be found sitting on one of them, puffing on a pipe and contemplating life, Faerun, and magic. He smokes tobacco into which cherries have been crushed, and it gives off a delightful odor. Diplomats who need to blow off steam or chat away from prying ears in the palace sometimes find their way here, too.

Lhoril's Alley

This winding passage links Duir's Alley with Waterdeep Way, running down the eastern interior of the city block bounded by the Way and by the Street of Bells, Buckle Alley, and the Street of the Sword. By day, it's a busy delivery area and garbage-piling place.

Named for the sorceress who met her death here, battling tanar'ri summoned by an over-ambitious apprentice, this passage is known to be haunted by the phantom sounds of running, staggering footsteps (origin unknown). They can be heard at any time of day, hurrying northwards from Waterdeep Way as if a man or heavily laden woman in boots was fleeing frantically with their last, failing energy. No

breathing is ever heard, and no magic or barrier seems to silence or stop this phantom—nor does it respond to the calls or actions of living beings.

The Prowl

This short alley loops eastwards off Alnethar Street, and also, by a side spur, links up with Cymbril's Walk to the south. It provides rear access to a row of shops and to a row of apartments that stand in the center of the block. The Prowl is named for the acts of an eccentric nobleman who used to loose his pet panthers to stalk around it, terrorizing the neighborhood (until one of the cats grew exasperated—or just hungry—one day, and ate him). This otherwise unimportant alleyway is the favorite hunting ground of a pair of skeletal hands that strangle folk from behind, leaving wither-scars graven deep into victims' throats where each finger has been. Some folk who have glanced into the alley at night but not entered have reported seeing two points of light close together in the air, like floating, glowing eyes.

This frightening killer doesn't strike often—four times a year, at most—and seems adept at evading detection whenever powerful wizards and priests come

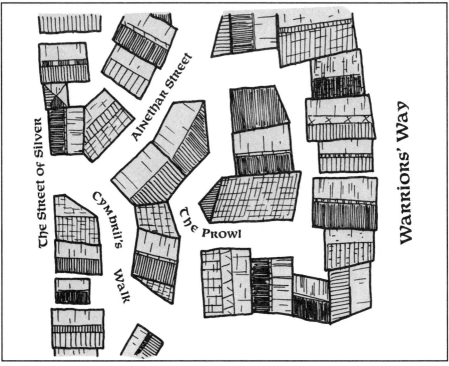

looking for it. No one is yet sure what it is—let alone how to destroy it. It only seems to be active in the hours of darkness, and never strikes at folk in buildings, but only out in the alleyway.[42] I recommend visitors avoid this area until news comes that this mysterious menace has been destroyed.

The Reach

This short side way runs north-west off Lackpurse Lane to the west of Dretch Lane, climbing a steep slope to reach a cluster of warehouses—including Crommor's Warehouse.[43]

It's named after the nautical term *reach*, and got the name after a group of sailors watched a companion, in icy winter weather, come out of one warehouse and slide—quickly and helplessly, arms windmilling just to stay upright—down it and across Lackpurse Lane into the buildings beyond, where he

---

[42] Elminster believes that the skeletal hands are undead—specifically a wichtlin, a being almost always encountered only on another world, Krynn (see MC4, the *DRAGONLANCE® Appendix*). He stresses he's guessing from descriptions he's heard and hasn't investigated this personally.

[43] Location #2 on the color map. See also *Waterdeep and the North* page 32. Two of the men you'll encounter here, Elminster tells us, fence stolen goods.

fetched up against a wall of crates with the inevitable crash.

It's a popular place for sailors to hang out these days, telling yarns of their lives at sea and looking for trouble. Don't approach unless you're looking for a fight—which is what I watched a trio of adventurers do, one evening, deliberately starting a brawl so they could smash heads against walls, hurl sailors down into Lackpurse Lane, and generally send teeth flying.

Sevenlamps Cut

This short cut-through links Swords Street and the Street of Silks, just south of Selduth Street. The alley is named for the seven ornate, everburning, magical lamps installed here long ago by a now-forgotten mage (some say Ahghairon himself).

This handy passage is not only safe and well-lit, it is a popular destination, day and night—for by some tradition whose origins are also now forgotten, this is the place where apprentice (not yet members of the Watchful Order, or visiting) wizards and starving or wandering underpriests in need of money gather to offer their services at spellcasting in return for coin. They cluster here in tiny knots of three and four, waiting for a chance to demonstrate their Art.

Wounded men have been known to stagger and crawl here after tavern brawls, leaving a trail of blood and hoping to buy healing—if they make it. This is the place to hire a spellcaster for a few days' aid if you're about to brave Undermountain's depths— or to have a curse removed or your friend who's been cruelly *polymorphed* into a pink frog changed back into his rightful form.

Shadows Alley

This long passage links the back doors of shops, grand homes, and apartments that face Piergeiron's Palace along the eastern side of the Street of Silks with Cage Street, Lemontree Alley, and Mulgomir's Way.

It's named for the undead that haunted it in earlier days, before a determined effort was made to root them out and destroy them (and block the sewer connection they retreated into, when priests came looking for them).

No shadows have been seen in Shadows Alley for almost 20 winters now, and today the alley is known more as a way for important visitors to the city and wealthy merchants to slip out of their lodgings and go in search of nighttime companionship and revelry without being seen. It is also known for the (illegal) duels often fought at night here by diplomats or young nobles who

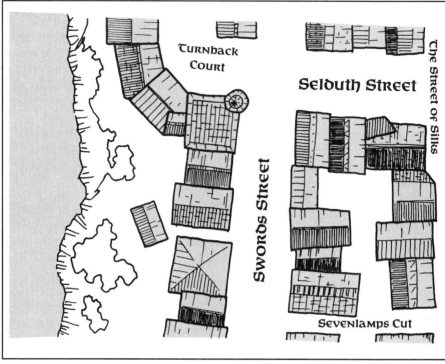

Turnback
Court

Selduth Street

The Street of Silks

Swords Street

Sevenlamps Cut

both think they'll win, and want to leave the body of their fallen foe contemptuously on the palace steps—or throw it into the spell defenses of Ahghairon's Tower, so as to confuse any detection magics used on it to determine who the killer was or to impair attempts at resurrection. In many such duels, magical cheating goes on—one or both parties employs hidden magic items or weapons—and such a release of Art almost always alerts city guard duty wizards at the palace and causes general mayhem as wizards and warriors rush towards the alley from various nearby barracks and guardposts.

Turnback Court

This westernmost extension of Selduth Street is a short stub that allows access to a few buildings nestled against the eastern cliff face of Mount Waterdeep. The reason for its name is obvious. Lit by bright lamps by night, it is a rallying point for city watch and city guard patrols.

The large building that walls off the north side of the Court, hidden from the view of most who pass on Swords Street by the bend in Turnback Court, is a warehouse that, I'm told, is owned by a mysterious organiza-

tion—the Harpers, perhaps, or the Red Sashes, or an arm of the Lords' Alliance, or maybe a cabal of wizards—and holds hidden a number of items of powerful magic, including (several locals whispered to me, on separate occasions) a small ship, that sails the sky instead of water![44] When I tried to investigate, I was politely told to be on my way or Piergeiron would have gained one over-inquisitive visitor to put onto a convict ship and send far, far away!

Zeldan's Alley

This narrow, winding way runs south from the Crawling Spider tavern, along whose south wall it connects with the Street of the Sword, past a pleasant little well of safe drinking water shaded by trees to circle around the southern interior of the city block bounded by the Street of the Sword, Waterdeep Way, Warriors' Way, and Buckle Alley. Along the way, it offers back door access to the Golden Key and other shops, townhomes, and apartments.

Zeldan was a short, puffing merchant who was a devout worshipper of Gond. He finally met his doom some 30 winters ago in the arms of an automaton that came to life too soon and too vigorously, and smashed him

through a wall it was supposed to raise him gently up to paint!

Unfortunately for all concerned, Zeldan built most of the warehouses and townhomes that fill the center of this block—and under cover of the construction, spent much of his fortune sponsoring priests of Gond who came to Waterdeep on ships from Lantan to build and install various experimental devices in this alleyway. Some of them still lurk, hidden beneath paving stones and behind walls, waiting for the unwary to trigger them. Some are harmless or do nothing more than make grinding noises and lurching movements (they were either faulty designs or have broken since installation)—but some are mechanical traps and killing devices that rank right up there with the most horrible killing devices that rich fiends in Thay and Calimshan have devised! A few still pop up from time to time, frightening, crippling, or slaying outright the folk who discover them. Be warned—and avoid this alleyway unless unavoidable business takes you there.

---

[44] When asked about this, Elminster merely smiled like an old fox just leaving a chicken coop, with feathers still stuck to its lips and said, "No comment" (a phrase I know he didn't pick up on Faerun).

Sea Ward

ea Ward is the wealthiest ward of the city. This district lies north of Julthoon Street and west of Shield Street, with a small eastern arm extending to the High Road along Vondil Street. Lashed by sea storms, it is almost deserted in winter, but in warmer months is home to most of Waterdeep's noble families, who play here with as much gusto as they do on their own estates.

The major avenue of this ward is the Street of the Singing Dolphin. The ward is notable not only for the many-spired and grand homes of the nobles,[1] but for containing the majority of the city's temples, which soar every bit as grand and haughty as the nobles' homes. Other notable landmarks include the Field of Triumph (a vast open stadium), the lush Heroes' Gardens (Waterdeep's only public parkland outside the City of the Dead), and West Gate, which leads onto the beaches where folk of strong hearts and tough skins brave the chilly waters whenever winter ice sculptures don't block access to the waves of the Sea of

Swords. Be sure to see the Lion Gate, the impressive carved entrance to the Field of Triumph, facing Gulzindar Street.

Also in this ward are the towers and works of many powerful wizards. Folk of importance who want to build opulent homes come here. Those with less snobbery and more lust or need for everyday power can be found in Castle Ward. Those with less money or less need to impress can be found in North Ward.

Truth to tell, except for the fading smell of the sea and lack of temples as one goes east, the visitor can see little difference between North Ward and Sea Ward. Nonetheless, the visitor should remember that the most pushy of Waterdeep's wealthier merchants crowd into the best addresses they can find in this ward. Some Waterdhavians devote their entire lives to attaining a Sea Ward address. Though citizens may joke about this social climbing, the visitor would do well to avoid talking on such sensitive things.

Watch patrols are very frequent. However, they are always polite and generally lightly armed.[2] Street violence, theft, and

---

[1] One correction for the maps in both FR1 *Waterdeep and the North* and the *City System* boxed set: the Tesper noble family is shown as owning *two* villas, #87 and #89. The more southerly villa, #87, is actually the seat of the Eagleshield noble family, who, Elminster says, appreciate our help in restoring their rightful recognition. Its floor plan, still mistakenly attributed to the wrong family, appears on Map 4 of the *City System* boxed set.

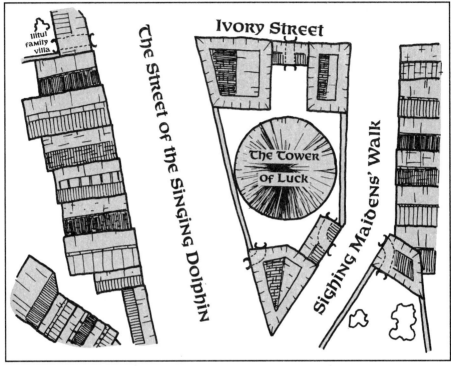

Map labels:
- Iiitul family villa
- The Street of the Singing Dolphin
- Ivory Street
- The Tower of Luck
- Sighing Maidens' Walk

vandalism of any sort is not tolerated in this ward. Unless well-dressed or a known Waterdhavian noble, and drunk, those who engage in such things are quickly handled by the city watch.

Landmarks

Many visitors to the city, if they can find good weather and time enough, go for a stroll in Sea Ward just to gawk at the griffons and other steeds being flown overhead, the proud architecture all around, and the wasteful display of wealth everywhere. The walk is apt to be thirsty. There are very few taverns in this ward. Inns stand thin on the ground here, too—and there are no guildhalls at all.

In evening, the setting sun blazes on many gilded domes and spires here. More ornamental things such as minarets, bell

---

[2] City watch patrols are detailed on page 17 of *Waterdeep and the North*. In this ward, four-sword patrols pass a given point about every 10 minutes and look in to a tavern or inn dining room every 30 minutes.

As detailed on pages 16–17 and 23 of the *City System* set booklet, six-man detachments of the city guard also patrol the ward. Typical patrol details are as given therein, on page 23. Reinforcements will be a dozen LG hm F3s to F6s clad in chain mail and armed with maces, long swords, daggers, slings, and a polearm. Guard patrols pass a given street location about every 30 minutes, but appear 1d4 minutes after a city watch patrol blows a warning horn in this ward.

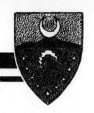

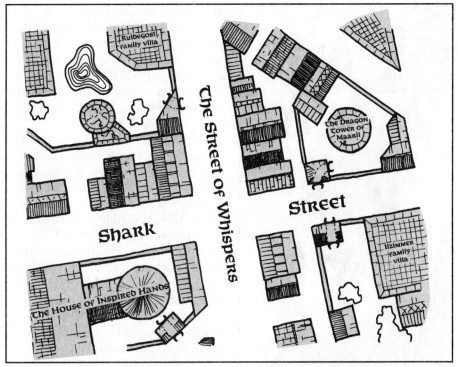

On the map: Ruldegost family villa · The Street of Whispers · The Dragon Tower of Maaril · Shark · Street · Ilzimmer family villa · The House of Inspired Hands

arches, and statuary crowd this ward than other areas of the city.

As in North Ward, most nobles' homes are behind walls, but most of the walled temple complexes welcome visitors—even those of other faiths, so long as they offer no blasphemy, and make offerings to the gods. The largest temple is the House of Heroes, dedicated to Tempus. It stands just north of the Field of Triumph stadium, and is rivaled in size by the Tower of Luck, the temple of Tymora. In Waterdeep, these two vie with the Spires of the Morning—the temple to Lathander, located in Castle Ward just south of the stadium—

and with the up-and-coming temple to Gond, the House of Inspired Hands.

The faith of Selune has always been important in the port city of Waterdeep, and the House of the Moon can be found off Diamond Street in Sea Ward. The city's wealth is demonstrated by its support for a walled and forested shrine to Silvanus and two mighty temples that could not flourish in smaller centers: the House of Wonder, dedicated to Midnight (formerly to Mystra), and the Temple of Beauty, given to the worship of Sune.[3]

Walled but less welcoming are

---

[3] Locations and clergy of these temples are found on page 29 of *Waterdeep and the North*.

the wizards' towers that rise in this ward: the Dragon Tower of Maaril, about which so many sinister tales are whispered; Naingate, abode of the famous adventuring mage Nain, once of the Company of Crazed Venturers; and Tessalar's Tower.[4]

There is also a strange sort of obstacle course, established by a crazed wizard to test the greedy, the venturesome, and others who wander into it. Known as the Blue Alley, this magical death trap is entered by either one of two blue-tiled passages that run into a large, windowless stone building on the north side of Ivory Street, just east of its meeting with Sighing Maidens' Walk. Vast treasure is said to wait there for any who can take it, but from what I heard, the place is studded with inescapable traps that claim almost all who enter, like those found in the wilder tales of dungeon exploration. Look down the alley, as I did—but be very sure of your favor with the gods before you step farther.

---

[4] On the color map, the Dragon Tower is #63, Naingate is #73, and Tessalar's Tower is #95. Chapter 7 of that work also details the three mages who own these homes and some of the strange magical features of the Dragon Tower can be found in the *Knight of the Living Dead* adventure gamebook.

Maaril has turned to evil, and his tower, sculpted in the shape of a rampant dragon, is a place that citizens of Waterdeep warn visitors away from. They say its steps lead up to chambers and winding stairs adorned with many trapped, enchanted creatures set as guardians and in torment. The steps also lead down to cellars where there are magical pools that speak and whose waters confer magical powers on those touching them—or dissolve flesh, bone, metal, and all in a moment of smoke!

The wraiths of Maaril's young female apprentices, their lives drained by his evil magic, wander the tower, attacking intruders. Everywhere lurks a webwork of Maaril's waiting, terrible spells. The unwitting can trigger their own doom with a single wrong step.

Maaril is said to ride dragons, to call them from the dragon's mouth balcony at the top of the tower—and to experiment with hatchlings, creating fearsome dragonet monsters.

Elminster confirmed that these things are true, but added dryly that, "It's just a stage he's going through. Know ye: Maaril will either grow up or be destroyed by the things he's playing with. If ye run afoul of him, thy best defense is that he's only about a tenth as powerful or as smart as he thinks he is."

Tespergates

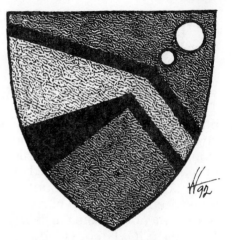

The Waterdhavian noble family of Tesper uses its walled city villa[5] to host parties—parties even common folk and outlanders are welcome to attend. The Tespers have an almost insatiable hunger for live music and the willing company of strangers who enjoy wrestling and other body contact sports. They host one all-night gathering every tenday. Rousing ball games and impromptu wrestling tournaments abound, with not a few bumps and bruises to the participants. To make sure that no one goes away in bad spirits, a 5 gp purse is presented to the best player.

The food tends to be simple—roast fowl, usually—but the ale and zzar flow freely. The only reason the common folk don't crowd into the villa until a guest couldn't breathe, let alone take a step in any direction, is that Tespergates is—haunted.

This keeps most Waterdhavians away. Everyone in the city has heard the tragic tale of the Tesper sisters, Silpara and Yulhymbra, who grew up playing with elven friends and proved to have a mastery of magic. Unfortunately, their family hated and feared magic at the time (this

occurred four generations ago). When this was revealed, they were ostracized, and the two sisters were soon slain by assassins sent by a younger brother, who feared they might use their Art to rule the family.

Their ghosts still haunt the house, drifting about its chambers and passages as silent but seemingly intelligent phantoms. If angered, they cast spells that create spectacular images and sounds, but do nothing more than attract attention. They are now considered to be both amusing party entertainment and a sort of household warning system, alerting the family to thieves, vandals, and crimes done in their halls.[6]

---

[5] The villa is #89 on the color map and the *City System* map. Map location #87, mistakenly labeled as a Tesper villa, is actually that of the Eagleshield noble family.

[6] Elminster reveals that a Harper mage, Nleera Tarannath, has been impersonating one of the ghosts for a year or so. This gives her a chance to pass on messages to Harpers at the parties—messages adventurers might well overhear and get drawn into an adventure. The ghosts seem to tolerate and even aid Nleera in her imposture.

The Fiery Flagon

Tavern

This odd, cramped place[7] stands on the west side of Seawatch Street, across the street from the House of Inspired Hands. A relic of the time when sailors lived on the mud flats north of Mount Waterdeep and the rich had yet to migrate north from Castle Waterdeep, it is famous among sailors up and down the Sword Coast, who throng to visit it when they make land at the city.

The Place

I found the wide, iron-barred door of this dark, ramshackle place late at night. I thought it was just on the edge of the ward, not in its depths, but I walked past tall house after tall house.

When I came at last to the Flagon, I couldn't believe how small it was. Inside, it descended in a series of steps, opening into a cellar level larger than is above-ground. Yet there is scarce room for all the fish, flotsam, and ships' gear that crowds the place.

As I went in, water shone back at me from tanks of sullen, gliding blackjaws, moon-faced clearfins, and the dangerous kgrench. All around were nets, blown-glass floats, anchors, and wave-worn figureheads.

The awesome skeleton of an eye of the deep hung overhead. Lamps set in its eye sockets cast an eerie, flickering glow over all.

The Prospect

The interior of the Flagon is not at all the slick, expensive watering hole one expects in Sea Ward—for that, go to Gounar's or the Ship's Wheel. Yet unlike the rough bars of Dock Ward, the place felt safe, like a refuge from the storms of the sea. It even creaks and groans just like a ship when winds blow high. It was full of sailors eager to spin yarns of the sea's mysteries over plentiful drink and the freshest fish to be had in the city.

The Provender

Food in the Flagon means cheese, grapes, bread, and lots and lots of seafood—seafood hauled live and dripping from tanks all around the place, and cooked, swiftly and expertly, in front of your eyes. Sailors can bring their own catch to be cooked, too, but the wise guests leave their palates in the care of the four cooks, grizzled old seamen who know just what will make a particular fish or deep-sea creature taste the best. Try the fried sea snake!

The People

The proprietor is a fat, weathered

---

[7] On the color map, this place is #61.

old man named Ulscaleer Anbersyr. A retired sea captain, he seems to know everyone and is said to have fabulously rich pirate treasures hidden away somewhere in the city. Some told me he quietly supplies pirates with food and gear as well as fencing goods for them.[8]

The Prices

The ruffians and lowlives are kept out by the prices. The splendid but simple meals are 7 sp/plate, and drink goes by the tankard: 3 coppers for rough ale, 5 coppers for good ale, 1 sp for zzar, and then steeply upwards for wine and spirits, up to 14 gp for the best firebelly whiskey.

Ulscaleer is proud of the fact that you can't drink even the finest wine out of anything but a tankard in his place. He has little use for dandified nobles and snobs of any sort.

Travelers' Lore

The Flagon's damp cellars are said to have a hidden tunnel, that winds down a long away by stair and ladder shaft to caverns near to a strange, lawless place in the depths called Skullport.[9] Ulscaleer, I was told, charges 5 gp to open the stoutly barred, magically protected[10] door that seals the cellar off from the top of the

tunnel. All openings are performed by a half-dozen armed men. Ulscaleer keeps some sort of magical wand at the ready during such openings. Much illicit trade passes this way, with the Lords of Waterdeep being none the wiser.

I also heard something about a Sea Ghost—a dripping wraith of a drowned pirate, festooned with seaweed, that pursues those who meddle in the affairs of pirates. Regular patrons told me, however, such talk was just nonsense put about to scare off the overly inquisitive.[11]

---

[8] Elminster says these tales are true.
[9] And so, he affirms, is this tale.
[10] It turns spells as a *ring of spell turning*, sounding an alarm gong whenever this defense is activated.
[11] Elminster's not so sure this is only empty words!

Other Places of Interest in Sea Ward

If one tires of opulence and isn't hungry to brave the dangers of the sinister Dragon Tower of the wizard Maaril or the fool-swallowing Blue Alley, what else is there to do in Sea Ward? Perhaps, gossip? Yes, the Street of Whispers didn't get that name for nothing. But gossip's a game visitors play to learn what to see and where to go. One has to be a resident to really *enjoy* gossip.

You can also shop. You can spend a *lot* of money very quickly and easily in Sea Ward. We've all seen overpriced goods, so I've tried to pick out some outstanding or useful establishments.

Shops

Aurora's Realms Shop "Singing Dolphin" Catalogue Counter

This is the Sea Ward outlet of the famous Faerun-wide all goods retail chain. It occupies the third shopfront north from the corner of the Street of the Singing Dolphin and Grimwald's Way, on the west side of the Dolphin.

It has six guards who work in shifts of three and three, and who wear sparkling weapons

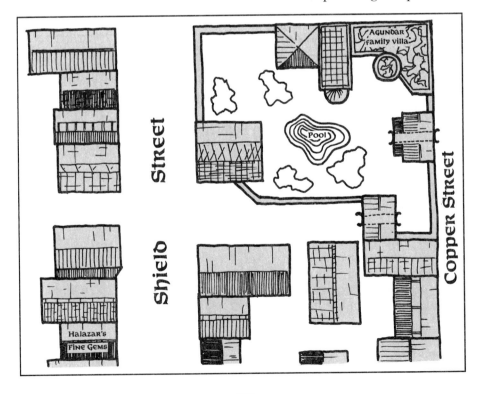

and finery; a handsome male counter clerk of impeccable taste and great tact, Orloth Theldarin; and a service mage of many rings, airs, and grand entrances, Saerghon "the Magnificent" Alir. Saerghon thinks himself the greatest mage in Waterdeep, but hasn't even opened all the tomes and scrolls he's acquired down through the years.

Halazar's Fine Gems

This shop has a glistening black front kept shiny with magic. In its center gleams a single sparkling gem the size of a man's head (an illusion). Those touching the gem feel a wrenching shock as the magic temporarily drains them of a small amount of energy to sustain itself.[12]

Inside are truly the finest gems one can find for sale, exquisitely cut and mounted, displayed in glass cases with severe simplicity, and sold for precisely *four times* what they'd fetch anywhere else. Waterdeep being what it is, the gems *do* sell, as folk proudly boast of how much they paid. The security[13] arrangements are confidential, but powerful.

---

[12] Halazar's is location #50 on the color map. The illusion magic drains 1 hp, which can be recovered in any normal manner, to power itself.

[13] Rumors of gargoyles, Elminster hints, are not unfounded.

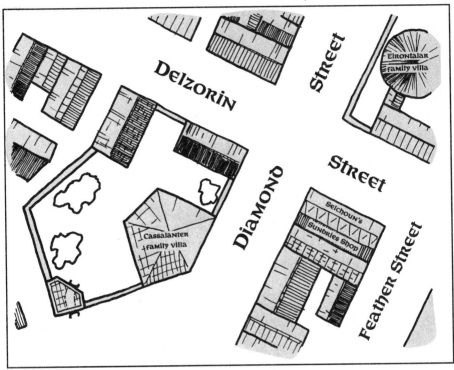

Proprietor: Stromquil Halazar, Guildmaster of the Jewellers' Guild is the proprietor. He is a tall, aristocratic, sneering man of soft words and watchful eyes.

Selchoun's Sundries Shop

This shop has those tourist knickknacks that travelers swiftly grow to hate (such as toy wooden shields emblazoned with the words: "I Saw Waterdeep—and Survived!") but it is also the only place in the entire ward where you can buy string, and thongs, and kindling, and flint, and clay pipes, and carrysacks, and—you catch my thrust? Very useful to the visitor.

Proprietor: Osbrin Selchoun, a fat, very short man with a rolling gait and a cheerful, huffing nature, is the proprietor.[14]

Taverns

Gounar's Tavern

This is one of the most brightly lit taverns you'll ever see. It gleams and sparkles with mirrored glass and cut glass faux

---

[14] Location #85 on the color map.

gems everywhere to catch and throw back the many *glowing globes* that hang in the air. It's bright because citizens go here to be seen and to survey each other as much as to relax over a drink.

The words *slick* and *on display* come to mind. On the other hand, if you want to be noticed in Waterdhavian high society, this is *the* place. Expect to pay 6 gp/glass for drinks and double that for quality wines. If bought by the bottle, drinks are 25 gp and up.

Proprietor: Doblin Gounar is the proprietor. Doblin is a coldly egotistical hard nose—the sort you hate on sight.[15]

The Ship's Wheel

Located on a corner just inside West Gate, this place is a little less high-nosed and a lot less clean and bright than Gounar's. It's also probably the safest tavern you'll ever see. Old men come here to watch each other's hair fall out over drinks that cost 4 gp/glass or 10 gp/bottle, with double those prices for fine wines.

Adorned in the front lobby with a gleaming ship's wheel large enough for a titan (of all the city's taverns, only Gounar's and the Wheel *have* front lobbies), this is the place for those with too much money or too many years to want to go to Gounar's.

Proprietor: Olhin Shalut is old, affable, and full of himself, but wealthy. He is always armed with a lot of magic items.[16]

Inns

Dacer's Inn

Located south of the temple of Gond on Seawatch Street, this fine old inn caters to rich sailors who want to stagger to bed from the Fiery Flagon as late as possible and to the constant trade of pilgrims and others visiting the temple. As a result, it is a very prosperous place that is well-built and incorporates all the innovations and improvements that Gondfolk suggest, such as dumbwaiter shafts that bring hot food to each room, sliding bolts recessed into every room door, alarm gongs on each floor, pumped water on tap in each room, and suchlike, and avoids a lot of the more ostentatious frills that some places north of Mount Waterdeep indulge in.

Dacer's is a quiet, luxurious place to stay, and is almost worth the 8 gp/night per head it costs to stay there (stabling and simple meals are included). Only water and zzar—at 12 gp/bottle—are available to drink. Dacer's will send runners for food you order from street vendors or cooks

---

[15] Location #55 on the color map.
[16] Location #51 on the color map.

61

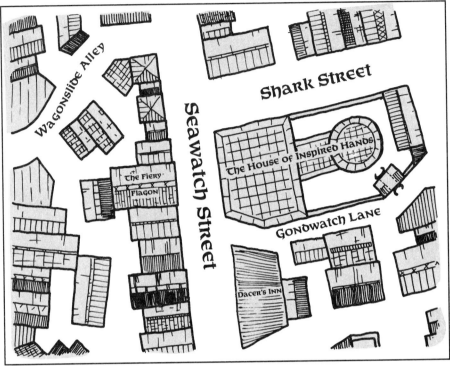

elsewhere, and have it delivered to your room, a rare luxury that is most appreciated on wet days!

Proprietress: Amasanna Vumendir is a dusky-skinned, agile hostess of few words but a keen intellect. She orders her staff about with hand gestures.[17]

Maerghoun's Inn

Located on the west side of the Street of Whispers, just north of Diamond Street, this old, opulent inn of scented purple hangings, flickering lamps, and dark wood paneling is much favored by young couples and by Waterdeep's paid escorts. No food or drink is available, but you are free to bring it in or have it delivered. Utmost discretion is observed. Each room has inner curtains, so that staff can bring things or do things in one part of a room without seeing or being seen by the guests in another part of the same room.

Maerghoun's is notable for its large round beds, complimentary purple silken house robes, and soundproofing. Extreme privacy is the watch word. The inn is used by many to conduct sensitive business deals.

---

[17] Location #59 on the color map.

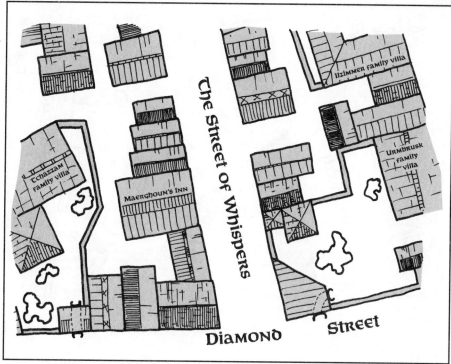

Proprietor: Yuth Sammardoun, the proprietor, is a cynical, crafty man with white hair but dark eyebrows who's seen it all—and lived because he said little about it and continues to do so.[18]

Pilgrims' Rest

Located in the triangular northwestern angle of the intersection of Diamond Street and Satchel Alley, this is the humblest of Sea Ward's inns and the cheapest. It's usually crammed with faithful worshippers who have come to the city to visit one of the temples (hence its name). There's actually nothing special about this place—which means that it would be a first-class inn anywhere else in the whole of Faerun. One can get a private room for 9 gp/night, with stabling and a solid evening meal included in the price. A two-share (two double beds, usually rented to two couples) is 6 gp/bed per night. A common room (8 beds or more) is 4 gp/night per person.

Proprietor: Balaghast Brightlingar is a grim, hard-working ex-warrior, whose gruff manner conceals a sincerely kind heart,

---

[18] Location #58 on the color map.

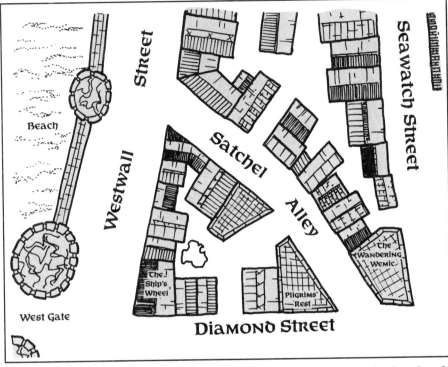

Beach

Westwall Street

Satchel Alley

Seawatch Street

The Wandering Wemic

The Ship's Wheel

Pilgrims' Rest

West Gate

Diamond Street

eager to lend a helping hand to anyone in need.[19]

The Wandering Wemic

Located in the angle between an alley and two streets, this large, recently opened inn offers ample, airy, well-lit rooms, new furnishings, clean surroundings, high rates, and an efficient, numerous staff—including bouncers to keep undesirables out. The 10 gp/room per day rate includes stabling, a valet service for cleaning and repairing clothes and boots, and a bottle of wine per head per evening, but no food. It provides a good place for wealthy merchants who want no trouble over a place to stay.

Proprietor: A big, easygoing man, Cheth Thanion is far more alert than he seems. He never forgets a face or anyone doing him out of money.[20]

Festhalls

The House of Purple Silks

Standing on the west side of

---

[19] Location #52 on the color map.
[20] Location #53 on the color map.

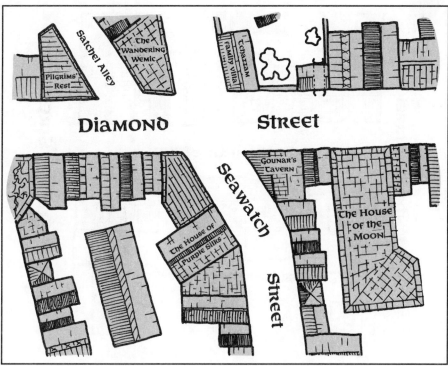

Seawatch Street, just south of its intersection with Diamond Street, this is one of the most famous pleasure palaces of the Sword Coast. For decades, its name has been synonymous with decadent dalliance. Its trademark is the sheer purple silks worn by its ladies.

Inside, it's a series of warm, carpeted rooms crowded with cushions, bold guests, and bolder staff ladies. Not a place for the bashful. Highly recommended. Rumored to have contraband hidden inside some cushions, and under certain areas of carpet.

Proprietress: The proprietress, Jathaliira Thindrel, is petite, pert, and always bustling about. A guest who insisted on her company at his every visit described her as having, "a shrewish temper overlaid by a passionate nature." She is in her forties, but still energetic and good-looking, and is reputed to be a shrewd investor and very rich.[21]

Alleys

Sea Ward's alleys are the playground of the rich, famous, reckless, and utterly undisci-

---

[21] Location #54 on the color map. Elminster says Jathaliira is *very* rich—and a close friend of Khelben "Blackstaff" Arunsun. She can call on magical aid whenever desired and also has a hired band of fists (a dozen bouncers).

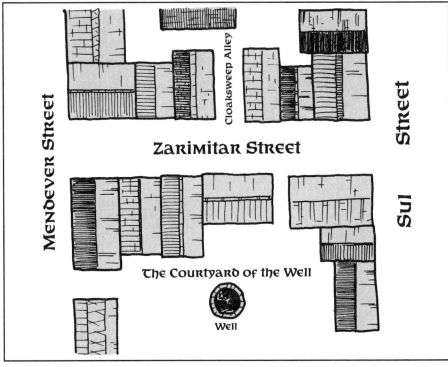

Cloaksweep Alley

Zarimitar Street

Mendever Street

Sul Street

The Courtyard of the Well

Well

plined—but they are clean and either short or wide, offering the armed and careful person plenty of fighting or running room.

Cloaksweep Alley

This wide, very short passage runs north off Zarimitar Street due north of the Courtyard of the Well. Its name comes from an incident involving the long-ago wizard Milist Samblin of the Many Cloaks—who, when set upon by thieves in this alley, used a cloak that swallowed them whole in one flap. They were never seen again![22]

Today, the alley is notable as the usual vending place of a nameless old man who sells ear oil. Made of the fat of adders boiled down into oil, it is thought by many to be a cure for deafness when poured into the ears. I shudder at the very thought.

The Ghostwalk

This crescentiform alley branches

---

[22] Elminster believes the cloak was a magical device that *teleported* those caught in its folds elsewhere—too far away for the thieves to ever return to Waterdeep. He also warns strongly against trying the ear oil!

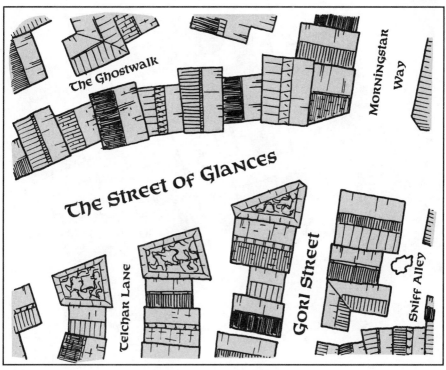

off the southern half of Murlpar Street and curls around the interior of the city block it's found in, providing delivery access and garbage storage for the businesses and homes located here. It boasts several shadow-tops (climbing trees that local children spend much time playing in). It's also known to be the place where the ghost of a long-ago noble rake, a harmless but frightening phantom, walks. He carries a drawn sword and whispers, "I've killed him! I've killed him!" as he staggers along, his own fresh blood welling out and down him until he's entirely covered—and fades away.

Gondwatch Lane

This alley runs along the southern wall of the House of Inspired Hands, Waterdeep's temple of Gond. The temple's main entry gate opens onto it, and it is named for its use by locals to watch the latest explosive or otherwise entertaining results of inventions dedicated to Gond.

If inventions seem too dangerous to operate within the temple, they're often tried here. Things can get quite dangerous! Locals are generally unconcerned, and stand watching while food vendors circulate among them.

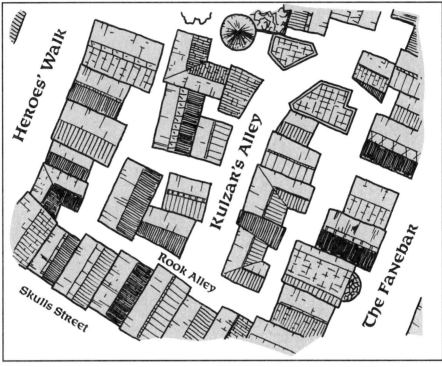

Kulzar's Alley

This alley runs south from the Wallway to join with Rook Alley. It is named for a famous local sailor, who dwelt here before his death some 70 winters ago. Kulzar was master of a ship appropriately known as the *Lost Luck*, which ran aground on shoals near Waterdeep one stormy night and broke up. Kulzar, a man of terrific strength, swam his personal cabinhold treasure ashore chest by chest through the crashing surf, and is reputed to have hidden it somewhere in or under this alley.

Many have looked, but Kulzar's gems and coins have never been found. Any folk who try digging for them will attract the attention of the city watch, who'll require that they replace the paving stones when they're done and forbid any tunneling towards the city wall. Diggers will also attract the attention of certain old sailors, who'll shadow the treasure-seekers in hopes that they'll discover Kulzar's "jools" and can then be robbed.

Moarinskoar Alley

This alleyway curls around the

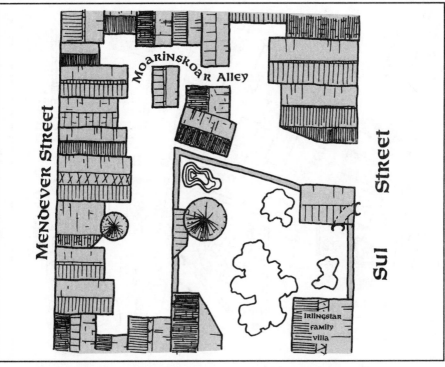

interior of the city block bounded by Mendever, Vondil, Sul, and Delzorin Streets, and is named for a famous ancestor of the Irlingstar noble family, whose villa is partly encircled by the alley. Moarinskoar rebelled against the family hopes and dictates, and ran away to sea to become a famous shipmaster. After a long, successful trading career on the Sword Coast, he turned pirate—and is said to sail his ship still, as a wight commanding a zombie crew. *The Moonwind*, his fast caravel,[23] is now a ghost ship, still seen scud-

ding along the Sword Coast. Moarinskoar tries to board all the ships he meets. If a ship is bound for Waterdeep, he does not attack, but demands that it deliver a message to the Irlingstars: "Tell my mother I love her, but I'm not ready to come home yet." Local lore whispers that when he does come back, this peaceful alley will become a killing ground haunted by his undead crew!

Moonstar Alley

This back alley curls around the

---

[23] Ship types and statistics are detailed on page 36 of FR5 *The Savage Frontier*. The Irlingstar villa is #93 on the color map.

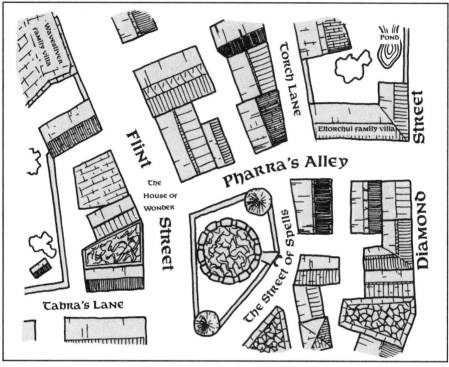

walled villa[24] of the noble family for which it is named. Of old, Waterdeep's first temple to Selune was located on this site. Known as the High House of Stars, it was burned to the ground by raiding worshippers of Bane. Selune's faithful never set foot on the desecrated ground again, building their present temple a block to the west. Local rumor holds that the cellars of the burnt temple still hide magic and wealth, buried under burned rubble—and that they can be reached by stairs and shafts now hidden under the paving stones of this alleyway.

Pharra's Alley

This alleyway is named for the first magistress of the House of Wonder (the temple to Midnight, formerly to Mystra, which the alley passes), who died more than 120 years ago. It is a busy shortcut route used by merchants and their delivery carts, and is often crowded with would-be wizards coming to the House of Wonder to try and hire on as an apprentice to a wizard. Some are anxious to impress everyone with their magic or are just very, very nervous—and they have been

---

[24] Location #66 on the color map.

known to let fly wildly with magic, endangering passersby.

They vanish hurriedly, though, when the Circle of Skulls appears. This spellhaunt, as wizards call it, is all that is left of some early priests of Mystra who tried to devise their own means of immortality—and achieved only a lich-like state.

These eerie skulls are always seen floating in a circle, arguing among themselves in hollow, echoing voices. They spit spells from their empty mouths or hurl beams of fire from their empty eye sockets when angered by those they encounter, but are unpredictable and may help someone with information instead of attacking. They seem tied to Pharra's Alley, and never appear anywhere else in the city, though the information they pass on indicates that they must be able to see and hear things in other parts of Waterdeep.

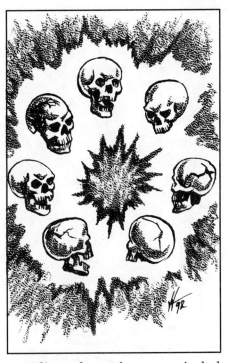

Prayer Alley

Running south off Aureenar Street at its eastern end, this alleyway hooks around inside a city block to parallel Phastal Street, to the south, for much of its length. It is named for those caught in it in more lawless days by thieves. Such unfortunates didn't have a prayer of escape due to the length of the alley and its lack of side exits.

A disused warehouse encircled by it (located just east of its lone tree) is sometimes magically replaced by an infamous vanishing shop that deals in magic, spell components, weird artifacts, and objects from other worlds and planes. This place, rarely seen these days, is known as Whistlewink's Revenge, after the crazed old wizard who runs it.

Roguerun Alley

This narrow alley runs up the interior of the westernmost city block on the north side of the Street of Glances. A famous inn, the House of the Flying Horse,

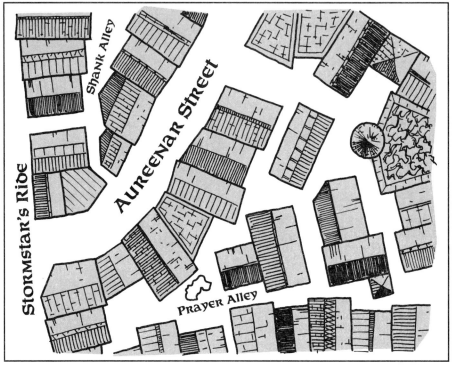

once backed onto this alley. The inn was used by smugglers as a clearinghouse for fencing stolen goods and was ultimately destroyed in a spell duel between rival wizards. A treasure of unclaimed smugglers' loot is still said to lie hidden somewhere around or under this alley, which got its name from the number of times smugglers ran full tilt down it to escape city guardsmen raiding the inn.

Rook Alley

This alley, just north of Skulls Street, curls around the inside of the city block entered by Kulzar's Alley.

It is named for a notable thief, the Rook, who flourished about 50 years ago and had his secret headquarters here. He died fighting in it when discovered by officers of the city guard. The Rook's hold was a series of old crypts—the old burial grounds that give Skulls Street its name— that he tunneled down to from this alley. The tunnel, blocked off with stones, is said to still exist, along with his treasure. It is guarded by undead from the crypt who attacked the last folk brave enough to unseal the tunnel.

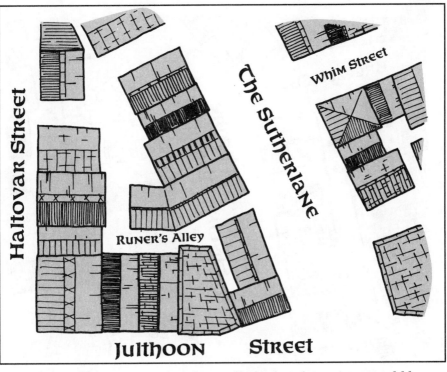

Haltovar Street

Whim Street

The Sutherlane

Runer's Alley

Julthoon Street

Runer's Alley

This short, three-branched passage winds through the triangular city block that stands between Julthoon Street, Haltover Street, and the Sutherlane. It is named for the Runer, a minstrel who slept here for years.

A wizard once mistakenly thought Runer's pipes were enchanted and his song a magical attack, so he used a *dispel magic* on the minstrel. It stripped away Runer's magical disguise, revealing him to be a missing noblewoman, Shrylla Manthar.

This eccentric free spirit had fled when her parents told her whom to marry, and escaped discovery for almost 30 years. Unmasked, she refused to return to her house and station and lived on in this alley, becoming known as Shrylla of the Spiders. Her long, fantastically coifed hair hid not only needle daggers and lockpicks, but a poisonous spider trained to defend her.

Feeling death coming, she climbed Mount Waterdeep to see one last dawn and died there. Her body was not discovered for months among the rocks—and the spider lived on in her skull, using one empty, staring eye socket as its door.

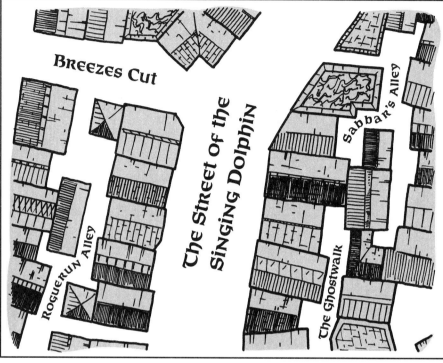

Breezes Cut

The Street of the Singing Dolphin

Sabbar's Alley

Roguerun Alley

The Ghostwalk

Sabbar's Alley

This tiny, dogleg alleyway opens eastwards off the Street of the Singing Dolphin, just south of Aureenar Street.[25] It is named for Sabbar, an unscrupulous wizard who dwelt at its innermost end until he disappeared, some 80 winters ago.

Sabbar was known to hurl fireballs at boys who ventured into this alley to play, and was infamous for once maliciously transforming buckets of raw, live fishbait worms into the sem-blance of well-cooked, spiced beef roasts, just before guests were served at a feast.

Nowadays, this alley is the gathering place for a local street gang, who can sometimes be hired to watch or follow a person by anyone bold enough to contact and pay them.

Satchel Alley

This shortcut runs northwest from Diamond Street. It was named for the bags of gems and valuables that jewelers used to

---

[25] On the FR1 *Waterdeep and the North* map, Aureenar Street isn't labeled. It's the major street south of and curving parallel to the Street of Lances, in the extreme northern tip of Waterdeep. It's shown on the *City System* maps and the color map in this accessory.

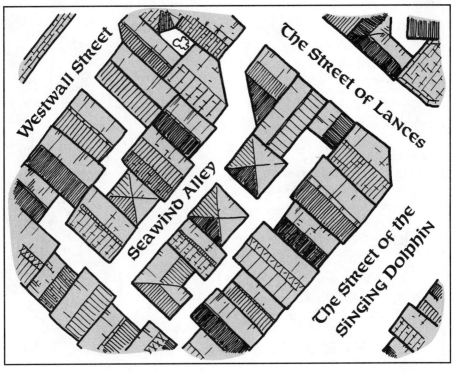

carry along it before waiting thieves made the trip too dangerous (in the days when Waterdeep had a Thieves Guild). It's now a place where the coaches, carts, and mounts of the travelers staying at the inns all around it load and unload their passengers and cargo, and as a result is well-paved with dung.

Seawind Alley

Running south from the Street of Lances, this alleyway offers rear access to the buildings in its city block. Usually shrouded in sea mist, it once led to a now-vanished inn, the Banshee at Bay (other, unrelated inns also bear this name in Cormyr and in Amn). The inn was destroyed, over a hundred winters ago, after everyone inside it was found dead of some unknown disease. Their restless spirits are still said to haunt the alley, though few have seen anything eerie in recent years.

Shank Alley

This alley[26] circles the interior of a triangular city block north of

---

[26] On the *City System* maps, this alley is mislabeled as Shark Alley.

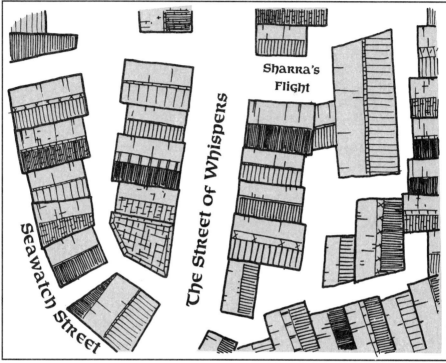

Aureenar Street and east of Stormstar's Ride. It is named for an antiquated sort of knife known as a shank, wielded by thieves who used to gather in this alley.

Today, it is a crowded place stacked with fish crates where many city birds gather to feed. Local youths and visitors skilled with a sling or hurled sticks and stones kill the birds to sell to cooks throughout the city or for their own meals.

Sharra's Flight

This wide courtyard opens east off the Street of Whispers and connects with Moonstar Alley. It is named for Sharra of the Invisible Dragon, the famous archmage who roused Neverwinter in a long-ago coastal war by using a spell to bring her cry into every bedroom of the city: "Awake, and to arms! Awake, or the princes of Sundul will come for us in our beds!" Due to her efforts the forces of Neverwinter rose up, defended their city against the naval attack, and followed their foes home to destroy the Calishite realm of Sundul.

Sharra created this route when still an apprentice to

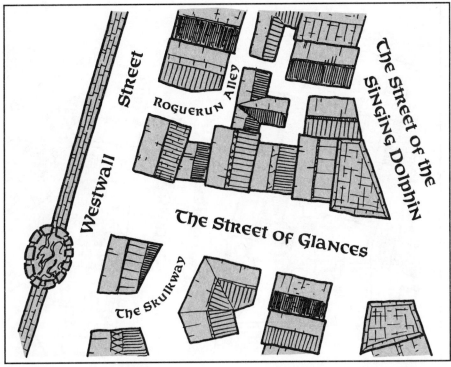

Street

Roguerun Alley

Westwall

The Street of the Singing Dolphin

The Street of Glances

The Skulkway

escape being caught in a magical battle between rival mages of power. She blasted down a building and ran through the space she'd just cleared. The open space has remained that way ever since. It is today used by several street vendors, who cram their stalls into it, selling candies, sweets, exotic liqueurs, eel pie and rare delicacies of the deep, and cut-rate jewelry to passersby.

The Skulkway

This short passage cuts across the southern corner where the Street of Glances meets Westwall Street. It was literally used to skulk past the noses of the city guard when they established a stationary watch at the cross-roads against smugglers. At the time, the Skulkway was occupied by a building—or so all but the smugglers thought. It was actually an empty shell, with holes in each wall large enough for a cart to be driven through. The holes were covered by illusions created by an enterprising wizard, and during the day doors were rolled across the openings under the cloaking illusion to avoid unintentional discovery of the magic.

This lasted until one day the building vanished—illusions,

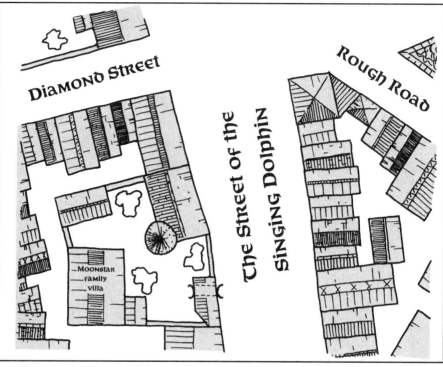

stonework, roof and all. Some claim the smugglers fought amongst themselves, and destroyed the place. Others think the Lords—or a powerful wizard acting for them—made the building vanish. The cause of the disappearance was a hot topic for arguments among local citizens. None knew the truth.[27]

Sniff Alley

From the north end of Gorl Street, this alley curves east and then north to meet the Street of Glances. Named for the smell of the fishbone pile that was located here until the Lords tightened laws about garbage, this is today a pleasant, paved back way with a tree, benches for relaxing under its shade, and a small handpump of cool water for public use. It's a good spot for the visitor to rest in for awhile—but it also seems to be a favorite meeting place for whispered conversations amongst shady characters. Try very hard to look uninterested and hum or yawn to indicate that you're not listening if you're getting the eye.

---

[27] Elminster told us, with a gentle smile, "We should ask Khelben about that. He grows restless from time to time, like all the rest of us."

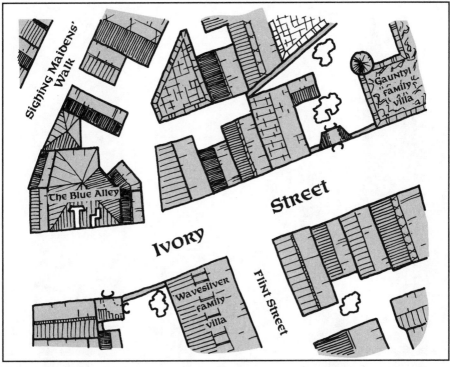

Labels on map: Sighing Maidens' Walk · Gauntyl family villa · The Blue Alley · Ivory Street · Flint Street · Wavesilver family villa

Wagonslide Alley

This alley links Westwall Street with Seawatch Street through the block bounded by Diamond Street on the south and Grimwald's Way on the north. Its name comes from the steep, slippery slope leading up it from the west that has made many a wagon slip down it in wet or icy weather. In winter, sea rime is almost unbelievably fast to freeze here.

To improve traction, the stones of this street are laid loose, so they sit unevenly. Tripping is easy if you go too fast or don't look down. Under many of the stones are small hollows or pits, some undoubtedly dug by children playing in the street. Locals told me that not only are messages often left under certain stones, but some of them conceal magical weapons left ready by thieves who operate in the city from time to time. These are invisible weapons cached in plain sight under the stones—but, since they are invisible, no one can see them. Horridly clever, eh?

It is certain that whenever I went up or down this alley, I could feel the heavy gaze of eyes from windows above, where old men sit seemingly all day with nothing to do.

North Ward

orth Ward is the quietest ward of the city. This district is home to most of Waterdeep's wealthier middle classes and lesser noble families. It is an area of quiet neighborhoods dominated by private, walled noble villas. Little of interest meets the visitor's eye, but local talk says much plotting and partying goes on behind closed doors in this reach of the city—intrigue that affects trade, wars, and wealth as far away as Thay. Yet, unless you come to the city already in the know as a member of this or that guild, cabal, merchant alliance, or underground network, there is actually little in North Ward for you to see.

Aside from folk strolling to or from their homes or private parties, this area practically shuts down at dusk. It is often so quiet that a man talking in the street can be heard by others outdoors several streets away!

Watch patrols are frequent, but are polite and lightly armed.[1] Rowdiness and street violence of any sort are not tolerated in this ward unless one is noble or well-dressed and drunk. Those who engage in such activities are quickly and roughly handled by the city watch.

Landmarks

The only widely known ward landmark is the Gentle Mermaid,[2] whose fame as a gambling hall has spread up and down the Sword Coast. A more interesting evening can be spent at the Misty Beard tavern,[3] a refined but often lively drinking spot staffed largely by exotic and monstrous beings from all over the Realms. The ward is dominated by the ornate walls, spires, wrought iron work, and balconies of many walled villas and grand houses, but only the lucky or privileged visitor sees more of these than can be glimpsed from the street. Two noble families, the Hawkwinters and the Roaring-

---

[1] City watch patrols are detailed on page 17 of FR1 *Waterdeep and the North.* In this ward, four-sword detachments (more often female officers than in any other ward of the city) pass a given point about every 15 minutes, and look in to a tavern or inn dining room about every 40 minutes.

As detailed on pages 17 and 23 of the *City System* set booklet, the city guard also patrols North Ward, in six-man detachments. Typical patrol details are as given therein, on page 23. Reinforcements will be a dozen LG hm F3s to F6s clad in chain mail and armed with maces, long swords, daggers, slings, and a polearm appropriate to the situation.

Guard patrols pass a given street location about every 50 minutes, but appear in 1d6 minutes when a city watch patrol blows a warning horn in this ward.

[2] Location #114 on the color map.

[3] Location #155 on the color map.

horns, often give large, splendid parties at their villas.[4] I'll give you what I can recall of these splendid houses. My memory is rather spotty, though, as the delicious wines served were both plentiful and strong!

Only two guildhalls stand in this ward: the House of Crystal[5] and the House of Healing.[6] The House of Crystal houses the headquarters of the Guild of Glassblowers, Glaziers, & Speculum-Makers, where one can buy the finest crystal balls and mirrors, ranging in prices from 1 sp for a curved ladies' handglass to 600 gp for a sphere of perfect crystal as large around as a small shield. The House of Healing is the headquarters for the Guild of Apothecaries & Physicians, who do very well here as an emergency hospital and vendor of medicines and potions. The House of Healing is a place many tragically diseased folk or their agents come specially to Waterdeep to visit.

Several shopkeepers in this wealthy, clean district, however, are heads—spokemasters—of their respective guilds. Darion Sulmest of Sulmest's Splendid Shoes & Boots[7] is the public contact of the Order of Cobblers & Corvisers. (His boots and shoes *are* splendid, too. I'm wearing a warm, springy pair of his lifelong swashboots right now, and they are worth every single copper of the 12 gp they cost me. Pairs not guaranteed to last as long as the wearer can be had for 8 gp or less.) Shalrin Maerados of Maerados Fine Furs[8] is Gentleman Keeper of the Solemn Order of Recognized Furriers & Woolmen. And Relchoz Hriiat of Hriiat Fine Pastries[9] speaks for the Bakers' Guild.

There are also whispers about stolen goods (and even smuggling!). The largest and most exotic things, they say—ships and golems, for example—can be bought and sold through a certain noble resident in the ward. I was unable to contact him, and dare not reveal his name here, for fear of spreading malicious, "bladed" tonguework. Discreet word can be left for him at the Grinning Lion tavern.[10]

---

[4] The Hawkwinter family villa is #151 on the color city map, and the house of the Roaringhorns is #145.

[5] On the color city map, the House of Crystal is #104. Its mirror-bedecked facade dominates the west side of Copper Street, just north of the Market.

[6] Location #117 on the color map.

[7] The shop is #111 on the color map.

[8] Location #112 on the color map.

[9] Location #134 on the color map. In all cases, relevant guilds and noble families and something of their current doings, interests or fees, and current heads, are covered in the *Waterdeep and the North* sourcebook.

[10] Location #135 on the color map. A certain fat man sitting on a barstool almost every moment the Lion is open, Hala Myrt, is eyes and ears for the noble Orlpar Husteem, who deals largely in spices, scents, wines, and various potions. His house is #160 on the color map.

The Gentle Mermaid

*Tavern, Gambling House, &
Festhall*

Like the unrelated Blushing
Mermaid festhall in Dock Ward,
the Gentle Mermaid is a place of
luxury, offering no accommodation save for a few dungeon cells
reserved for debtors, sharpers,
and thieves. It *does* boast the
largest and richest gambling
rooms in all Waterdeep—perhaps
in all Faerun.[11]

Its large, carpeted central
gaming chamber has a soaring,
pavilion-like roof, through which
slowly shifting lights play in a
soft, continually changing show.
The room holds two dozen or so
circular, cloth-covered tables,
where Waterdeep's wealthiest
play at dice and cards.[12]

The atmosphere here is refined, relaxed, clean, and free of
danger. Many an old noble
matron plays solitaire, or two
dowagers may sit and gossip, sip
their favorite drinks, and both
play solitaire.

The attentive staff of over 20
bouncers, reinforced by unseen
but watching wizards[13] (via
wizard eyes), ensures that guests
aren't disturbed by thieves,
ruffians, beggars, or harassment
of any sort. This is a place to see
and be seen, to meet people, but
not to do business—unless it can
be managed without bothering
anyone, or you'll be ejected.

The Place

Alone in the interior of a city
block bounded by the High Road
and Copper, Sulmoor, and Hassantyr's Streets, the Gentle Mermaid is
a huge stone pile of turreted and
balconied splendor. Its exterior is
the result of several rich merchant owners with more wealth
than taste adding their ideas onto
an already ostentatious but abandoned noble house.

Within, everything is carpets,
tapestries, curtains, and hangings.
Soft lights, subtle perfumes, and
magical heat dominate the rooms
and passages to make the Mermaid a place of cozy warmth,
active the night and day through,
with evening the busiest time.
Many come to lose money at the
gaming tables—or spend it to
enjoy the company of the charming and beautiful escorts of both
genders on the Mermaid's staff.

The upper floors have been

---

[11] On the color city map, the Gentle Mermaid is #114.

[12] For an unusually quiet view of this chamber, see page 63 of the *Knight of the Living Dead*
adventure gamebook.

[13] These wizards are senior members of the Watchful Order (mages of 8th level or higher), hired at
the princely rate of 77 gp/shift. A day and a night consists of four six-hour shifts. There are two wizards
per shift, equipped with wands, rings, scrolls, and items they expect to be effective in quickly and
decisively quelling any disturbances—such as hotheaded outlander mages who start magical duels.

turned into a labyrinth of lounges, cozy bowers, private rooms, and secret passages which are used by staff and by certain famous clients who wish to avoid being seen. At least one such passage enters the Mermaid underground, running from the rear of a nearby shop. I couldn't learn which shop.

The Prospect

The Mermaid prides itself on serene, above-snobbery luxury in creating a home that nobles will prefer to their own. Unpleasantness of any sort is stamped out, swiftly and ruthlessly, and the wealthy are encouraged to spend as much time losing money at the gaming tables as they wish. The less wealthy are encouraged to drift about watching—before being deftly chosen by escorts who steer them upstairs to a lounge where each guest can choose a companion to while away a pleasant time with.

The Provender

Table fees are a gold piece a seat. This entitles a guest to a starter glass of whatever sparkling vintage is being served at that table and to as many snacks from passing silver platters as they're bold enough to take. The canapés consist of crab rolls, smoked salmon and silverfin daggers (slivers of fish, served on slices of

lemon or lime), pickle and cheese skewers, olive or nut cups, and spicy sausage finger rolls. They are utterly delicious!

Wine and spirits of all sorts may be had, but they are dear: 1 gp/glass or 12 gp/bottle, regardless of what is being drunk. Escorts sell their time and company for 60 gp for an hour to 10 times that for an entire evening, depending on the escort's fame, whim, and beauty. The Mermaid takes 20% of all fees collected.

The People

The Mermaid has over 40 efficient, hard-working escorts, a dozen of whom are male. In the past at least one doppleganger has been ferreted out of their midst. The Mermaid's owner now interviews and auditions each escort carefully. Beautiful folk of wealthy or refined breeding and merry, sensual natures are desired. Waterdeep attracts many such folk—and the Mermaid ignores the past of any staff, so long as they perform suitably while on duty.

There are two dozen or so security staff (bouncers), under the command of Housemaster Eiraklon Marimmatar, who sits with the watch wizards while his second in command, Ulthlo Relajatyr, marshals and directs the staff on the floor. There's a very old Mermaid joke: "More

than just looking? Look down, then. The escort on the floor will help you."

The Mermaid was founded and for a long time owned by Lady Shaeroon Brossfeather, a colorful old dowager of strong will, wit, and intelligence who sponsored poets and other free thinkers and speakers, had many dear—er—friends, and backed unusual causes, getting herself loved by the common folk and disowned by her kin in the process. She died recently. Ownership of the Mermaid passed to the mysterious Jhant Daxer, a caravan owner and moneylender little known in the city.[14]

The Prices

A guest who only gambles for part of an evening can expect to pay out 12 to 15 gp in fees and usually lose two to three times that. Large wins are rare. Small wins occur just often enough to keep guests coming back for more.

Tipping is common. Some regular guests give triple a table fee to get a seat at their favorite table. To get a table alone or to get control of who sits there, such as the noble matrons playing solitaire, costs 14 gp, but that includes a personal waiter or waitress whose gender is of the guest's choice. To get the use of one of the curtained, private

---

[14] Jhant is only a front for Xanathar, the beholder crime lord (detailed in FR1 *Waterdeep and The North*). Anyone mixing with him or the Mermaid will arouse Xanathar's entire organization.

gaming side chambers costs double that. Each holds one table. A dozen of these private gaming side chambers open off the main gaming room.

Travelers' Lore

Several tales cling to the Mermaid involving guests who have mysteriously disappeared—and a few lucky winners who staggered out burdened by many gold pieces. The two most interesting tales are also the darkest: the death card and the haunted chessmen. These are not popular topics of discussion in the Mermaid. Those inquiring over-

boldly can expect to swiftly see the street outside.

The death card is still drawn from time to time, though no staff member ever puts it in a deck, nor has it a place in any game. It is thought to be the result of an ancient wizard's curse, and consists of a card that appears in any deck used in the Mermaid. Its face consists of a laughing skull on a black field.

A chilling laugh is heard as the card is uncovered, and a spectral, cowled figure rises up from the card, flying about and swinging a scythe. It attacks the being who drew the card, and its weapon *can* slay. The touch of almost any spell makes it and the card disappear. The watch wizards are always alert for the appearance of this Hooded Death.[15]

The haunted chessmen are now destroyed or hidden away. They are a set of pieces of unknown origin, used in the strange game brought to Waterdeep by wizards who learned it, Realmslore generally attests, on other worlds. These chessmen moved about the board of their own accord when unattended. In their own eerie games, captured pieces toppled over and changed forms to resemble living folk—whose death they foretold. What animated these grim gaming pieces, and where they are now, none can or will say.

---

[15] The Hooded Death's powers change from time to time, but most who have seen it say it seems to be a wraith (an undead creature— see MC1) armed with a scythe (2d4 damage, 6' arc reach).

Hawkwinter House

The city villa of this quietly powerful Waterdhavian noble family[16] is the site of many splendid parties.

On a strategic corner location in a block of fine merchants' houses and luxury apartments,[17] the walled Hawkwinter compound consists of three spired, balconied stone houses made in the likeness of miniature castles—with crenelations, gargoyle-shaped downspouts and arched windows only found in the uppermost reaches of the walls. The only exceptions to this design lie in the tall-peaked tiled roofs, which shed copious snow down onto passersby in winter. Some folk believe the downspouts are real gargoyles that the family can release to defend their home. These are kept immobile by strong enchantments controlled by the Hawkwinters.

These miniature castles are linked by winding garden paths, overhung by many old, carefully tended trees, hung with lamps.

When parties are thrown, many-hued *driftglobes* light every corner of the gloomy halls, passages, and cellars of the castles, and perfume is added to the lamps amid the trees.

Musicians play in chambers here and there, and mages are hired to perform minor illusions—either of languid beauty in the early evening or of mystery, danger, and spice later, when those who celebrate until the dawn chase each other around the balconied rooms and dungeons. Oh, yes, these castles have dungeon cells. They cells are very clean and lit with red torches for show, but functional—and, I

---

[16] Traditionally a strong arm of the city guard and troops fielded by the Lords of Waterdeep, the Hawkwinters hunt and breed highly prized war horses on extensive country estates north of nearby Amphail. They spend much of their time there, and make most of their money selling horses in peacetime. In times of war, they serve as mercenary generals and guides, hire out their own cavalry, and work as high-priced, lightning-fast troop outfitters.

Their best mounts are black with silver manes and tails. A rare few have blue eyes that glow in the dark—they have 120' infravision and, some warriors swear, a rarer few can even *see invisible creatures and items* as auras, within 70'. Wizards are especially eager to purchase Hawkwinter horses. They are bred to accept spells hurled nearby and from their backs calmly.

[17] The villa is #151 on the color map. Apartments in the same block rarely fall vacant. When they do, rooms are typically 35 gp/month and up, with the first season (six months) paid in advance.

doubt not, used from time to time.

Conversation and tales from afar are valued to stave off the boredom that threatens nobles, so adventurers and those newly arrived in the city are welcome as guests. The doors are not open to all, though. Waterdhavian nobles invite a select list of folk: usually Piergeiron, out of courtesy, although he but rarely attends such fetes; other nobles with whom the family is on speaking terms; mages and other fashionable or powerful personages, such as guildmasters; and the occasional very successful merchant in some sort of dignified trade.

These guests are expected to bring their spouses or an escort, and from two to six guests each—who may be anyone, such as the aforementioned adventurers and other walking entertainment. Those with ideas of slipping such feasts (elsewhere in Faerun, the term *crashing* is often used) are warned that nobles' doorwards and bouncers are mighty, experienced, quick, and reinforced by magic and might of arms that even successful adventurers respect—from a safe distance.[18]

Want to get invited? Let it be known around the city that you're newly arrived and either an adventurer of import or that interesting things befell you that you can tell or, even better, show something about. With a smile or two from the gods, someone will invite you. A young, ardent female escort invited me to the party I attended, on the condition that I wear a rather humiliating outfit and address her in an extremely deferential manner. In the interests of seeing what would otherwise be denied me, I agreed—and was treated to a wild evening of flirtation, drink, splendid food,[19] and gossip.

As to the goings-on, let me say merely that on such occasions, the nobles of Waterdeep *are* ruled by their whims. Fancy costumes, exotic food and drink, even more exotic entertainment—let me tell you, tales you may have heard in your local tavern of the decadence and wild ways of Waterdeep are all true.

---

[18] There are presently four F12s in the Hawkwinter ranks, and even the slightest Hawkwinter maiden can call on the gargoyles and on more than two dozen magical crossbows that wait behind walls both inside and outside of the castles.

Elminster assures us the gargoyles are real and 100% loyal to those of the family blood. Once loosed, they must taste blood before they can be commanded back into station. When commanded by word and will, the magical crossbows appear (stone panels slide aside) and fire two heavy quarrels per round, at THAC0 7, for normal damage (1d4+1 vs. M). Their activator must be of the family blood and need only speak the correct word within 90' of a concealed bow and mentally select the target or targets. The word is different for each crossbow. A bow can fire at up to two targets per round.

[19] Waterdeep boasts many hire-cooks, notably Brazaun of Baldur's Gate and Kathliira Salarth, who descend on your kitchens and whip up fantastic hand-food for feasts if you stock your larders beforehand to their specifications. Noble families pride themselves on having kitchen staff who can outshine these justifiably famous culinary artists.

As to the gossip: At parties, nobles can meet—to exchange items, for example—without eyes noticing or tongues whispering, but rarely conduct important business. That's what they have large walled houses with many closed doors for. They *do* use parties to meet with, manipulate, and arrange future meetings and business with underlings, outsiders, and newcomers. I saw more than two adventuring bands hired in the time it took me to drain a tiny glass of firewine at the feast I attended.

Also, such parties are the only place that outsiders and common folk are likely to hear nobles gossiping about nobles firsthand.

The alert listener can learn a lot from a tone of voice, raised eyebrow or lip, or when and how long someone pauses when they are speaking.

The folk who attend Hawkwinter parties are eccentric and powerful—and, if they're noble, up to something all the time. The scent of masked danger is always in the air.

Truly, a Waterdhavian noble's feast is something all should enjoy. If you manage to acquire an invitation to one, by all means go out of your way to ensure that you get to go. However, I plan to attend my next one in my own clothes—or at least in a slightly more dignified outfit.

The Misty Beard

Tavern

This interesting place stands on a corner hard by the east wall of the city, where its noise and crowding create as few problems with the refined neighborhood as possible. Its signboard depicts a laughing bearded sailor, with beads of water glistening in a rainbow all over his beard.[20] Minor enchantments make these droplets gleam, sparkle, and change hue from time to time.

The Beard is famous up and down the Sword Coast because it is staffed largely by exotic and monstrous beings from all over the Realms: halflings, lizard men, killmoulis, myconids, faerie dragons, spectators, and even, in the kitchens and cellars, skeletons and zombies[21] under the command of other beings. There are also shapeshifting and illusion-using creatures on staff. As one regular patron put it, "You never know just what you'll see—and for most of us, it's the only time we're every likely to see some of these creatures."

Their presence attracts a lot of thrill-seekers, and many visitors of the creatures' own kind. All are welcome, in an uneasy truce enforced by the magical powers of the wand-wielding owners.

The Place

This clean, well-mannered tavern (in such mixed company, all folk tend to be extra polite) is a solid-looking stone building with large arched windows, downspouts carved into the likenesses of beautiful winged maidens, and a steeply pitched slate roof. It rises four floors above the street. This was once a tavern known as the Cat and Songbird, but its owners were members of the Thieves Guild, and perished bloodily in an assassination attempt on the gathered Lords of Waterdeep.

---

[20] This place is #155 on the color city map.
[21] These creatures appear in Volumes 1, 2, and 3 of the *Monstrous Compendium*.

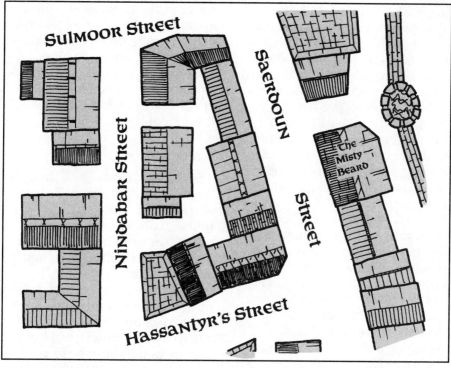

Sulmoor Street

Saerdoun

Ninoabar Street

Street

The Misty Beard

Hassantyr's Street

The Prospect

The interior of the Misty Beard is a well-lit jumble of booths and cozy chairs salvaged from sales all over the city. The rooms all open into a central well, where various stairs curve and zigzag up and down, and winged waiters dart from bar to table with single glasses. The waiters are sprites, who are hired here for month-long shifts, by which time they're usually sick of the city and flit home.

The Provender

Food in the Beard tends to be of the breadstick and cheese dip variety. The garlic butter is justly famous, and a wonderful gooseberry jam is made on the premises. The fruit is brought in from High Hill, the owners' estates northeast of the city. There is also very good sausage and morkoth soup, which varies in ingredients. Morkoth soup is one of those simmer-all-day, throw-in-whatever's about concoctions. The food is filling, but bland. The varied clientele hold little seasoning in common high regard.

The People

The half-elven mages who own the place are two wand-wield-

ing[22] sisters, Allet and Vindara Tzuntzin, who once ran the Black Gryphon inn in Elturel. Their monstrous friends and visitors were not welcomed in that city, so they sold out and came to cosmopolitan Waterdeep, where they soon tired of making beds, so they turned their inn into a tavern. The tavern's name refers to a private joke between them, involving a bet, a Waterdhavian sailor, and some magic.

The bartender at the Beard is Munzrim Marlpar, a dignified, fearless lizard man of unusual height and intellect. He was outcast from his kin in the Marsh of Chelimber because of those features. He's usually to be found deep in conversation with a beholder-like, deadly looking spectator floating behind the bar: Thoim Zalamm, who is something of a philosopher, and sometimes drifts out over the rooftops of the city on dark nights to spy on the endlessly entertaining doings of humans.

The Prices

The Beard has a more varied and well-stocked cellar than anywhere in Waterdeep except perhaps Piergeiron's Palace itself. The many drinkables run from 3 sp/tankard for ale and 4 sp/jack for zzar (the bargains) up to 12 gp/tallglass for most wines and exotic drinks. Bottles are always six times the price of a glass. Meals are 1 gp/head for as much as you want to consume in one evening from what's on the menu that night.

Travelers' Lore

There are many tales of the parties—and occasional brawls—at the Beard. The two sisters are quick to use their wands to keep racial fears and hostilities from erupting into full-scale slaughter, and this promise of safety is enough to attract a steady stream of the curious. A rare few citizens are comfortable drinking at the Beard as regulars, but it is a very popular place for low-income merchants to use to impress out-of-town visitors and a common neutral ground meeting place for merchants and others engaged in difficult negotiations. A few private rooms can be rented for short periods at 10 gp/hour. Some nights things turn into raucous sing-alongs—and as one Waterdhavian told me, "Until you've seen a spectator and a faerie dragon dancing on air together and struggling to harmonize— well, you've not seen Waterdeep!"

---

[22] Each carries at least six wands on her person, one or two sheathed openly at her belt, and the others hidden down boottops, up sleeves, and so on. They own many, many wands, but a typical carried assortment is as follows:

Allet: *enemy detection, frost, magic missiles, misplaced objects, negation*
Vindara: *fear, fire, flame extinguishing, illusion, lightning, paralyzation, polymorphing.*
The *wand of misplaced objects* is detailed in the *Tome of Magic*. All others can be found in the *DMG*.

Other Places of Interest in North Ward

Homes

The High House of Roaringhorn

This city villa of the Waterdhavian noble clan famous for its brawls, parties, and swashbuckling, pranksome approach to life is used to host a seemingly endless succession of feasts. Almost everyone is welcome. The Roaringhorns delight in breaking the heads of vandals and would-be thieves. Although such gatherings can be so crowded and noisy as to resemble a herd of oxen milling about, the down-on-their-luck of Waterdeep can often get food and drink at one of these festive gatherings and meet to conduct shady business, too—though it's a bit like whispering secrets in a room full of listeners.

Their hospitality has made the Roaringhorns deeply loved among the citizenry of Waterdeep. Old men and street youths alike have been known to leap to the defense of a drunken Roaringhorn in Dock Ward at night. But their behavior has reduced this once-fine, huge walled villa[23] to a well-worn shambles of torn and stained tapestries, splintered furniture, and empty rooms.

The Roaringhorns seem not to care and never run short of funds. If it's ambiance you seek, their home is like an abandoned hold stripped bare—but there's always fun to be had there at least two nights in a tenday. The family's never short of volunteers when it announces mercenary hirings, either.

Shops

Aurora's Realms Shop Catalogue Counter

This is the North Ward outlet of the famous Faerun-wide all goods retail chain. Located next to the House of Healing in a narrow but grand old home converted to luxury apartments above the shop, Aurora's North fronts on the High Road. It has four guards who work in shifts of two and two, a stunningly beautiful but sharp-tongued

---

[23] Location #145 on the color map. A partial floor plan of the everyday part of the villa appears on Map 9 of the *City System* boxed set, along with those of several other noble family villas.

counter clerk, Phandalue Tarin-thil, and a service-mage, Quirtan Ondever, who delights in acting mysterious and sinister.

Maerados Fine Furs

This shop sells stylish and well-made furs—winter cloaks, vests, and caps for all, and year-round fashions for the lady of taste, breeding, and deep pockets. Secret pockets are standard in such garments, as are concealed push-daggers. Furs can be per-fumed to order, but philandering nobles frown on this—it leaves a distinct scent trail to who one has been with.

Rumors speak of a guardian in the shop. One of the furs is really a living beast—some say a great cat, others a sort of sly furry cloaker—that preys on intruders when the shop is closed.

Proprietor: Shalrin Maerados, the Gentleman Keeper of his guild, is the proprietor. He is observant and soft-spoken. He adventures in his spare time and conceals several weapons on his person and in his shop.[24]

Hriiat Fine Pastries

This shop is a bustling place. Locals line up here when the smells tell them a fresh batch of something is ready for eating.

Hriiat's place (say *Hur-REE-atz*) is known not just for sweets, but for savory pastries, notably the bite-pie or the meal loaf. Among the sweets, the hand-sized al-mond-and-apple sugar tarts, at 1 cp each, are especially fine. Bite-pies made of pork, beef, or cur-ried mixed meats run to 2 cp each, and mixed fish bite-pies cost only 1 cp each. The meal loaf, a Hriiat original, is an egg-shaped stuffed roll as long as two man's hands full of a stir-fried mix of cooked vegetables and meat doused in a spicy mushroom sauce that visiting merchants trot across the city to get.

All these wares are made for eating in the street as one walks. Hriiat sells fine cloth belt-towels for this purpose. Hriiat food is a hearty treat not to be missed!

Proprietor: Relchoz Hriiat, the public contact for the Bakers' Guild, owns and runs this shop. He is short, stout, and jolly. He is always sampling his wares and offering bites to customers.[25]

Sulmest's Splendid Shoes & Boots

Footwear here can cost as much as 10 times the going rate else-where in the city, but any repairs to a Sulmest product are half the

---

[24] Location #112 on the color map.
[25] Location #134 on the color map.

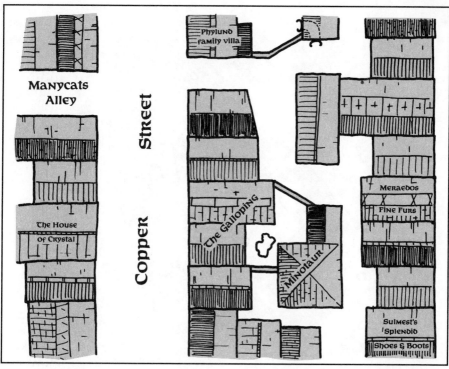

going rate, and many boots can be bought with lifelong guarantees of free replacement for any reason save loss due to theft. Men's shoes, slippers and boots for both sexes are made to custom fit the customer's foot. Off the shelf sizes are much cheaper than custom work, going for only twice the average cost. All work is stylish—so much so, I'm told, that Lady Galinda Raventree once attended a nobles' party clad only in her thigh-high Sulmest boots!

Proprietor: Darion Sulmest, the sarcastic and handsome spokesman for his guild, is the proprietor. He is a touch snob-bish but always interested in tales of adventuring.[26]

Taverns

A Maiden's Tears

No tavern in this ward competes in prices with those elsewhere—drink is dear, and rowdiness strongly discouraged. Nobles with a taste for brawling, color, or danger walk to more southerly wards for their fun. This place, named for the old Sword Coast legend that the best wine is the tears of a maiden whose suitor

---

[26] Location #111 on the color map.

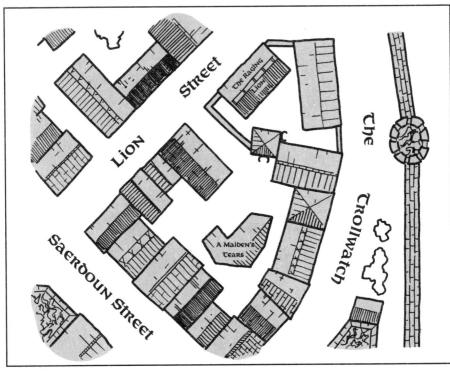

turns away (or is slain), is quieter than most.

Soft lighting, deftly quiet service, and curtained booths make this a perfect and popular place for meetings—both for private intrigue, and encounters with ladies of the evening. Once you're seated, it is rare to even see other patrons, and the snoring betrays just how many unhappy nobles come here to drink zzar until they fall asleep.

The Tears is rated highly for its privacy and quiet. Some will find it a excrutiatingly boring place to lift a cup.

Zzar is 4 cp/jack. Wines go up from there to 20 gp/glass for Tashlutan dragonstongue. No menu is offered, but all drink orders include complimentary salted crackers, garlic-and-cheese-melt breads, and celery.

Proprietress: Zobia Shrinsha is the proprietress. She is quiet, watchful, and shy—like a little girl speaking to strangers.[27]

The Grinning Lion

Tucked away inside a block of homes and businesses just north of the big bend in Golden Ser-

---

[27] Location #154 on the color map.

pent Street, this place, adorned with battle trophies (or faked battle trophies) from all over Faerun is as raucous as taverns get in North Ward. An old joke claims the Riven Shield Shop sends all shields beyond repair here, to hang on the walls.

The music is loud, with male and female dancers in fantastically styled and revealing mock armor swaying and pirouetting among the tables. Real, if broken, weapons hang on the walls everywhere, so disputes are swiftly discouraged by the bouncers. Grasping a patron's upper lip is an effective way to tow him to the door, one told me.

Food consists only of platters of fried onions and eels. I'm told you get to enjoy them, but I couldn't get past the revolting look and smell.

Folk really come here to drink—and drink they do, copiously, at a price of 3 cp/tankard of zzar and upwards. Most wine is 2 sp/glass.

I'm told that a certain fat man on a stool at one end of the bar can help visitors buy and sell goods that are rather "warm." The only such patron I spoke to was very rude and emphatic in his rejections.

Proprietor: Unger Farshal, who owns and runs the Grinning Lion, is bald, close-mouthed, and dangerous-looking.[28]

Inns

The Cliffwatch

At the northeast corner of Endcliff Lane and Nindabar Street stands this rambling old inn—recognizable for its exterior galleries. These are continuous balconies running the entire length of the outside, a feature seen in Dock Ward and South Ward, but rarely in this well-to-do district.[29] By night, find it by going to the Endcliff Tower on the city wall, and head west down the narrowest lane you can see. It's on the first corner on your right.

Inside, it's well worn, even shabby—but the cheerful, understanding keeper makes up for this. He's quick to hide warm goods or wanted folk, direct adventurers or visitors to where the oddest things can be found in the vast city, and to chat about rumors, treasure tales, and doings in the city in the old overstuffed armchairs in front of his roaring fireplace. For folk wanting only a comfortable, home-like place to stay, this is one of the best lodgings in the city.

Oh, by the way, tales of secret passages leading down to smugglers' storage cellars and thence to navigable reaches of the cellars are true. But the kindly

---

[28] Location #135 on the color map.
[29] Location #156 on the color map.

keeper advised me not on investigate too far unless I felt confident of my ability to defeat a beholder!

Proprietor: The amiable, but otherwise unremarkable, proprietor of the Cliffwatch is Felstan Spindrivver.

The Galloping Minotaur

Widely known among travelers, this inn has begun to slip in its service, relying on its name and convenient location[30] for market vendors and for shoppers to keep its rooms full. And they are full; it's rare to find lodgings here, because the keeper has instituted the city's first system of advance bookings. Merchants valuing the guarantee of a place to stay in the city have gone for it to such an extent that the Minotaur has expanded to take in a former warehouse behind and a storefront beside the original inn. The cheaper rooms are located in the former warehouse, above the stables and below the servants.

Inside, this place is all bustle. Errandboys and newslungs (youths who arrive every hour or so, and for a handful of coppers from the innkeeper bellow out the current news to all in the salon) are always coming and going, merchants full of their own importance are always striding in all directions ("at

once," as one serving maid dryly put it), and the mutter of business dealings fills the entire ground floor. The ground floor is given over to a lobby, the salon, and four private, rentable meeting rooms. The salon is an open lounge used by most guests and those they have dealings with. Servants tend the private rooms by means of passages behind the paneled walls in answer to the tug of a bellpull. Be warned that they can easily eavesdrop on what goes on within. All in all, a noisy, overpriced place—rather like paying high gold to sleep in an army camp.

Proprietor: Waendel Uthrund, a beady-eyed, sardonic man who is always alert, is the proprietor.

The Raging Lion

This little-known, fine old inn is highly recommended. Dominated by dark wood paneling, thick but worn carpets underfoot everywhere, and a strict rule against open flames of any sort including smoking, it is a quiet refuge from the bustle of the city, being as close to the east wall as one can get.[31] Light is provided by an assortment of *glowing globes* of different hues.

Dwarves and at least three bands of lady adventurers have adopted this place. Some live here

[30] Location #110 on the color map.
[31] Location #153 on the color map.

98

permanently, helping the proprietor keep order, and others use it as a base between expeditions into the northern Sword Coast. The Swordmaidens in particular are an impressive sight as they stride through the halls or dining room in full armor.

All rooms have their own bath and garderobe, and all have doors that can be locked and barred from within. All have locking bar-grates on the windows that can be swung up out of the way from within only. All have canopied four-poster beds of the sort usually reserved for nobility or royalty.

The ground floor is given over to kitchens and to a dining room where one can choose between beef, pork, or goat stews nightly, each available either highly spiced as favored in the South or more moderately seasoned (which is more to my taste—I like to taste what I'm eating first, and the spices second).

During my meal, I found something that led to a very interesting adventure—about which I'll say only that in the better wards of Waterdeep, always check the underside of any chair or stool you sit in (if, and only if, you can do this unobserved by others!). Messages, coins, gems, weapons, and other valuable objects are often stuck, wedged, or fitted into recesses there for someone to pick up at a later time.

Two dwarves seem to live in the dining room, whittling little chains and lock mechanisms from various exotic woods, and sipping beer as they while each day away. I believe they take messages from dwarves, to pass on to other dwarves who come here to find them. Their names are Ilmairen and Jaerloon. They merely smiled when I asked their clan. They told me many interesting tales of the city in exchange for a tankard or two—including some things about a curious cult, embraced by some nobles of Waterdeep, that once used this inn as a place of worship.

Their temple still exists, as a cellar now crowded with casks, potatoes, mushroom frames and the like, but it was once a place of frenzied dancing and sacrificial offerings to Kambadlan, the Black Tortoise of Night. I must admit I laughed at this, but after I was shown the temple and the burnt bones still on its altar, my mirth left me hurriedly.

This is the origin of the seldom-heard Waterdhavian oaths: "By the Black Tortoise!" and "By the shell of Kambadlan!" The cult is now extinct—I believe. Yet something of its dark and dangerous mystery still clings to this old place—or perhaps some other plots lurk here?

Proprietor: The tall but stout proprietor of the Raging Lion, Lhaerhlin Masram, is impassive-faced but affable.

Alleys

North Ward's alleys are by far the safest of any ward of Waterdeep. Children have been known to safely play unattended in them on bright moonlit nights. Lantern guides tend to be lone men or youths and sometimes even maids, and the alleys have a reputation more as a place for drunks to snore away the night undisturbed, than places to be avoided due to danger.

Black Dog Alley

This short way circles around the interior of a block of buildings due south of Farwatch Tower, linking up with Watch Alley. It is named for the silent phantom of a black dog that is seen padding steadily along here on many nights. The hound wears a spiked hunting or war collar, stands as tall a goat, and has blazing red eyes. It looks at no one directly, and simply walks through people and objects alike.

Catchthief Alley

This short, narrow passage runs north off Golden Serpent Street, along the east wall of the Helmfast noble family villa com-

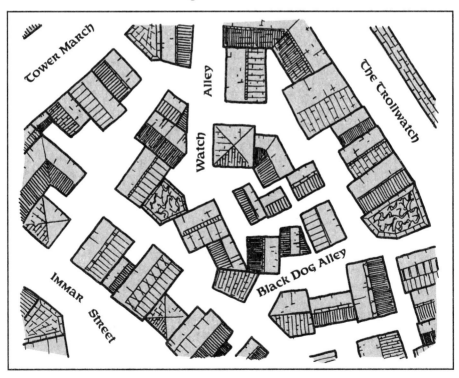

pound.[32] Its name comes from its site as the downfall of the infamous thief Uluryk Malogh, who was slain by a hail of poisoned arrows here many winters ago after he killed the heads of two noble houses in a tavern brawl and taunted their kin by revealing himself as an agent of the banished Thieves Guild, who had been ordered to bring about their doom.

He escaped into the sewers and cellars of the city, which he knew as few others do, but the Guild thought him insane and a risk to themselves, and sent agents into the city to slay him. The agents of the Guild caught him in this alley. Some folk swear they have heard the ghostly, bubbling whisper of his last words, pronouncing a curse on all traitors, and lamenting that the poison *burns* so.

There are persistent rumors that he made an extensive map of the cellars and sewers, detailing traps, barriers, and locks. If it exists, it has never come to light.

The alley is also notable for the fact that much of it was once destroyed by a wyrm bursting up from below! There is an old legend in the city of a dozen or more dragonets that once hatched early and ate their way to freedom, escaping from an importer of dragon eggs into the city sewers. They dined on rats, thieves, and other skulking monsters, growing slowly in size and powers. This tale has probably grown a great deal in the telling, but a single dragon undeniably broke out of some cellar, cell, or sewer below the widest part of this alley some 70 winters ago and flew away over the city to escape into the nearby mountains to the north. Its origin, if it was learned at the time, has been forgotten.

Manycats Alley

This way crosses two city blocks and winds through the interior of a third, running between and for the most part parallel to Julthoon Street and Traders' Way. It passes just to the south of the Adarbrent noble family villa,[33] and is notable not only for the many cats that roam it (for which it is named), dining on leavings from several butcher shops located along its run, but also for the many carved stone heads that adorn buildings along the alley.

The carved heads are of both sexes and many races and are very lifelike—leading some fanciful folk to claim they are petrified, severed heads of once-living beings. Whatever their origin, it is widely believed in the city that the heads speak aloud from time to time, uttering cryptic messages.

---

[32] Location #144 on the color map.
[33] Location #106 on the color map.

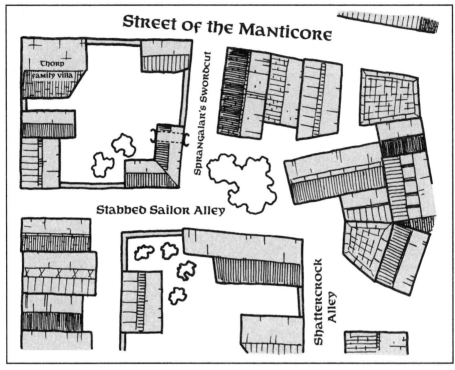

Street of the Manticore

Thorp family villa

Sprangalar's Swordcut

Stabbed Sailor Alley

Shattercrock Alley

Shattercrock Alley

This short alleyway circles south from Stabbed Sailor Alley only to meet with it again, encircling the Margaster noble family villa.[34] It is named for a famous incident, many summers ago, when a wizard—Phantamos of the Purple Cloak, who went on to become mighty in Art, a legend across the North—was learning to fly by means of magic and swooped wildly *through* a huge cart of crockery being pushed along this alley to make delivery to a shop here. For many years a tavern, the Wizard with Wings, backed onto this alley, fronting on Suldoun Street, but it burned down of suspicious causes a decade ago. A fine shop offering spectacular hats, wigs, and body-manes to ladies stands on the site now.

Stabbed Sailor Alley

This alleyway links Vhezoar Street with Whaelgond Way. At its midpoint stands a clump of magnificent shadowtop trees of great age and height (some 90'), that shade the streets around and provide a home to nesting birds.

---

[34] Location #129 on the color map.

This alley links with Shatter-crock Alley and is linked to the Street of the Manticore to the north by a tiny alleyway known as Sprangalar's Swordcut.

The Swordcut and Stabbed Sailor got their names in the aftermath of a bloody street fight, years back, when citizens fought with followers of the Cult of the Dancing Bear and either destroyed it or drove it under-ground.[35] The alleyway is a busy but safe delivery route today. Its shade makes it a favorite stroll on hot, sunny days.

Trollskull Alley

A narrow, little-known passage winding through the interior of a city block just north of, and parallel to, the eastern end of Delzorin Street, this alley's dead-end is a favorite night haunt of gambling gangs—bored, wealthy youths who waste their money on dares and games of chance. By day, it is safe and crowded with carts of garbage and delivered goods for the businesses that back onto it. By night, it is the turf of aggressive youths of both sexes—who often pelt the city watch with stones.

Watch Alley

A short passage that runs due south from Farwatch Tower before looping back to meet itself, this lane serves as an assembly point for city watch patrols and a quick route south for them—hence its name. It is as safe as an alley can be, except for a curious thing, as yet unexplained: From time to time, single, severed, bloody, bare human feet are found lying in it.[36]

---

[35] The Cult of the Dancing Bear was born seven or more generations ago, when Waterdeep celebrated the Festival of Dancing Bears once a year. This barbarian custom preceded the city—the nomadic human tribes of the north simply shifted the place of their annual gathering to Waterdeep.

During the festival, the barbarians came down to the city with pelts and horns to sell and trinkets, good swords, and much beer to buy. They danced far into the night, and the greatest of their dances was the Dance of the Bear. In this dance, a hunter danced with a captured bear, holding its attention (and claws) by skill and stratagems so it would not menace the crowd around. The hunter wore bear-claw gloves tipped with a drug, and if the bear was scratched deeply enough, it would be affected, falling ever so slowly asleep. Many hunters were killed in this dangerous dance, and Waterdhavian worshippers of Malar took it up after the barbarians stopped coming, dancing with a trained bear or even a man wearing the preserved pelt, claws, and head of a bear.

The Cult of the Dancing Bear is presently led by Urinborm, who is secretly a specialty priest of Malar, as detailed in the *FORGOTTEN REALMS® Adventures* hardcover sourcebook, and is a small, underground faith. Its followers are marked, usually on some part of their body normally hidden by clothing, by the parallel scars of the raking claws of the bear. The faithful meet secretly at least once a month, usually in a cellar somewhere in the city. Rituals involve drinking the blood of animals, dancing with the Bear (Urinborm, in costume), dedicating any hunting activities to the Bear, and mock-fighting fellow cult members with bare hands and teeth until blood is drawn. Cult members are trained in aggressive attacking behavior, and to enjoy a bloodlust. They fiercely avenge any slight or attack on any member of their fellowship, and try to run down in a hunt by night at least one visitor to the city a year..

[36] Elminster says this is an old Thieves Guild punishment, and may herald their return to the city. It comes, he said dryly, from a bad pun about defeating your opponents.

Trades Ward

f all the wards in Waterdeep, this ward has the least community feel. You certainly can't tell by walking through the streets where it ends and South Ward or Dock Ward begins.

Trades Ward is almost entirely given over to commerce. Middle-class workers and merchants dwell and ply their trades there. The ward wraps around most of the City of the Dead, running out from its walls along Andamaar's Street to the High Road, down that broad street to Snail Street, and down Snail Street to Shesstra's Street, where it turns east. The boundary jogs south at Book Street to Drakiir Street, runs east along it to the Way of the Dragon, keeps to the north side of Telshambra's Street as it runs on east to the High Road, and there jogs north again to turn east at Sahtyra's Lane. It takes in Caravan Court and then follows Belzor's Walk northeast to the city wall. The city wall, and those of the City of the Dead, make up the rest of its boundaries.

Inside this area are many landmarks the visitor won't want to miss. Besides, it's almost impossible to travel anywhere in Waterdeep without passing through Trades Ward. Its streets are always busy. On dark nights, so many lighters are at work here that it looks like a sea of bobbing stars from afar.

Watch patrols are very frequent.[1] The protection of property is paramount in this ward—theft and vandalism are the worst evils. Crowding, pushing, shoving, and cursing are commonplace at the day's height.

Landmarks

The congested streets make walking while looking up in this ward—or even stopping for a good look—hazardous at most times of day. This is quite a pity, because there's a lot to see.

The first thing that strikes one's eye is the tallest building: the Plinth, a temple at which all faiths can pray. No person can be barred entry from it. In fact, in winter its warmth keeps a lot of poorer citizens alive.

This mighty tower stands like a

---

[1] City watch patrols are detailed on page 17 of FR1 *Waterdeep and the North.* In this ward, four-sword patrols pass a given point about every 10 minutes and look into a tavern or inn dining room every 30 minutes. As detailed on pages 18, 19 and 23 of the *City System* book, six-man city guard detachments also patrol the ward. Typical patrol details are given therein on page 23. Reinforcements will be a dozen LG hm F3s to F6s in chain mail and armed with maces, long swords, slings, daggers, and a polearm. Guard patrols pass a given street location every 45 minutes or so, and appear 1d10 minutes after a city watch patrol blows a warning horn in this ward.

needle-like, tall and thin pyramid with the top cut off. The flat roof is a landing place for aerial steeds used by the wealthy and powerful. At many levels on the Plinth's sides are balconies. City laws forbid sacrifices of intelligent beings to any god, but a lot of folk leap or are helped to fall from these heights each year.

The next most prominent features of the ward are three open spaces—the Court of the White Bull, where livestock is bought and sold; Caravan Court, which is usually a dust-shrouded melee of cursing, whip-wielding drovers, bawling beasts of burden, and creaking wagons and carts; and Virgin's Square, where warriors gather to await hire.

There are plenty of inns and taverns in this ward, but aside from the Plinth, no temples. There are also countless shops, most rising three floors above the street, with apartments above the stores—but only one mage's tower.[2] I'm sure many wizards of middling powers dwell here, but there's only one of power and wealth enough to erect a traditional wizard's tower who has elected to stay in Trades Ward.

The main feature of this ward are the many guildhalls—a wearying list of places that vie

---

[2] Mhair's Tower, home of Mhair Szeltune, Lady Master (head) of the Watchful Order of Magists & Protectors (Waterdeep's wizards' guild) is location #171 on the color map. It's a conical stone tower on the east side of Spindle Street with an oval, mithril and copper front door.

for the attention of passersby with large replicas of whatever goods the guild produces, gilded lettering, and grand facades. These are working headquarters, and many folk travel a long way to get inside them, to deal with the guilds. The guildhalls are: the Citadel of the Arrow, headquarters of the Fellowship of Bowyers & Fletchers;[3] Costumers' Hall, of the Order of Master Taylors, Glovers, & Mercers;[4] the House of Song, of the Council of Musicians, Instrument-Makers, and Choristers;[5] the Office of the League of Basketmakers & Wickerworkers;[6] and the House of Cleanliness, of the Launderers' Guild.[7]

This ward is also home to the Old Guildhall, headquarters to the Cellarers and Plumbers Guild;[8] the Zoarstar, headquarters of the Scriveners, Scribes, and Clerks Guild;[9] the House of Textiles, of the Most Excellent Order of Weavers and Dyers;[10] the Guild Paddock, of the Stablemasters' and Farriers' Guild;[11] Cobblers' & Corvisers' House;[12] the House of Light, of the Guild of Chandlers & Lamplighters;[13] Stationers' Hall;[14] and Wheel Hall, of the Wheelwrights' Guild.[15]

The Zoarstar, in particular, is always crowded. Aside from all those who need letters written, gawkers are always peering through the windows at the maps, charts, and architectural renderings on display on easels at its front. One such map is always an overall view of the city, as a kindness to visitors. Go there if you get lost. The Zoarstar is on the northwest corner of Quill Alley and Wide Way, northwest of the Court of the White Bull.

Shoppers should explore at night in a leisurely manner with a lighter and a group of armed friends, then traverse the ward in an organized shopping route by day. It's often said you can buy *anything* in Waterdeep. A walk around Trades Ward will have you believing that. (I'll admit I let the "guaranteed" unicat familiar go even before its illusory unicorn horn started to fade. It stopped clawing me and hurried back to its shop to be sold again.)

---

[3] Location #174 on the color map.
[4] Location #176 on the color map.
[5] Location #181 on the color map.
[6] Location #183 on the color map.
[7] Location #185 on the color map.
[8] Location #186 on the color map.
[9] Location #189 on the color map.
[10] Location #190 on the color map.
[11] Location #195 on the color map.
[12] Location #199 on the color map.
[13] Location #200 on the color map.
[14] Location #202 on the color map.
[15] Location #205 on the color map. In all cases, the guild owning the headquarters, and something of its doings, fees, and current heads, is covered in the *Waterdeep and the North* sourcebook.

The Bowels of the Earth

Tavern

This rough, rowdy tavern stands on the southeast corner of the intersection of Snail Street and Simples Street, just west of Virgin's Square.[16] It is a cheap but cozy dive popular with mercenaries and adventurers. If you're a mercenary or an adventurer or are looking to meet or hire one or the other, you must go to this place—if you're male, that is, and look like you'd be trouble for someone in a fight. Lady adventurers are usually bold enough to go in—but they sometimes have to empty the place with their fists or spells to win the respect they need to stay and enjoy themselves untroubled!

The Place

The Bowels is an old stone building that leans noticeably to the north into Simples Street. The windows are covered with stout wooden shutters, barred from within, because they long ago lost all their glass and screens. The tavern fronts on Snail Street, where its hanging signboard vividly depicts a pile of manure transfixed by a spade. Local children and drovers alike play an old, old game by flinging spadefuls and handfuls of dung at the sign, trying to make it stick to where the pile is painted.

The Prospect

Inside, the Bowels of the Earth is chiefly memorable for being *dark*. Hooded candlelamps at each table provide the only illumination. It's easy to imagine a blade being drawn in stealthy silence and sliding in and out of a man's ribs without warning until he crashes forward onto his table—and I'm sure it's happened here a time or two. The place is a haunt of the Shadow Thieves, it's said, the place where the thief Moriath of the Company of Crazed Venturers met his end at their hands.[17]

There are several private, rentable rooms off the taproom. They are Spartan cubicles furnished only with lamps hanging on chains above built-in benches and tables. Behind the bar are the kitchens, and beside it is a door leading to the alley behind the tavern. Stairs lead up to a cesspit/jakes at the back of the place, a set of former bedrooms crammed with stores, and a dust-filled attic. Stairs behind the bar lead down to a low-ceilinged cellar crowded with kegs as tall

---

[16] This place is #198 on the color city map.

[17] For more about this tavern, see Blazidon One-Eye's entry on page 50 of FR1 *Waterdeep and the North* and the adventure entitled "The Unmourned Passing of Roungoze Haballanter" on page 64. Blazidon owns the Bowels of the Earth and often sleeps in its attic.

as a man and about as fat around as any four men. Even before you find the trapdoor behind them, you can smell that this place is connected to the sewers.

So why do adventurers, who can often afford better, come to this dump? Well, the prices are low, well-banked fires keep it warm in winter, and in the close darkness there are always tales being told back and forth—tales of taming and flying dragons, of hewing liches and baatezu limb from limb, and withstanding the hurled magic of archmages or beholders. The listener can visit far, exotic corners of Toril—from fabled Evermeet to the chill ice of the Great Glacier, and from the depths of the Deep Realm of the dwarves to the unrelenting heat of Zakhara, the Land of Fate—without ever leaving the safety of his or her chair.

But more importantly than that, listening quietly and perhaps smoking in the darkness are usually one or more who have come to hire adventurers or simply mercenary swords for a task. They sit, and listen, take their measure of the speaker, and may lay down a coin for a hire-sword to take up and so enter their service.

The Provender

Food in the Bowels is simple fare: coarse, rich dark rye bread in

circular loaves, served to accompany slabs of cheese, sausage, and fowl pâté. There's also soup—usually a thick concoction of peas and lentils simmered with all the meat scraps, fat, and bones that have come within reach of the place.

To wash all that down, there's lots to drink—in quantity. The selection isn't great. All that burns going down and isn't well thought of can be had, but if you want fancy wines, walk elsewhere.

The People

Regular patrons are hard to recognize in the darkness—which is just as well for the city guard undercover agent who's usually listening here or for Mirt the Moneylender, the colorful and stout ex-mercenary.[18]

The bald-headed proprietor wears a gold earring and is almost as wide as he is tall (in other words, about five feet in each direction). His biceps are as large around as a fat man's thigh! This gentle giant is capable of snatching an unruly guest off his feet one-handed and hurling him across the taproom to strike the door so hard that it flies open

and he sails out a good 10 feet into the street—and bounces. No wild tale—I saw this myself. This bartender, Ongamar Talthloon, is (thankfully!) slow to anger.

The Prices

Drink goes by the tankard: 1 copper for rough ale, 3 coppers for good ale, 7 cp for zzar, and 1 sp to 6 sp for wine and spirits, depending on quality. A plate of food is 1 cp. A bowl of soup is 1 cp, but free with a plate of food.

Travelers' Lore

The Bowels of the Earth has so many tales connected to it that I could fill another book this size, but there's one that every traveler finds interesting: The tavern has been owned by more than one wizard in the past—and it's said in the city that there's still magical treasure hidden in the place somewhere. Many folk have stealthily cast detection spells—only to find that the entire place radiates strong magical auras—layer upon layer, so that a *dispel magic* doesn't clear things! So far, only one magical ring has been found—in the bottom of one of the wine kegs, when it rotted through.[19]

---

[18] You won't find Mirt, or Khelben "Blackstaff" Arunsun either, for that matter, in the "Folk of Waterdeep" appendix at the back of this book. Elminster refused to say anything about either of them. He did say something like, "The safety of all the Realms is too important to jeopardize just to sate thy curiosity."

[19] Try chipping into the stone roof pillars that hold up the ceilings in the taproom and cellar, Elminster advised sarcastically with a grin. Just one small matter, he added: Remember that they're holding the place up, and you're in it! Oh, another warning: The pillars reflect back all magic cast at them, 100% on the source.

The Inn of the Dripping Dagger

Tavern & Inn

This cozy old inn stands on the east side of the High Road, south of Selduth Street and north of the Coffinmarch.[20] It's well-known as the favorite watering hole and resting place for hire-swords, and has a reputation for jovial horseplay that keeps the more timid merchants and pilgrims away from its doors.

The Place

This tavern has a fieldstone street-level floor pierced by a few squat, iron-barred arched windows. A row of iron and amber-glass lamps run along its front, illuminating the hanging dripping dagger signboard and the entry door, which is covered with many bloodstains and weapon scars. The owner used to leave all the weapons that had sunk into it in place as grisly, bristling adornment, but they started proving too handy for those wishing to snatch up a weapon and work a little mayhem, and the city watch asked him to remove them.

The timber upper floors have necessitated a no smoking/no fires rule except in the taproom. They contain two floors of comfortable rooms, an attic with a secret closet for hiding incriminating things (such as bodies) from the city watch, and a flat roof with several carved stone griffons on it, which serve to give pigeons something to adorn and people using the roof to look for the watch or just to enjoy the city view something to lean against. If folk visiting the Dripping Dagger use aerial steeds, the griffons have rings set into them for the easy tethering of mounts.

There is a stable behind and a little south of the inn reached by a passage off Spindle Street, and a few gnarled old trees that one can relax under. This back alley is frequently full of fighting men at practice.

The Prospect

Inside, the inn has a dark, low-ceilinged taproom like many a tavern. A stair beside the bar leads up to the inn rooms, and there is a private dining room around behind the stairs that has been used for many war councils and private business meetings down through the years.

The place is simple, but comfortably furnished and welcoming. The warrior guests seem to relax completely here, and laugh, joke, and play at dice, cards, or board games with easy, lazy enjoyment. Songs and play-acting, wherein one hairy warrior gets

---

[20] This place is #168 on the color city map.

Floorplan of the Inn of the Dripping Dagger

Cellar

Street Level

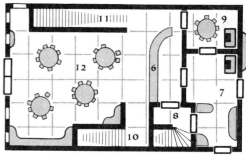

Second Floor

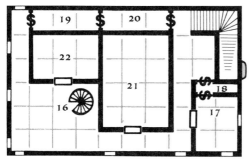

Third Floor

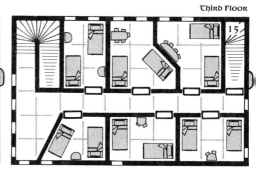

Attic

Roof

1	Ladies' Jakes
2	Mens' Jakes
3	Stairs From Taproom
4	Storage Cellar (Wine Casks, Broken Furniture, etc.)
5	Strongroom (Stairs from Pantry connect here; also, via secret doors, there is access here to the navigable sewers of Waterdeep
6	Bar
7	Kitchen
8	Pantry (Stairs to Cellar)
9	Private Dining Room
10	Stairs to Cellar (Jakes)
11	Stairs to Upper Floors
12	Taproom
13	Linen Closets
14	Stairs to Upper Floors
15	Stairs to Attic

16	Iron Spiral Stair to Roof
17	Office
18	Secret Closet (Weapons Storage)
19	Secret Storage
20	Secret Storage
21	Storage Room
22	Storage Room
23	Flat Roof
24	Penthouse
25	Storage Hut (Awnings)/ Chicken Coop (for Fresh Eggs, Daily)
26	Washing Lines

Scale: 1 square = 5 feet

Secret Door		Window	
Door		Chimney	

up and lisps and flirts his way through an imitation of a noble lady or mimics a pompous merchant met during the day, are common.

Laughter rings often around this taproom. I can see why guests love this place so and become regulars. Those who are not fighting men are greeted affably and treated with courtesy, rather than being made to feel unwelcome or out of place. On my first visit, I saw three hulking mercenaries on their knees on the floor solemnly playing orc

Welcome to the Dripping Dagger
All Prices are per Person, per Platter or Bowl

For The Hungry

Roast Ox (cooked with onions or leeks—garlic optional) .... 1 sp

Venison (marinated in red wine and spices) .... 2 sp

Veal (always fresh) .... 2 sp

Goat (in red wine) .... 1 sp

Pork (chops or ribs) .... 1 sp

Bacon (raw to crisped, as you prefer; thick-sliced and served on a bed of parsley, with rolls) .... 6 cp

Rabbit (cooked in red wine with butter and chives) .... 4 cp

(Melted cheese 1 cp extra)

Hot Sausage and Sauce (your choice of sauces and how spicy) .... 5 cp

(Sausages also available to go—2 cp/small, 5 cp/large, or 1 sp/coil)

Quail (if available) .... 4 cp

Pheasant (when available; steamed with wine) .... 5 cp

Eels (done in our own white sauce) ... 3 cp

Tripes (cooked with onions in a wine gravy) .... 3 cp

Herring, Pan-Fried .... 4 cp

Longfin and Other Pleasures of the Deep (when available fresh; served with sauces and your choice of greens) ...... 6 cp

Cooked Beans (mild or hot-spiced) ...... 3 cp

(Salt pork chunks 1 cp extra)

Eggs (done to your taste, in sausage and breading nests):

Goose .... 5 cp

Duck .... 5 cp

Chicken .... 4 cp

Exotic Fowl (when available) .... 6 cp

Lighter Fare

Cold Meats (served with lettuce or endive) .... 4 cp

Stew (mixed meats and vegetables) .... 3 cp

Soup (fish and vegetables, seasoned) .... 2 cp

Soup (mixed meats) .... 5 cp

Pasty (meat and vegetable, hot-spiced or mild) .... 1 cp

Pork Pie (hot-spiced or mild) .... 1 cp

Steak and Kidney Pie .... 1 cp

(Pies available cold or packed in ice and leaves for travel.)

To Drink

Prices by Tankard or Tallglass, and then by Bottle
(Hand Keg or "Half-Anker" for Beers)

Ale	1 cp	4 cp
Stout	2 cp	8 cp
Mead	3 cp	12 cp
Zzar	6 cp	1 sp
Sherry	7 cp	1 sp
Almond Brandy		
(Moonshae)	7 cp	1 sp
(Mintarn)	6 cp	1 sp
Fruit Liqueurs (apricot, cherry, gooseberry, peach, pear)	4 cp	1 sp
Whiskey	1 sp	1 gp
Firewine	1 gp	9 gp
Elverquisst	4 gp	20 gp
Fine Wines and Exotic Drinkables	1 sp	1 gp

squash with a little boy as his mother looked on in pleased amazement.

The Provender

The menu at the Dripping Dagger is typical for a good inn, and I've reproduced it in full here (page 113). I would hope that those planning to open their own establishments elsewhere will take their measure of its simple breadth and prices!

The People

The proprietor is Filiare, a jovial, middle-aged ex-mercenary who's Blazidon One-Eye's chief competitor in the business of getting mercenaries hired. Many folk come here seeking hireswords in a hurry, and Filiare is known to all and trusted by most. He has lots of spare weapons and gear given to him by fighting men who never came back or who paid him in goods when they lacked coin, which he will sell or rent to adventurers. He has also known to trim his prices a bit for guests thin in the purse.

Filiare presides over a staff of four waitresses, four chambermaids, six kitchenfolk, and four hostlers (in the stable behind).

The Prices

Food prices are as given on the menu. A room rents for 5 sp/day from highsun to highsun, with stabling included, or 20 sp/ tenday. Bedroll (bunking on the floor of the attic with others) is 1 sp/night. A bowl of soup, a mug of ale, and a round loaf of bread are included with bedroll service.

Travelers' Lore

Many famous mercenaries and companies have stayed here while in Waterdeep. By common consent, the inn is neutral ground where rivals and sworn enemies stay amicably—or at least tolerantly—together. Before they built their own keep (since destroyed), the Company of Crazed Venturers lived here, and it was always their favorite place to drink. Longtime regulars still talk about the time they used a *wish* spell to *teleport* back from disaster in a nearby dungeon and shattered the bar with their arrival. Unfortunately, they appeared without any of their equipment—and closely followed by their *teleporting* foes! (If you should meet with a former member of the Company, this is *not* a good topic to discuss.)

Many other tales are linked to the Dripping Dagger, but I'll tell only one other. Alusair Nacacia, princess of Cormyr, when still a slip of a girl, gave her lady attendants and guards the slip while her father was meeting with Piergeiron. She wandered in here and was happily playing with the warriors in the taproom while the city watch and city guard were frantically turning the city

upside down searching for her and dreading having to report her disappearance to Khelben to get magical aid in tracing her—whereupon her father was sure to hear of her disappearance. After the Dagger's patrons had mock-wrestled with her, tossed her from hand to hand until she was quite winded, let her sip strong things that she'd always been forbidden to taste, and disarmed her and showed her how to do it to someone else, they were in the midst of showing her how to throw daggers when the city watch came in. It's a good thing the watch's lead officer was swift—Alusair had just flung a dagger at the battered inside of the front door when he opened it. The most astonishing thing, he remarked later, was that no one in the Dagger knew that she was a princess.

Her father's later dry comment was that the most astonishing thing (to him) was the number of unsuitable jokes and sayings she'd learned in a brief hour or so. Her lifelong habit of muttering "Stop me vitals!" under her breath comes from this childhood visit to the Inn of the Dripping Dagger. When she turned up missing much later in life, the first place Cormyrean agents in Waterdeep were ordered to check was (of course) the Inn of the Dripping Dagger.

Other Places of Interest in Trades Ward

In the crowded streets and byways of the Trades Ward, the determined shopper or enterprising merchant can spend a summer or two without poking his nose everywhere or doing business with everyone. I've done my best to set down here some of the shops and sights of universal interest—or at least those of note to the casual passerby, rather than to the dedicated shopper.

Earlier, I spoke of such landmarks as the Plinth and the open squares and courtyards—and it bears repeating that to visit the closest thing Waterdeep has to a bazaar (an open air market, crowded with many everchanging stalls) the Court of the White Bull is your place. It's named, by the way, for a now-vanished tavern, famous in its day, that sprawled over much of where the court now lies and was destroyed in a mighty explosion in the infamous battle between the archmage Thongalar the Mighty and the evil mage Shile Rauretilar and his apprentices

In the spellstorm that befell here, Shile and his apprentices all perished, and the very fabric of Faerun was rent, so that Azuth the One appeared to set things right. Even today, it is said that magic sometimes goes awry in the Court—and for that reason, magic items, scrolls, components, and demonstrations are all forbidden in the Court.[21]

The White Bull tavern was in turn named for an albino bull born on this spot to an astonished caravan owner in the days when this area was an open field for livestock and caravan assembly. He took it as a good omen.

Caravan Court, to the south, is a popular spot for loafers and old men to sit (many bring stools or crates for the purpose) and watch men sweat and curse, animals bellow and thunder about, and the generally frenzied, often dangerous, activity as caravans are formed or broken up. However, not counting the ever-passing confusion of the High Road and the Way of the Dragon—watching those thoroughfares is itself a spectator sport of long tradition—the most interesting of all these open spaces is Virgin's Square.

This space is, of course, not a square at all, but roughly round in shape. Waterdeep's womenfolk often come here to gasp at and give the eye to sinister-looking men from all over Faerun who swagger about Virgin's Square fully armed, hoping to attract

---

[21] Treat the Court and the streets for roughly a block around it on all sides as a wild magic area. If your DM lacks the *FORGOTTEN REALMS® Adventures* sourcebook, he or she simply use the *wand of wonder* table in the *DMG* or devise his or her own random magical effects. Whenever magic is unleashed, it will go wild on a roll of 4 or 8 on a d12.

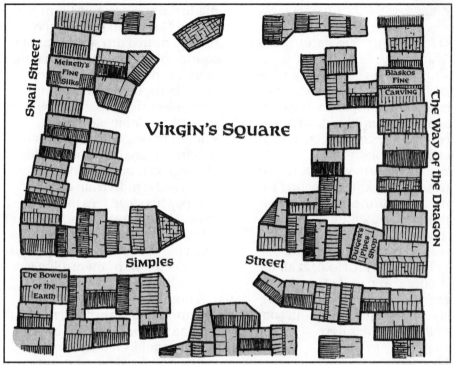

Snail Street

Meireth's Fine Silks

VIRGIN'S SQUARE

Blaskos Fine Carving

The Way of the Dragon

Dulger's Pipes Shop

Simples   Street

The Bowels of the Earth

mercenary employment. Here
Blazidon One-Eye sits on a crate
most days, matching hireswords
with employers.

The square is named for a local
legend that tells of virgin men
and women being sacrificed long
ago to dragons on this site, before
there even was a City of Waterdeep. Some Sword Coast barbarian tribes do have legends of a
Dragon God that keep them from
raiding Waterdeep, where great
dragons are said to lair on Mount
Waterdeep. According to these
folk, if they ever fall under the
gaze of the Waterdeep dragons,
the wyrms will come devouring
among them to make up for all

the virgins not given to them
down the ages since the nomadic
barbarians stopped coming here.
Interestingly, there are much
newer legends in the city of
dragon hoards hidden somewhere in Mount Waterdeep, and
still not recovered by either the
city guard, which inhabits caverns and passages in the mountain, linked to Castle Waterdeep,
or the smugglers who use buried
Skullport, below.

There is yet more lore linked
to Virgin's Square. A mimic once
somehow reached it and took the
shape of a statue. It remained
undetected for two winters until
the continuing disappearances of

street drunks in the square on every dark night prompted an investigation. The statue seemed strangely unfamiliar to the sculptor who had fashioned it—and a sewer beside it was discovered to be completely filled (to a depth of over 60 feet) with the real statue—covered by a huge heap of bones!

This was after two of the city watch, not really expecting to find anything amiss, carelessly prodded the statue with their spears, and in response, it reached out and ate them.

Take a careful look at all the statues you pass, I guess. I'll look at the alleyways of this ward later, after I tell you about some of the buildings here.

Homes

The Snookery

This is the house of the noted Captain-at-Arms (weapons tutor) Myrmith Splendon.[22] It's a rambling old place with stone walls and barred windows. Its exterior doors are covered with plating made from old armor, hammered flat. From inside, there is often a muted din similar to the sounds of a foundry, as Myrmith's students repair weapons they have damaged, or modify those they wield, or simply use them on each other. Some have been known to practice the knack of driving an adamantine sword *through* armor plate for days.

Here Myrmith trains all who can pay his steep fees in advance[23] in the use of weaponry of all sorts; he has mastered an amazing variety of weapons and has specimens of them all here for daily use.

Those planning on robbing Myrmith's house are warned that no one knows just what he does with his gold, that the snooks (griffon-like animated stone statues, something like gargoyles) which adorn the roof of the house are intelligent and formidable guardians. Not only would robbers have to contend with the snooks, but at least seven magical *flying daggers*[24] also steadfastly guard the place.

---

[22] Location #170 on the color map.

[23] Myrmith can use any weapon the DM desires and can train a character in the use of it thoroughly or assist warriors in improving their overall battle skills enough to allow them to advance a level in expertise. His fees are 190 gp/level per week. His skill is such that training, even when the house is full of students learning simultaneously, will take the minimum time necessary.

[24] As Myrmith's wizard friends are continually experimenting with and improving on the snooks, the DM is free to improve upon the powers of a gargoyle in any way desired. All snooks (there are at least 6 active at all times) are LN in alignment, and unshakably loyal to Myrmith. Even magic cannot turn them against him.

Flying daggers are fully detailed on page 115 of the *Campaign Guide to Undermountain* book (in the *Ruins of Undermountain* boxed set). Myrmith's version of these self-animated flying weapons are AC5; MV Fl 21 (A); HD 1+1; hp 9; THAC0 17; #AT 2; Dmg 1-4; get no attack bonuses but are considered +2 magical weapons for purposes of what they can hit; cannot be affected by any type of magical or psionic control except by Myrmith; and are immune to *magic missile* spells and all lightning or electrical-based magic, which they reflect back 100% on the source!

118

Shops

Aurora's Realms Shop "High Road" Catalogue Counter

This is the Trades Ward outlet of the famous Faerun-wide all goods retail chain. Located on the northwest corner of the meeting of the Street of the Tusks and the High Road, this shop has six guards (shifts of three and three), a stout, motherly matron of a counter clerk named Orgula Samshroon, and a tall, kindly service-mage called Dhaunryl Zalimbar.

Belmonder's Meats

This shop is always busy. From when the place opens at dawn to when it closes at dusk, the four counter clerks and five butchers here are kept hopping chopping and wrapping meat for all they're worth to satisfy the endless lines of customers crowding in for fresh meat. By far the most popular meat counter in the city, Belmonder's has two side counters: one sells skewers of sizzle-cooked meat scraps (a popular walking meal for those one the go) and the other sells whole sides of meat to buyers for inns, other eateries, noble families, and wealthy folk. At night, a security force of 20 experienced and well-equipped hireswords guards the unloading of meat wagons. A meat wagon arriving in the city is escorted to a warehouse by a city watch patrol and/or a member of the Guild of Butchers. The night runs from warehouses to the various butcher shops have similar escorts.

There are tales of corpses found hanging on hooks in the ice chambers here and murdered men delivered packed in the wagons with the other meat under the ice and straw, but the throngs of shoppers love the place and have never been put off by such outrageous whispers. Smoked and well-aged sides are brought in from Belmonder's own estates northeast of the city near Rassalantar. The butchers will also cut up a carcass for you if you bring one in. This task takes about 20 minutes and costs 3–10 gp, depending on the size and difficulty of the job.[25]

Proprietor: The proprietor, Morathin "Hooks" Belmonder, is a burly, hearty man with a strong stomach and a good eye for meat. He is Second Knife of, and public contact for, the Guild of Butchers.

The Golden Horn Gambling House

This ornately gilded palace of gleaming black polished marble stands on the east side of Snail Street, dominating the curve

---

[25] Location #188 on the color map.

where it sweeps sharply east near its northern end.[26]

I could barely see inside this place—and what I could see was red and plush: red carpet, red sofas, red cushions, dancing girls wearing sheer red silk gowns (that were high cut and low cut!), and even a red-painted ceiling.

The lamplight is kept dim, I suspect, to hide as much of the cheating from the customers as possible. If any notice and object, the 16 bodyguards in the place converge like thirsty stirges, and the disturbance is quickly and quietly removed.

My advice to those who don't enjoy losing great sums of money is to stick to the four-hand card and dice games where you play against the house and three other patrons. And try to find out early on which one of the other patrons is the house antic (undercover agent)! It's worth one visit, just to be overwhelmed by all the red coziness—and to see the sensual dancing.

If you do win big—once a year or so someone does, I'm told— you'll have the mystery contents of the golden horn, which hangs above the huge open hearth, added to your winnings. But be careful: I expect the horn holds coins treated with a slow-acting paralyzing agent or a *polymorphed* monster, so these folks can quietly get their money back!

Proprietor: The Golden Horn's proprietor, Hahstoz Baerhuld, is a dark, silent, expressionless man who seems to glide silently around the place.

Thentavva's Boots

This old, narrow shop on Vellarr's Lane is adorned with the carved stone images of frolicking nymphs and pegasi.[27] Inside, the crowded interior smells strongly of leather. Here a man considered by some to be the best cobbler in Waterdeep makes custom footwear for all.

His thigh-high, sleek, pointed-toed ladies' boots are famous and eagerly sought after, even at the steep price of 10 gp and the waiting period of at least nine days, but the shop is also full of slippers, walking boots, and the like. Thentavvan work is of the best quality, known for lasting many years and surviving mud and wet well.

Proprietor: Thurve Thentavva, the cobbler supreme and proprietor of Thentavva's Boots, is calm, bespectacled, and unflappable.

Orsabbas's Fine Imports

Here you can pay far too much money for things you never

---

[26] Location #196 on the color map.
[27] Location #177 on the color map.

expected to see on sale in a shop—things from far away in Faerun. This shop caters to the homesick, with perfumed hangings from Calimshan, a spear from Tethyr adorned with the skull of a royal family member, rock rubble from Mirabar, and much, much more.

Nobles needing costumes for feasts often come here to rent or buy authentic pirate garb from the Sea of Fallen Stars, barbarian furs from the far, frozen North, silken robes from Thay, and even Bedine robes and headgarb from the depths of Anauroch. Others come for disguises.

This shop, on Vellarr's Lane just east of the Street of the Tusks,[28] is entered up a steep flight of stone steps. The main floor of the shop, a dozen feet above the street, is adorned with a large, arched window inset with a border of varicolored glass. At night, it

glows slightly due to powerful spells on it that deflect all missiles and blows, preventing its breakage.

Inside, the observant visitor will notice a curious sight on the windowsill: a scattering of small, knobby bones, yellowed with age. They are a legacy of Waterdeep's more lawless days, when most thieves snatched by night, rather than wore guild livery and stole by contract and moneylending.

There was a scything blade trap built into the sill of this window. The trap may still function when set. The present proprietor will not say, though he will talk about the bones.

The window's excellent location as a means of entry resulted in more than one late-night scream. On many a morning, the shopkeeper would get up, draw his sword, go downstairs to unset the trap, and open the window—

---

[28] Location #179 on the color map.

only to find the remnants of an unlucky or unskilled thief's hand there on the sill.

Orsabbas fills special orders (where customers request specific items from certain places), but the fees are steep, and the wait may be long—as long as an entire season in some cases.

Proprietor: Ildar "the Duke of Darkness" Orsabbas is the proprietor. His nickname comes from the masked, sinister guise he wears to nobles' feasts.

Riautar's Weaponry

This shop fronts on the High Road just east of the Street of the Tusks[29] and is crowded with an assortment of ready weaponry, most of it secondhand. It is notable as the source of the best arrows, bowstrings, and long bows in Waterdeep, made on the premises by the owner. Their superlative workmanship is admired and coveted by all archers who see them.

A relic of Waterdeep's past can also be seen on the roof of this shop. The crouching, fanged female figure with the spread wings is not a carved ornament, but a petrified harpy. She dates from the long-ago War of Five Wizards, when five mages battled their way across the city in one terrible night, vying for

supremacy in the Wizards' Guild of the time—and destroying most of the city in the process.

This harpy, along with two others, was *teleported* to Waterdeep from afar by one of the wizards, and another wizard promptly petrified them all. The other two harpies plunged to the street below. There they shattered—and crushed the wizard who had summoned them. It is rumored that some mage in the city frees this harpy to fly—and kill, at his command—from time to time, and then forces her back into her customary pose and stone shape, but this has never been proven to be more than a flight of fancy.

Proprietor: Zarondar "the Nimble" Riautar, public contact for the Fellowship of Bowyers and Fletchers, is the proprietor.

The Riven Shield Shop

This shop is famous up and down the Sword Coast for its large and varied assortment of secondhand arms and armor—including many famous relics of fallen or retired adventurers. The most famous items are either not for sale, or command very high prices (thousands of gold pieces). There are, however, many serviceable, unhistoried used weapons here, from tiny daggers used

---

[29] Location #180 on the color map.

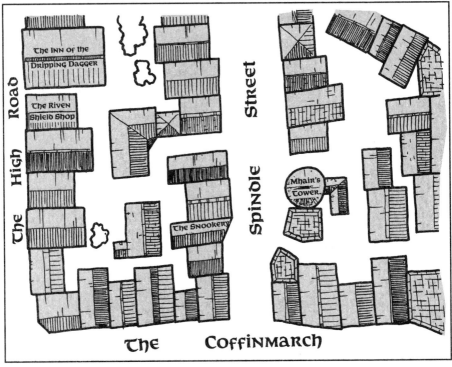

The Riven Shield Shop — The Inn of the Dripping Dagger — High Road — Street — Spindle — Mhain's Tower — The Snookery — The Coffinmarch

by noble ladies to the heavy broadswords favored by barbarians, that are useful to anyone in need of a weapon. Scores of these sell each day.[30]

No one is tempted to steal the more valuable pieces. It is widely known that some of the magical shields hanging from the rafter beams contain magically imprisoned monsters that can be released to fight as an ally of the shield-wearer. It is also well known that one of the items in the shop (no one is quite sure which one, and the proprietor neglects to say) is an alert, always vigilant, sentinel.

Proprietor: Delborggan the Blade runs the Riven Shield Shop. He is a grizzled, one-eyed ex-adventurer.

---

[30] Location #169 on the color map. Currently, the shop holds such wonders as the Horrible Hammer of War (functions like a *vampiric ring of regeneration*); the Spear of Lochal, which has some strange magical powers and is believed to be only a part of a larger, more powerful magic item; the Helm of Bolarr, which allows its wearer to see even in pitch darkness and with *infravision*—and to perceive any foe struck by the helm-wearer within the last turn, who is still within 400 yards of the helm, even if the foe is invisible, disguised by magic, has changed form, or is hidden behind a solid barrier; the Shield of Many Meteors, which attracts and harmlessly absorbs all *fireballs, minute meteors,* and similar fire magic effects into itself; and many others. The Horrible Hammer of War was wielded by the half-ogre Klarargh Skullbold, leader of the adventuring band known as Wrath Rampant, until he was slain by the city guard while trying to set fire to a tavern in Dock Ward.

Saern's Fine Swords

This shop stands on the southeastern corner of the meeting of the High Road and Burnt Wagon Way.[31] It's an old, massively built stone place with bars on all the windows, crenelations on the flagstone roof, and a narrow, exposed, iron-bound door overlooked by arrow slits—in short, a miniature fortress.

It holds a large stock of swords, including a few made by Szwarharba the Swordsmith, the famous craftsman of Tethyr, who before his death some 90 winters back had learned how to forge blades that could be bent around almost in a circle without breaking or becoming permanently angled out of true. Swords are not made to fit the user here, but they are sharpened (including overall lightening by shaving the blade thickness). The large selection means that most shoppers will be able to find a sword that is reasonably suitable to their reach and strength. A good long sword costs about 20 gp, including the 1 gp city fee, and a fine dagger about 4 gp.

Piergeiron has a deal with the proprietor of this shop: Should the city militia ever need to be called up quickly and reinforced with volunteers needing arms, the city guard will empty the shop of arms, take it over as a rallying post, and pay the owner (who will be allowed to stay in residence with his staff if he desires) 90,000 pieces of gold on the spot.

Few clients know the quietly polite owner of the shop is a warrior, and fewer still know he has invisible weapons stashed all over the shop in plain view, ready to defend himself with. One is a *sword of dancing* and another is a *sword +4, defender.* The shop has at least three staff on duty at all times—one of whom is an out-of-uniform city guard officer, who notes the names and descriptions of those who buy particular weapons.

Proprietor: Zygarth "Slayer" Saern runs Saern's Fine Swords. He is a tall, gaunt, smiling man who can tell the age, quality, and condition of steel at a glance.

Taverns

Felzoun's Folly

This many-windowed tavern is a noisy, crowded, casual place, where many merchants and shoppers grab a quick tankard and a bite. Its exterior presents an awning-festooned, three-story face on the northwestern corner where the mouth of River Square opens into Salabar Street.[32]

---

[31] Location #175 on the color map.
[32] Location #193 on the color map.

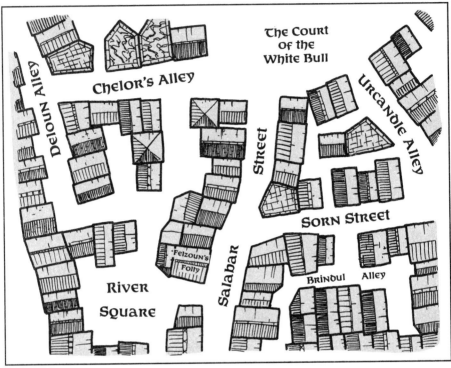

The Court
of the
White Bull

Chelor's Alley

Deloun Alley

Urcandle Alley

Street

Sorn Street

Salabar

Felzoun's Folly

Brindul Alley

River Square

A bite here means a sausage roll or chicken-and-cheese pasty augmented by fresh asparagus with melted butter (when in season) or fresh whole oysters. Those with strong stomachs eat oysters raw here by tradition. The standard fare costs 4 sp each—a real bargain. The seasonal delicacies are 6 sp/plate.

There's little variety in drink here. Ale is 1 sp/tankard, stout is 2 sp, and wine and zzar are both 4 sp/tallglass. There are usually six white wines to be had, including sweet Neverwinter Nectar, and three reds.

I've heard rumors that stolen goods can be fenced here, but could learn nothing more.[33] In all the din and confusion, I suspect wholesale *wars* could be fought here, with no one the wiser!

Proprietor: Felzoun Thar, the bristle-bearded, fearless dwarven host, is always bustling busily about the Folly.

Inns

The Gentle Rest

As a rule, a traveler spends more than one might expect to be at the center of it all in Waterdeep

---

[33] Elminster reminds us to consult page 32 of *Waterdeep and the North* for more on this matter.

when taking accommodation in Trades Ward. This inn is by no means an exception to that practical expectation.

Located on the north side of the High Road, just west of where it begins to bend westwards to meet Waterdeep Way, this inn rises five full floors above the street. It is large and well-appointed.[34] And for the money being asked, it should be—the rate is 6 gp/room per night!

No meals are included, but there's house wine and hot water for baths. A copper sitting-tub is provided in each room, as well as a—noisy!—stoppered floor drain. Well-tended tabling is also part of the room fee.

Proprietor: Torst Urlivan, the proprietor, is a tall, withdrawn, dignified man who dresses as if he were the wealthiest noble, but smells strongly of horse.

Gondalim's

This large, comfortable old inn stands in the angle where Winter Path and Burnt Wagon Way both meet with the High Road.[35] It's a worn but comfortable place, and because of its massive construction, it's also very quiet. You'll seldom hear noises from other guests at night.

Rooms vary from 2–7 gp/night, depending on the size and amenities. The top-priced rooms are actually large suites, sleeping up to 10 people in comfort. In all cases, stabling and dawnfry—or morningfeast, as they call it more formally here—are included. In all, it is a nice place to stay and very central.

When crossing the lobby between the room stairs and the dining room, observant visitors may see a dark stain on the door leading to the kitchens—as if something spattered against it just above halfway up and ran down it to the floor. The stain isn't poor housekeeping. Some 70 winters ago, the princess Shaerglynda of Tethyr was murdered on that spot.

She died from a swordthrust that pinned her to the door—and the dark stain was left by her life's blood. It can't be cleaned away, and it never fades or disappears. Even when the door is replaced—and it has been, at least twice—the bloodstain slowly reappears by itself.

Proprietress: Shulmeira Gondalim is the proprietress. She is the granddaughter of the founder. She is a short, slim, unspectacular but charming woman of young age. She presides with quiet expertise over a staff of old, large, stoop-shouldered and shuffling, but calmly capable, servant women.

---

[34] Location #191 on the color map.

[35] Location #173 on the color map. Elminster confirms that the bloodstain tale is true.

The Grey Serpent

This sleek, fairly new, expensive and high-class establishment stands on the east side of the Way of the Dragon, not far north from its intersection with Drakiir Street.[36] Rooms here are a stiff 6 gp per night (single or double), but the furnishings are so clean and luxurious that this place outshines some noble villas I've seen! Stabling and very fine house wine, but no food, is included in the room fee.

By special arrangement, apprentices of the Launderers' Guild and the Order of Master Taylors are always on hand to whisk garments away for cleaning, alterations, or repairs. This is a cool, private place—but truly the lap of luxury.

Proprietor: Orlpiir Hammerstar runs the Grey Serpent. He's a man with dwarven blood in his past, I was told. However, when I met him, he appeared very tall, thin, and austere, with a cultured voice and a beaky nose. The dwarven blood must be rather far back in his ancestry.

The Unicorn's Horn

This fairly new inn occupies the most strategic location in Waterdeep: the northeast corner where the High Road meets Waterdeep Way and turns north.[37] As you might expect, room fees are as high as a halfling after several kegs: 10 gp to 25 gp per night! There's even an Imperial Suite of rooms on the top floor (the sixth) that costs 40 gp per night. Its windows command magnificent views of the city on three sides.

The furnishings are opulent, but not very tasteful. Huge tapestries and heavily gilded, massive pieces of furniture are everywhere. The canopied beds are the only comfortable place to sit in the entire inn.

Servants carry your bags, stable your mounts for you, bring a light evening meal with wine to your room, and hot spiced wine and hot water for a bath in the morning—but that's the extent of the service. There's a locked, guarded warehouse for wagons, carts, and coaches available as part of the room fee.

All in all, it is impressive, but not relaxing, or worth the money. Stay somewhere cheaper, and go to a nobles' feast if you want to be overwhelmed with haughty luxury instead.

Proprietor: Quendever Ilistrym owns and runs this inn. He is a haughty, effete man of excellent cheekbones and breeding, but little energy or competence that I could see.

---

[36] Location #204 on the color map.
[37] Location #178 on the color map.

128

Alleys

Trades Ward's alleys are crowded, often highly scented passages usually crammed with garbage, delivered and stored goods, or just empty crates. They are always busy and may not offer much faster travel than the larger streets they wind among. Many a brawler has found that close quarters here prevent the use of a favorite but large weapon or can cause an inglorious collapse of boxes on top of himself!

Atkiss Alley

This short passage links Quaff Alley with Virgin's Square. Many men habitually slip through here in livery or finery. Cutpurses sometimes lurk here to prey on them, but city watch patrols are quite frequent.

Blackhorn Alley

The northernmost of the passages cutting through the city blocks that stand between the High Road and the Way of the Dragon, this alleyway is named for a long-dead cobbler of some note, Alsible Blackhorn, who lived on it. Today, it is a constant haunt of brown rats big enough to make a (disgusting) meal of—and some poor folk do just that, hunting them with clubs and hurled, empty crates.

Brindul Alley

This crescent-shaped alley lies between Sorn Street and River Street. It is the frequent haunt of a dangerous apparition—one more often encountered near the docks in older days, but seen here since a few winters ago: the Hand That Sings.

The Hand has been seen more than once in Brindul Alley or floating in the ways nearby. It is an animated human hand with a mouth in its palm. The strange apparition all too similar to the sign of cursed Moander, the ancient and evil god who never sleeps quite soundly enough.

The Hand is said to snatch valuables it fancies—especially magic—when it encounters them, and to occasionally attack folk in the darkness, strangling them or tripping them into fatal falls. Most often, though, it seems to take no notice of those who do not bother or follow it, merely drifting along, eerily singing old and fragmentary Sword Coast ballads and love songs as it wanders through the night.[38]

Chelor's Alley

This short passage runs due west from the Court of the White Bull. Lit each night by many lamps set in the windows of the upstairs home of the man it is named for (a merchant who just loves candles), it is used as a rendezvous by those who need light enough to read by (to check maps or contracts, for instance), and by city watch and city guard patrols who need to examine evidence.

Dark Alley

This narrow, winding passage runs east off Buckle Street, just south of, and parallel to, River Street. Overshadowed by tall buildings on all sides, it is gloomy even at highsun and is pitch dark by night—a favorite mugging spot, used by half a dozen or more local thugs at once. Not a place to go near after dusk.

Deloun Alley

Reached from Chelor's Alley, this back-of-the-shops delivery route is always crowded with crates, barrels, and the like. By night, rats of both the human and rodent sort lurk here, where crates can easily be toppled onto, or to block the escape of, surprised victims.

Hunters' Alley

This narrow passage runs east from the Way of the Dragon. It continues the route of Soothsayers' Way. It is named for two brave brothers who roamed the Realms when yet young. One became a lore lord of the Realms, and the other currently aspires to dukedom. As in their company, those who traverse this way generally have a wild but ultimately safe journey.

Lathin's Cut

This short passage links the Plinth and Jelabril Street to the High

---

[38] Statistics of the Hand that Sings are left to the DM. It is suggested that the Hand be based on the undead crawling claw (see the monster of that name in Volume 3 of the *Monstrous Compendium*). It will wield any magic items it can hold, and has a whimsical personality—quick to anger and attack, but not vindictive. It does not hold grudges.

Road. It is named for the man who leveled his own house to create it for the greater convenience of the devout. Both citizens and visitors used it as a landmark, shortcut, and rendezvous.

Mhaer's Alley

This short passage has grown into a proper street that links Wall Way along the southern edge of the City of the Dead with Spendthrift Alley. It has the greatest concentration of shops in the city where you can buy thread, cord, rope, wire, and trimmings for clothing.

Spendthrift Alley

This former alley long ago grew into a major local street, but retained the feature that created its name: the ongoing bazaar of stalls and street vendors, selling everything cheap. This shoppers' gift from the gods never closes. By night, this route is brilliantly lit, and the trading goes on. *The* place to go for small trifles, buttons, laces, and whatever you can't find elsewhere. It is apt to be crowded. Beware thieves.

Quaff Alley

Stretching west from Atkiss Alley to the rear of the Golden Horn gambling house, this short passage is named for its traditional use by drunkards, who drink here until they pass out, and snore the night away. In winter, the city watch spreads straw here for burrowing-bedding, to keep these unfortunates from freezing to death. Many a thief or adventurer has hidden among it temporarily.

Quill Alley

Now a proper street, this passage is the traditional neighborhood of scribes, cartographers, and clerks. It is named for the feathers that most people of letters use as pens. You can still hire many here.

The visitor will see many exterior staircases winding up and down the sides of the rickety old buildings along this lane. Children love to play among them, and so, by night, do thieves.

Spoils Alley

A behind-the-shops way running westerly from the southernmost end of Quill Alley, this innocent-looking passage is where the Thieves' Guild of old used to divide up the street takings of a night's work. Now it's a box-littered backwater—but it still used for shady meetings. It's an especially good place to change clothing or don a disguise.

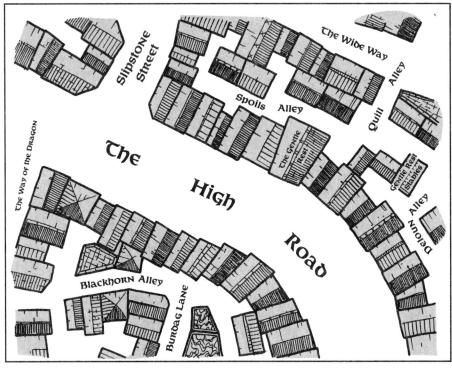

Theln Lane

This short cut-through links Irimar's Walk with Andamaar's Street at the north end of Trades Ward. It's an echoing, bare passage overhung by balconies where hard currency girls dwell, lowering rope ladders to clients. Theln was a "businessman" who lived and died long ago in one of the buildings on this alleyway.

Tsarnen Alley

Running east off the Way of the Dragon to Burdag Lane just north of the Plinth, this passage and Lathin's Cut provide a short-cut through the blocks of buildings. Thieves often preyed upon the traffic here in older days—but Tsarnen the ranger made it his business to bodily dispose of them in a quite unpleasant manner one summer before the Thieves' Guild was overthrown. (Tsarnen had had a very bad expience with muggers early in life.) The thieves moved to safer hunting grounds after a short time. These days, with Tsarnen long in his grave, the passage is not quite as safe, but watch patrols and, by day, pilgrims and priests pass along it often.

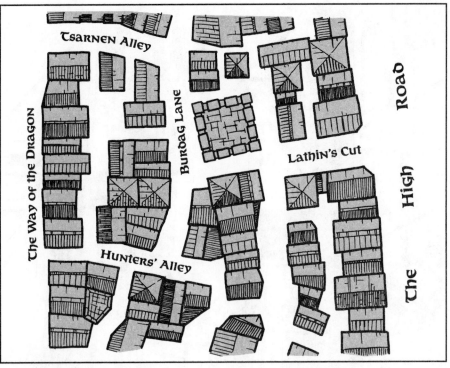

Tsarnen Alley

Burdag Lane

The Way of the Dragon

Lathin's Cut

Hunters' Alley

Road

High

The

Tuckpurse Alley

This alleyway runs east and south from the eastern end of Spendthrift Alley, linking it to the easternmost end of Vellarr's Lane. By night, it's very dark and a favorite working ground for thugs, some of whom use children to trip or snatch at passersby. There's a very large rain barrel partway along this alley just behind Thond Glass & Glazing that you should beware of. Its gutter was diverted long ago, and it is used by thugs who crouch inside it, watching for prey through knotholes.

Urcandle Alley

This short passage links the Court of the White Bull with Sorn Street. Urcandle was a person (just *who* has been forgotten), but today this alleyway is where you'll find ropes, cables, harness, reins, drovers' whips, spare wagon wheels, and the like for sale. If your cart or wagon needs a spare part, this is the place to look. There are other places in the city that sell such items (notably in South Ward), but the shops along this route have the greatest concentration of such vendors in one area.

Southern Ward

any of the common folk of Waterdeep dwell in Southern Ward. This homely, friendly, busy, and largely poor area is the forgotten ward of Waterdeep. It is sometimes referred to as Caravan City, after its major activity. In it warehouses, stables, and coach sheds stand in plenty to serve the bustle of overland trade in and out of Waterdeep. Be warned: Native Waterdhavians call it just South Ward. Anyone using the longer term is marked instantly as an outsider.

There's little of interest for the casual stroller to see, and the security of trade goods dictates both the presence of guards and their reluctance to let visitors gawk at what's inside warehouses or wagons.[1] Still, South Ward does have landmarks, and some hidden pleasures, too.

Landmarks

This is the first part of the city seen by most travelers entering it overland from the south. One of the city's smallest wards and probably its least socially and politically important and influential one, South Ward is the ordinary side of Waterdeep.

From Southgate onwards, the broad street known as the Way of the Dragon forms the southern and western boundaries of South Ward. The High Road, the closest thing Waterdeep has to a main street, bisects it.

South Ward's eastern boundary is the Trollwall. Its ragged northern boundary consists of Telshambra's Street, a little bit of the High Road, Sahtyra's Lane, Caravan Court (all of which is deemed to be in South Ward), and Belzer's Walk. Some call Belzer's Walk simply Belzer's, but locals sharply correct those who do.

South Ward is dominated by large, tall, old stone, mud brick, and timber warehouses. Crowded among them are three- and four-floor-high tenements, most with shops at street level. Trees and even bushes are few, dust (or mud) is plentiful, but everything

---

[1] The private guards at every establishment (typically a dozen or so LN F1s and F2s) can call on the law, who will come running at any sound of shouting or clanging metal, such as a guard beating his blade on his shield. All the guards know this.

City watch patrols are detailed on page 17 of FR1 *Waterdeep and the North.* They pass a given point about every 20 minutes and look into a tavern or inn dining room about every 40 minutes.

As detailed on pages 20 and 23 of the *City System* boxed set booklet, the city guard also patrols South Ward in six-man detachments. Typical patrol details are as given on page 23. Reinforcements will be a dozen LG hm F3s to F6s clad in chain mail and armed with maces, long swords, daggers, slings, and a pole arm appropriate to the locale. Guard patrols pass a given street location about every hour in South Ward, and arrive 2d8 minutes after a city watch patrol blows a warning horn.

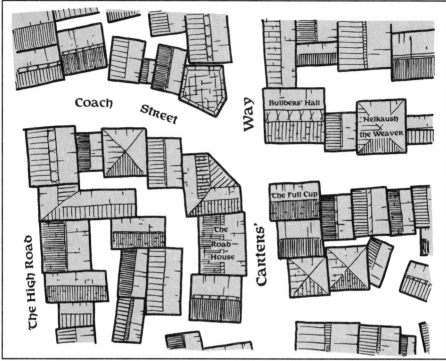

Coach Street · Way · Builders' Hall · Nelkaush the Weaver · The Full Cup · The High Road · The Road House · Carters'

else is kept clean, and the streets are always busy. The predominant sound in South Ward is the rumble of cart wheels. The smell of this part of the city is not of fish from the harbor, but is provided by the dung of the draft animals. Most of the stables are merely covered pens, although sometimes a multifloored building provides the cover.

The best-known places in the Ward are Caravan Court; Brian the Swordmaster's smithy and shop;[2] the house of the kindly wizard Kappiyan Flurmastyr;[3] Metalmasters' Hall,[4] headquarters of the Most Careful Order of Skilled Smiths & Metalforgers; the House of Good Spirits,[5] headquarters of the Vintners', Distillers', and Brewers' Guild; the magnificent, gargoyle-adorned edifice of the Stone House[6] of the Carpenters', Roofers', and Plaisterers' Guild (or, as I heard one merchant call it, "that great pile"); and the Jade Dancer[7] tavern and festhall. The House of Good Spirits is also a working inn, and

---

[2] On the color city map, Brian's smithy/shop is #207.
[3] Location #218 on the color map.
[4] Location #225 on the color map.
[5] Location #214 on the color map.
[6] Location #206 on the color map. Its floor plan appears on Map 7 of the *City System* boxed set.

it can be found from afar by following the strong almond scent of the zzar made there. Locals also use the lesser known taverns as landmarks, along with the other guildhalls in the ward: the Coach & Wagon Hall,[8] headquarters of the Wagonmakers' and Coach Builders' Guild; Saddlers' and Harness-Makers' Hall[9] of the guild of the same name; Builders' Hall[10] of the Guild of Stonecutters and Masons; and the Road House,[11] headquarters of the Fellowship of Carters and Coachmen.

I found that the most interesting places in South Ward were hidden away or that most visitors and Waterdhavians alike pass them by. One was the Moon Sphere, a magical sphere of blue radiance that appears in Dancing Court only when the moon is full and allows any folk inside of it to fly or dance on air. Another was the Old Monster Shop, which fronts on the Jar, and sells monsters for the hungry, the bored, and the vengeful.

[7] Location #208 on the color map.
[8] Location #216 on the color map.
[9] Location #217 on the color map.
[10] Location #219 on the color map.
[11] Location #222 on the color map.
The guilds and their doings, fees, and current leaders are described in the *Waterdeep and the North* sourcebook.

Kappiyan Flurmastyr's House

The unassuming house of the wizard Kappiyan Flurmastyr is a popular destination in South Ward. Many folk wanting potions find their ways to Kappiyan's house.[12] The house sits at the northern entrance to Anchoret's Court and has easy access to the safe drinking water well there.

An arched wooden door with a brass strike-gong and a brass nameplate that says "Kappiyan" leads into a small, neat, richly appointed two-story building. Fine furniture, rugs, and vivid, skillfully painted landscapes crowd a cozy home. Save for the homonculous that answers the door and the stone golem hung with cloaks and hats in the entry hall, the ground floor looks like the abode of any well-off, unpretentious merchant or widow.

On the upper floor, however, you'll find a large spellcasting chamber at the head of the stairs, three bedrooms (one for Kappiyan, one for an apprentice, and one for guests), a wardrobe room, a bathroom, and a spellbook-lined study lit by a tall brass brazier with a cast snake coiling up its standard. The rooms are richly paneled in polished wood, and all of the large, oval beds levitate, floating silently at whatever height anyone touching them wills them to be at.

Kappiyan's current apprentice told me there are guardian creatures and magic—especially flying wands that Kappiyan can trigger from afar—all over the house, but the only wand I saw was hidden behind a secret panel in the wall of the wardrobe. If you rap three times[13] on a certain panel there, it drops open to reveal a cached, silvery wand[14] for use in emergencies. These are fortunately few. Those living near told me Kappiyan is a quiet, kindly neighbor.

An expert maker of potions[15] who testily insists he is not

---

[12] This place is #218 on the color city map.

[13] In the same round.

[14] Information given in the *Knight of the Living Dead* gamebook, which contains descriptions of Kappiyan, his abode, and his apprentice Shalara, suggests this is a *wand of teleportation.* Thrice per day, and at a charge cost of 1 per being per use, the wand can unerringly *teleport* the wielder and/or any beings touched by the wand or the wielder to any location on the same plane. Unwilling beings cannot avoid this effect, but the wielder must make a successful attack roll to touch them. Multiple beings and nonliving material carried, touched, or within 10' of the wielder and not in the direct possession of another creature that are willed to accompany the *'ported* beings are all brought along. The trip can deliberately be to a midair location, and the wand then confers a *feather fall* effect on all the things it moves—so the user could *'port* to a hostile location, appear above defenders, and cast spells or trigger other items while descending.

[15] Kappiyan's prices tend to be twice the XP value of a potion in gold pieces. Exceptions are the magical drafts that ensure longevity (which he can't make, and has no supply of), allow etherealness and aid in treasure finding (three times their XP value), any potions of control (eight times their XP value), and healing or curative potions of any sort (which he gives out for half their XP value).

running a potion shop, Kappiyan is too kind-hearted to turn the world away, and so is always selling potions to folk who turn up at his door. The proceeds fund his researches. Kappiyan is a refiner of small and elegant magics, not a wizard bent on ruling the world. He is kind and easily moved, and is always helping hard-luck cases. Those who are cruel or who use magic to govern others make him very angry. He has been known to appear without warning and use his own magic to deliver sharp lessons to such folk.[16]

Kappiyan's kindness and soft heart have led him to help many eager students of the Art. Over the years, he has aided a long succession of maidens in becoming sorceresses.[17] His current apprentice is Shalara, a friendly lass born to merchants in Amphail.

Kappiyan looks like most folk

think a good wizard should. He's tall, thin, white-bearded, and always clad in dark robes covered with runes and symbols.

---

[16] Kappiyan is further detailed on page 53 of FR1 *Waterdeep and the North*. His staff is a *staff of power*. He is 86% likely to correctly identify any standard (that is, ones that are found in the *DUNGEON MASTER™ Guide*) potion that hasn't been doctored or mixed with something else. He can always tell when two or more potions have been mixed together, but not necessarily what the potions were.

Most of Kappiyan's enchanted gems have effects identical to *rings of protection* and *potions of vitality*. One commonly crafted sort requires a ruby, emerald, or black opal. It heals 4–16 points of damage/day, operating by itself with a visible flash and glow when its bearer is injured. Roll 4d4 when it first activates. If the total is higher than the hit points lost, the remainder waits for another activation, later in the day but is lost if it doesn't occur within 24 hours or 144 turns.

Kappiyan also makes *periapts of health, periapts of proof against poison*, and *greenstone amulets* (detailed in FR4 *The Magister* and many other Realms sources).

[17] Even Elminster was envious of the roster of apprentices Kappiyan had accumulated over the years. He's so kindly that young lasses trust him completely (and rightly). He has aided the following sorceresses of note, among many others, to become accomplished wielders of the Art:

- Cathliira of Elturel (CN hf W9)
- Ilphara of Amnwater (NG hf W10)
- Imbaerl of Baldur's Gate (CG hf W12)
- Larithmae of Almraiven (CG hf W12)
- Minthalue of Suzail (CN hf W9). When she came to Kappiyan, she was a famous Calishite exotic dancer. Tongues wagged furiously all over Waterdeep for over a year.
- Nesmorae of Callidyrr (CG hf W11)
- Phantrara of Priapurl (NG hf W8)

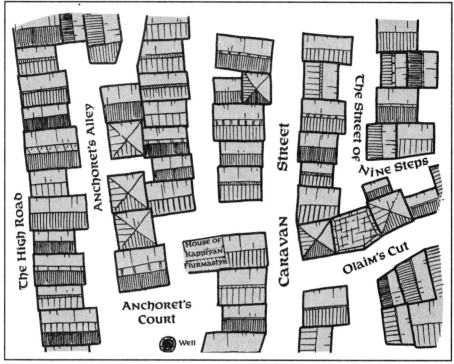

He's going bald, looks very distinguished, and always carries a staff. He can identify many potions by look and smell alone, and is especially skilled at turning gems into magical items that protect or aid their bearers.

Kappiyan lives with Shalara, who is perhaps 16 years old. She has dark hair and eyes, and is earnest and easily upset. She prefers to and wears pants and tunics, as do boys her age, for greater freedom of motion.

Spell battles in and around Kappiyan's house may be disappointingly few (to tourists, not neighbors), but this was not always so. Eighty years ago, one of Waterdeep's first nightclubs stood on this site. It was known as the Rusty Halidom and was destroyed one night in a magic fight between drunken wizards, who blew it apart with all the guests, wine kegs, and dancers still inside. There are still rumors of buried treasure being lost in the wreckage and paved over now in the alleyway outside the house. Shalara doubts such tales.

It is in the streets around Kappiyan's house that the Ghost Knight is most often seen.[18]

---

[18] This phantom, and the adventure connected with him, appears in the Undermountain Adventures booklet of *The Ruins of Undermountain* set.

The Moon Sphere

This strange, beautiful feature of South Ward appears only on nights when the moon is full. The Moon Sphere is a magical globe of blue radiance that appears in Dancing Court as the result of an ancient, powerful enchantment.[19]

The courtyard was left clear because of it, and the adjacent Jade Dancer was built to take advantage of it. For generations folk have come to Waterdeep to see it, and Waterdhavians have used it to relax and in courting each other.

The Place

Dancing Court is a smooth-finished courtyard paved in flagstones. Its central space is perhaps 60 feet across. In the midst of this a 40-foot-diameter sphere of translucent, vivid blue radiance fades into being as the rays of the full moon fall on the Court and fades away with waning moonlight.

By Waterdhavian law, no one is allowed to restrict access of anyone else to the sphere or charge any fee for admittance to its confines. And no one is allowed to cast any spell or unleash any magic within, or into, the Dancing Court for fear of disrupting the magic. By tradition, a city guard patrol, accompanied by a member of the Watchful Order (always a wizard of some power) keeps watch over the Dancing Court when the Sphere is present.

The Prospect

The Moon Sphere has existed for at least a century due to a powerful magic created by the goddess Selune. There have always been rumors that she, various avatars of her, or her agents reside in Waterdeep, concealing themselves among the common folk.

The ideal place of worship to Selune is open to the sky—on a bare hilltop or clearing in a forest. In a city, a rooftop or open space is preferable to an enclosed chancel. Because of this, many services at the House of the Moon take place on its roof, visible to all nearby. The Moon Sphere is said to be the sailors' temple, open to all. Whenever it appears, any sailors in the city sober enough to make the journey travel to it to extend a hand into the blue glow and whisper a prayer to the Lady to see them safe to their next port. The danger rating for the Sphere is for who you might meet with, around, or near it, not for the Sphere itself.

---

[19] The Moon Sphere is in the Dancing Court, the open space just west of the Jade Dancer (#208) on the color map.

come here to dance in the air and kiss on high, floating so only their lips touch. There are tales of even more ardent activities between intimate companions within the Sphere's radius.

Guests in the Jade Dancer customarily extend their festivities into the Court on nights of the full moon and drift or fly while drinking. The more daring even leap from the balcony of the Jade Dancer into the Moon Sphere. It is a mark of social daring and debonair nonchalance to do this without spilling even a drop of one's drink.

Travelers' Lore

There are many tales of dancers finding their true love in the sphere—even Piergeiron, High Lord of Waterdeep, is said to have first met his bride, Maethiira

What makes the Sphere attractive to those who do not worship Selune is its major magical property:[20] Living beings who enter it and will themselves to rise can fly about inside the sphere's radiant confines.[21] Traditionally, courting couples

---

[20] *Volo:* There are other powers. Even high-ranking priestesses of Selune don't know them all. Devout worshippers of Selune can be healed of wounds, poisoning, insanity, diseases, and magical curses by contact with the Sphere, but just how, when, and what rituals are involved remain unknown to me. The city guard patrols strongly discourage any experimentation intended to learn the secrets of the Sphere.

Elminster: Let's keep things that way.

[21] Elminster's assistance has given us these details:

Any sentient being can *fly* at will, with Maneuverability Class A and a movement rate of 7. Up to the flying being's own weight in worn or carried material can be supported. One person cannot drag another down by grasping them and willing descent. The Sphere's magic parts the two, so only one falls.

Descent within the Sphere is governed by conditions equal to a *feather fall* spell.

Beings who pass entirely out of the Sphere by means of their own navigation or who are forced out (and objects fired, hurled, or dropped out) fall to the ground below with normal speed and damaging effects. If they fall back into contact with the Sphere, its magic reasserts itself over their fall. The Sphere extends 30 feet above the Court at its highest point.

The Moon Sphere also affects magic cast within it. Spells of the abjuration, enchantment/charm, and greater divination schools when cast by a wizard of chaotic good alignment only and, when cast by a priest of Selune only, the spheres all, charm, creation, divination, guardian, healing, necromantic, protection and wards will have the fullest possible effects (maximum duration, etc.) when cast or triggered in the Sphere. The Sphere does the same thing to magic connected with starlight and moonglow (the powers of a *ring of shooting stars,* for example). Fire-based spells, however, are always reduced to the minimum possible damage (1 point per die) and effects.

Certain magics are twisted by the Sphere into wild magic results—hence the prohibition against magic. Adventurers are warned to curb any reckless behavior or tendencies while in Dancing Court or the Moon Sphere.

here.[22] Selune herself is said to sometimes appear, conferring powers, punishments, and *geas-*like directives upon folk. Her priestesses try to send at least one of their number to dance and pray in the Moon Sphere each time it appears.

There is also a ghostly tale about the phantoms of seven murdered princesses sometimes seen dancing in the Sphere. These young ladies, all of the royal house of Tethyr, were slain in Waterdeep some 80 winters back by a cruel host: their uncle, who wanted the throne.

After a night of joyful dancing with handsome young men in the Moon Sphere, which they found wondrous, the princesses were very tired. Their uncle replaced the pillows in their beds with mimic grubs (flatworm-like relatives of mimics who dissolve flesh by touch). The unfortunate girls were found dead in the morn, intact except for their heads, which had been eaten away to clean, bare skulls.

Many bravos and young blades of Waterdeep have spoken, down the many nights since, of dancing with pretty maidens in rich gowns. They are silent, but seem somehow sad, their eyes bright

with unshed tears—and their faces, when approached closely (for a kiss, perhaps), are instantly transformed into grinning skulls!

Certain powerful wizards of Waterdeep are also said to come here on rare occasions, when deep in thought, and drift about, staring at the stars as they ponder. It's the closest some folk of Waterdeep ever get to the great Khelben "Blackstaff" Arunsun, and, for that matter, his more sinister rival, Maaril, and the aged head of the noble house of Wands, Maskar.

There is also a rumor among wizards that the touch of the Moon Sphere can recharge certain items, if the right words are spoken.[23]

[22] Maethiira has been dead for almost 14 years. Piergeiron has not remarried and dotes on their daughter, Aleena, who is tall, grave, beautiful, reclusive, and said to dabble in magic.

[23] This rumor is true. Elminster refused to reveal the ritual, but did say that *wands of magic missiles* are among the items aided by the Sphere.

The Old Monster Shop

This little-known shop fronts on the Jar, a close that opens off Tilman's Lane not far from the Trollwall. There a stone warehouse sports a door marked with: "Beware Guardian Monsters Within." It is flanked by a pair of tall, massive, arched cart doors.

Inside, a nondescript-looking man named Feldyn Goadolfyn sells monsters to the hungry, the bored, and the vengeful.

The Place

This ugly, poorly built warehouse is littered with dust and rubble. It smells of animal dung and damp.

The upper floors are largely empty,[24] but visitors entering by the door are immediately confronted by a hungrily interested gargoyle perched on the swinging gate of a service counter.

Behind the counter sits Feldyn, who's usually examining a map or a worn copy of a crude monthly illustrated chapbook. He always appears calm, even bored. An adventurer who once saw him threatened with a cockatrice said he didn't even blink, but merely yawned and told the cockatrice-holder to state his business.

The Prospect

Shops where one can buy live monsters are rare anywhere in Faerun.[25] A surprisingly large number of folk make their ways as unobtrusively as possible to Feldyn's doors. His clientele include jaded nobles looking for exotic things to hunt, eat, or play with; those who want to create a sensation at parties or with traveling shows, or just acquire a wall trophy they can boast about; adventurers in need of practice; breeders and wizards needing live material for their researches, and so on.

In pools, cages, and a variety of imprisoning containers in his cellars, Feldyn keeps an ever-changing roster of monsters to sell to them. He also has a room of jugged, jarred, or coffered remnants, from horns and bottled gore to pelts and scales.

These valuables are guarded by a loyal (trained or magically controlled) staff of guardian monsters: four watchspiders,[26] two gargoyles (Feldyn controls them with a *ring of gargoyles*[27]), two mimics (a killer mimic that poses as a bar on the inside of the

---

[24] Feldyn makes a few coppers each month from selling guarded safe storage space to citizens, merchants, and fences of Waterdeep who deliver crated goods to him. He uses the three rambling, run-down upper floors of the warehouse to house these crates, and won't accept uncrated things.

[25] And in at least a dozen other worlds, Elminster added dryly.

[26] See "Spider, Subterranean" on pages 123–124 in FOR2 *The Drow of the Underdark.*

[27] Detailed in the Campaign Guide of *The Ruins of Undermountain* set.

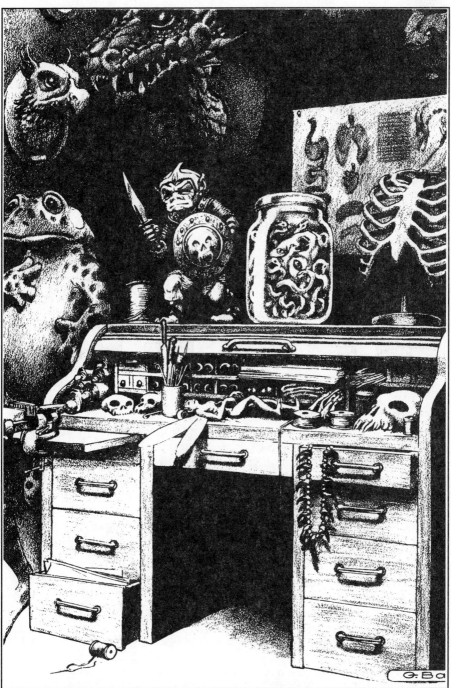

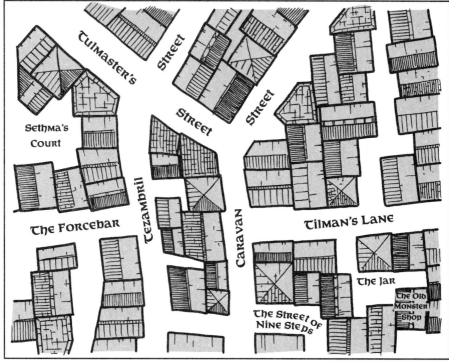

Culmaster's Street

Sethma's Court

Street

Street

The Forcebar

Tezambril

Caravan

Tilman's Lane

The Jar

The Old Monster Shop

The Street Of Nine Steps

cart doors, and a space mimic[28] that pretends to be the door at the bottom of the cellar stairs most of the time), and a female-looking stone golem known as Ouldra. In case of attack, Feldyn will flee to the cellars,[29] trusting to his *ring of spell turning* to keep him safe as his monsters spring to the attack.

The People

The owner of the Old Monster Shop, Feldyn, is evil, coldly calm, and unscrupulous. He gets even, but he does not hate. He uses his unremarkable appearance to adopt whatever disguises he deems necessary when following foes through Waterdeep. Whenever outside his shop, Feldyn is armed with a pair of golden lion *figurines of wondrous power.*

Feldyn will purchase monsters, including eggs and young. He does not like to handle magically transformed or petrified monsters (to minimize his personal danger). Badly wounded or dead beasts fetch very little from him.

He sometimes hires adventurers who have brought him lots of monsters to get specific monsters to order or to slay or kidnap folk

---

[28] In MC7 the *Monstrous Compendium SPELLJAMMER® Appendix.*
[29] If necessary, he'll duck through one of his *gates,* taking his best chest of accumulated treasure.

who have become his foes. Among residents of Waterdeep, his recent contacts have included the Company of the Bloody Banner, a fellowship of a dozen evil female half-elves, and the Weird Company, an evil adventuring band dominated by six wizards.

The Prices

Feldyn buys cheap and sells expensive. Most beasts go for at least 1000 gp. Prices increase with a creature's danger and rarity.[30] Monster parts are much cheaper—usually 40 gp to 250 gp, depending on what they are.

Whenever authorities look into his shop, Feldyn claims to be in business largely to serve the kitchens of Waterdeep, with a few noble patrons who love hunting as special patrons. He shows his selection of monster parts, keeps his guardian monsters (except for the golem) out of view, and gives out free copies of two of his most famous recipes: dragon soup and roasted cockatrice. Not being a member of the city guard, I had to pay 1 sp per recipe—but I've since been able to try them both, and the results were delicious!

Travelers' Lore

Some who live near the Old Monster Shop claim they've seen folk go inside it and never come out again—and also seen folk (and worse!) come out that they swear never went in.

Members of the Watchful Order who have too much drink say more. Some claim Feldyn has some sort of monster in the depths of his cellars that gives birth to other creatures. Others claim that he has several *gates* that link him to faraway places in the Realms.[31]

---

[30] As a rule of thumb, Feldyn's price in gold pieces will equal the listed XP value of a monster.

[31] Both of these tales are true. Feldyn has a deepspawn hidden in his cellar (a monster detailed in FR11 *Dwarves Deep*) and a row of unmarked closet doors that are actually the entrances to a webwork of two-way *gates* connecting his shop with:

- An Underdark cavern, near Menzoberranzan (a drow city detailed in the *Menzoberranzan* set)
- Somewhere in the jungles of Chult
- A ravine in the Stonelands north of Cormyr near the Haunted Halls (detailed in FRQ1 *The Haunted Halls of Eveningstar)*
- A glade deep in the High Forest (see FR5 *The Savage Frontier)*
- A knoll in the Sword Coast North, near Everlund (*The Savage Frontier)*
- A valley in Amn in the hills north of Amnwater (see FR3 *Empires of the Sands)*
- The edge of Anauroch near Spellgard (see FR13 *Anauroch)*
- A clearing in the Wild Wood (Demall Forest) in Alaron in the Moonshae Isles (see FA1 *Halls of the High King* and FR2 *Moonshae)*
- Somewhere on the third level of Undermountain, just outside Skullport.

Feldyn and his hired adventurers use these to gather monsters. They keep caches of food and gear hidden near most of their exit *gates.*

In his shop, Feldyn has over 56,000 gp, in bags of 100 gp each, stashed inside hollow pillars in the cellars. He also has a chest visible for the taking (containing 540 gold pieces and several false treasure maps) and his best chest. His best chest is a dark coffer high on a gloomy shelf above and inside a doorway on the cellar stairs that holds 12 rubies, 8 star sapphires, and 2 emeralds—each worth 5,000 gp—as well as 4 trade bars of silver, worth 25 gp each, and two *potions of extra-healing* in steel vials.

Feldyn's Recipes

Elminster warns that dragon meat should be properly prepared before eating (see page 82 of FOR1 *Draconomicon*) and that cockatrices should not be touched for at least three hours after death—and even then, gloves should be used to pluck out the larger feathers and throw them away. The large feathers sometimes retain the power to petrify for days.

Dragon Soup

6 large, ripe tomatoes
14 hot onions (or 6 shallots and 2 cloves of garlic)
1 pinch salt
1 handful dill
1 handful parsley
1 pinch black pepper
1 skin goat's milk
much clean water
dragon meat (ingredients listed do up to 10 pounds)

In a cauldron, bring water to a boil and with a ladle dip tomatoes in for the space of a short trail joke.

Take them out, and peel them with a sharp knife. Lay the skin aside. Stir the rest back into the water.

Chop the onions (and garlic, if used) finely. Stir this in too, adding salt, dill, and pepper to the pot.

Remove any scaly, inedible outer hide from the dragon meat. Cut the meat into manageable portions, and drop it into the pot—which must be at a rolling boil. Let boil while an inch is burned down on a thumb-thick candle.

Then, stop feeding the fire. As the pot cools, stir in the goat's milk and the parsley. Let stand until the fat and oil present in all dragon meat comes to the surface. Skim this off, and then reheat the mixture for dining.

Uncooked dragon meat keeps six sunrises. Cooked meat keeps for twice that.

He also tells me one pour is a measure achieved by tipping a shaken bottle upside down and then immediately upright again. A knife is an amount that stays on the blade of a knife. Merithian sauce is equivalent to a strongly spiced steak sauce. Nightcap mushrooms are found only in the Realms. Be very cautious with mushroom substitutions.

These recipes also show some time measures used by cooks in the Realms. The 16 verses of song called for (at least, as Elminster sang them) equal about 8 rounds, game time, and the space of a good sword-sharpening seems to be about 6 turns.

Roasted Cockatrice

1 cockatrice carcass

2 leeks

2 handfuls of morels (or 1 handful nightcap mushrooms)

2 plants (whole stalks, with hearts) celery or marsh lettuce

1 handful bean tubers (or marsh grass roots)

1 pinch thyme

1 pinch salt

2 pinches pepper

1 pouch flask's worth of red Lythton (or other semi-sweet) wine

2 pours hot brown Merithian sauce

2 knives of animal fat

In a skillet or upended iron shield over a small fire, chop and mix leeks with salt, pepper, bean tubers. Sizzle in animal fat until leek pieces grow soft. While the leek cooks, push it around just enough to prevent burning.

Cut off the bony head and neck of the cockatrice, which can later be boiled for soup. Slit the carcass up the breast, turning out the gizzard (with its sometimes-poisonous contents) and other organs.

The cockatrice need not be skinned. Its leathery, scaly outer skin protects the tender flesh during cooking. Don't let blood and fluids drain away or the bird will cook too dry. Tough or dried carcasses should be doused in diluted wine (1 part to 2 parts water) before roasting.

Stuff the carcass with celery and thyme. Put in the skillet atop sizzling leeks, roast for 16 verses of "The Unicorn and the Maiden," and turn.

When both sides are brown, turn the carcass so it lies with the flattest side down, and douse it with the wine. When bubbling and sizzling dies, baste the carcass with the brown sauce. Roast for the space of a good sword-sharpening, basting often and turning when needed to keep the color even.

The skin will crack and dry like old parchment, lifting and flaking away like wood ash when the meal is done. Take from the fire and let cool until it can be held for eating. Goes well with ale and greens.

The House of Good Spirits

Tavern, Inn, Winery & Head-quarters of the Vintners', Distillers', and Brewers' Guild

Located on the northwest side of the Rising Ride (at the crest of the small knoll for which that street is named) between the mouths of Juth Alley and Robin's Way, this complex of buildings is fronted by a timber, wattle and daub tavern. It extends north and west along Tornsar Alley as far as Buckle Street, where an alleyway offers access to the inn and its stables at the back of the tavern.[32]

The House of Good Spirits has always been a guild headquarters and a winery where sluth[33] and zzar are made. (Zzar is made from sluth by fortifying it with almond liqueur.)

Some 60 winters ago, a small brewery was added on the corner of the Rising Ride and Tornsar Alley, and then the tavern was opened. About four winters ago, the operators of the House expanded into an adjacent warehouse to open its doors as a 40-bed inn primarily for the convenience of visiting grape-growers and wine merchants.

Owned by the guild, this complex has enriched all guild members and now serves them as a home away from home base in which they can stay when their homes are overcrowded or being worked on, go for a quiet tankard when the working day is done, and house, entertain, and meet with business guests.

The Place

The entire complex still looks like a collection of warehouses and factories inside and out. Massive, exposed beams and bare mud brick walls are everywhere, and the lamp lighting is dim. Small passages, cozy nooks, odd doorways, and surprise steps up and down are numerous, and furnishings are bare-bones and workaday, but comfortable and ruggedly serviceable.

The inn, tavern, wine store, winery, and brewery are directly joined inside, but a narrow courtyard separates the stables from the rest.[34]

The Prospect

The House of Good Spirits boasts the best and cheapest selection of liqueurs and strong drink in the entire City of Splendors—even if, as a noble I overheard snootily put it, "You have to sit in the stinking brewery to drink its wares." Fiery blackthroat from

---

[32] This is #214 on the color city map.
[33] Sluth is dry, sparkling white wine.
[34] The Harpers novel *Elfshadow* describes an arrival (pages 114–117) and stay at the House.

far Lantan is as plentiful in its spacious cellars as is ruby-red elverquisst, beloved of the elves.

It is a comfortable, if disorganized, inn, most of the rooms sporting two single beds and bare board floors. There are no luxuries, but tired travelers will find it a comfortable place to sleep. The low prices attract a regular clientele of hard drinkers, but the staff[35] keep order. Brawls are frequent, but take place on the street outside, not within. Breaking one of the long, leaded windows of the tavern—or forcing another patron to do so by hurling him through it—costs a brawler 4 gp. During daylight hours, guild representatives are always on hand for those who want to deal in spirits. Private meeting rooms are available for conferences.

The Provender

The inn provides only a basic menu: roast boar, rabbit-and-smalls stew (fowl, vegetables, squirrels, and the like, always simmering in the kitchen), and cheese-and-mustard saltbread melts (small, circular loaves of very tasty bread).

The People

The guild staff numbers 40 or so, from Elguth the stableboy (an expert guide to the gambling houses and festhalls of Waterdeep) to Simon Thrithyn the innkeeper. The resident chief guild buyer and seller is Dlarna Suone. Her second is Gordrym Zhavall. Dlarna is the only sharp-tempered and sharp-witted person in the place. The others tend to be stolid, calm folk—even the seven burly bouncers, who are led by Mrorn "Black Bracers" Halduth.

The Prices

A room costs 2 gp/bed per night. If one person wants a private room, he must pay for two beds, but can invite a nonstaying guest to eat the second food share. This rate includes stabling for all mounts and all meals desired—just ask. Draft beasts are each 1 cp per night extra. The dining fare is restricted to the spare menu I listed. Also included is all the ale the guest wants to drink.

Wine and spirits are extra, and are sold by the bottle. Prices range from 2 cp/bottle for sluth made on the premises (a cut rate—outside the tavern, such a bottle sells for 8 cp) to 6 sp/bottle of house zzar. Prices then rise rapidly to a high of 33 gp/bottle for the finest, and with local unrest, very rare, Tethyrian distilled dragonsblood.[36]

---

[35] Staff acting as bouncers typically arrive as follows: 1d4 F2s in 1d4 rounds, an F1 a round after the first arrival, then 1d4 F2s and an F3 1d3 rounds later.

[36] A few popular wines and their prices per bottle: Neverwinter black icewine, 7 sp; Best Old Mintarn whisky, 1 gp; Wyvern Whisky, 2 gp (made in Nimbral—a wyvern's scale floats in every bottle).

Travelers' Lore

It is widely rumored that a large amount of treasure—a dragon hoard, brought back to Waterdeep by an adventuring company sponsored by the guild long ago—is hidden somewhere in or under the House. Would-be prospectors are warned that the staff take a very dim view of people who dig or pry at walls, floors, and ceilings.

The adventuring band, the Guild Adventuring Company (colloquially known as the Flying Flagons) all perished at Yartar, defending it against raiding orcs. This is remembered in the "Fall of the Company," written by the Company's bard, Felestin, and sent by spell to a comrade a day's hard ride distant as the adventurers fought their last fight.

These days, most guild members can recall only a snatch of the song. But visitors beware: If you laugh or offer disrespect when this stanza is sung, all the men singing with tears in their eyes are apt to rise up and separate you from your life.

*And no one will stand there to
    hear our reply,
And no one will come there to
    see heroes die...
Oh, raise flagons high
And swords to the sky
For guild and adventure
Die well when you die!*

The Jade Dancer

Tavern & Festhall

This raucous haunt of the young, free, and ardently romantic opens onto Dancing Court, sometime site of the eerily beautiful Moon Sphere, just north of Slop Street in the Tween Run (the local name for the alleys and buildings between the High Road and the Way of the Dragon).[37]

The Place

Built of timber and stone columns, its outer walls sealed by a slather-coat of plaster into which mud bricks have been pressed in slanting courses, the Dancer looks like what it is: a warehouse with a grand front tacked on. Its upper floors open onto a broad, two-tier balcony overlooking the Dancing Court, which boasts intricate ornamental wrought iron railings and potted fruit trees. Inside, minstrels play on a hanging gallery suspended from the ceiling on chains above a raised central stage where dancers and singers perform.

The stage and gallery dominate an open central well that soars up to a roof skylight. Interior balconies or promenades of the upper floors open onto the well and look down on the stage. Three large, wide-curving circular staircases rise around the well to link the floors. They provide good views of shows, and are often lined with standing patrons.

The kitchens, pantries, and staff quarters are hidden below ground level. The main floor is entirely given over to a bar, a ring-shaped dance area around the stage, and sturdily built, round wooden tables linked by floor-chains to quartets of plain, heavy-duty chairs for patrons.

The upper floors are devoted to large, plant-adorned drinking parlors on the Dancing Court side and festhall rooms (opening off the promenade) around the rest of their extent.

The Prospect

This clean, brightly lit, noisy place is beloved of young Waterdhavians wanting to be in the rush of new fashion and "in" behavior—and to be seen to be part of it. As most nights pass, the visitor can see and smell the steadily rising excitement. If half the too-loud, excited young boys swaggering around knew how to use the huge weapons they wave about, the nightly slaughter would make Dancing Court run red with gore.[38]

---

[37] The Jade Dancer is #208 on the color map.

[38] The chairs have been thoughtfully chained to the tables. Only an incredibly strong man (ST 18 or greater) can lift and hurl a table and four chairs as one—though many patrons swear they've seen it done.

The Dancer has a staff of expert, good-looking escorts who mingle with the patrons. Misguessing who is a patron and who is an escort has left many a visitor to the city with a face red and ringing from a hard slap. A hint: You can recognize an escort by the room keys worn around their necks on fine chains.

The rooms are not all for the use of escorts. Couples who find each other among the drinks can rent rooms. Those thinking of taking liberties with escorts or guests are hereby warned that the Jade Dancer also has as a bouncer a watchful wizard, Selcharoon Nrim, who wears a *ring of invisibility* and a *ring of jumping*, and ably wields a *wand of paralyzation.*

The establishment is named for its star dancing attraction: Jade, a magically animated, incredibly beautiful, life-sized jade statue, fashioned like a human female.[39] Usually found

---

[39] Elminster reveals that Jade is a special sort of *figurine of wondrous power*, mentally animated by the owner of the club, the sorceress Cathalishaera. It will crumble into dust if taken more than 200 paces from Cathalishaera or if Cathalishaera should die. She customarily keeps it in a *Leomund's secret chest*, and the tiny half of this item is carried on her person, avoiding the destructive effects of moving the statue too far away.

The sorceress customarily sits in a locked, hidden room during performances, seeing through the statue's eyes and moving it by will in response to the music and the calls of the crowd. She loves this work, but is too shy to ever dare dance in person.

dancing on the stage in acrobatic poses no human dancer with any dignity or nerve endings could endure for long, it begins an evening with no hair but grows illusory flowing hair as it moves—until a floor-length train of tresses flows behind and around it. The hair then vanishes, to begin growing again. The cycle takes about an hour.

The Provender

A wild variety of drinkables can be had here, from glowing amber dwarven *thorl beldarakul* (Old Trickster) to cool, minty green *shondath* icewine, favored by some elves and halflings. Among humans, Al & Tal's Slurp Syrup (well-spiked cherry syrup) is popular, along with Fool's Thirst-Quencher (a mix of six beers and winter wine), and, of course, zzar, which can be had at double strength. All drinks here are 5 sp for a handglass and 1 gp for a tall flagon.

To go with the drinkables, the Dancer staff serves free bowls of salted nuts, loaves of hot garlic-buttered bread (2 sp/round loaf), and skewered roast fowl two to a skewer for 3 sp/skewer. These are small plucked chickens with head, feet, and organs removed, cooked over an open fire.

The People

The proprietress of the Dancer is the seldom-seen sorceress Catha-lishaera, who relies on her bouncer Selcharoon and her staff of about 20 female and 12 male escorts, about half of whom are on shift on a given night, and the house staff of 10 bar and kitchen workers.

The best-known of the house staff is the fat, talkative, wise-cracking lady bartender, Khalou Mazestar. She loves to talk to guests at the bar and is a great source of jokes, information on current fads and interests among the swinging young of Water-deep, and gossip about who's involved with whom among Waterdeep's noble and monied families. She's especially envious of those people who can afford to festoon themselves with precious jewels, and never tires of hearing or passing on news of Lady Shanderplast's navel car-buncle or Lord Lunkoon's huge emerald earplugs.

The Prices

Aside from the bar prices already given, the Dancer charges 2 cp per glass or flagon thrown or broken, and 1 sp per plant eaten or destroyed, and 1 gp per piece of furniture set afire or de-stroyed. An hour's use of a room key runs 1 gp, with a maximum of 10 gp for use of the room the whole night.

Escorts charge 6 to 12 gp per visit to a room. No extra room charges apply, but the rate covers half an hour or less of the escort's

time. Those who want company for longer must pay multiple charges.

Travelers' Lore

Tales connected to the Dancer either have to do with love, legendary drinking bouts, or the Moon Sphere out front. The musicians hired to play here are very good. Come early for a good seat and the least amount of drunken drink-hurling at performers. Bards known up and down the Sword coast sometimes perform from the hanging gallery. Once, a few winters back, a sylph sang hauntingly mournful love calls and reduced the whole place to tears.

There are persistent whispers about the Jade Dancer being a transformed, trapped human female—perhaps a princess or noble lady. There are also tales of her occasionally taking a male patron up to one of the rooms— and that the men were never seen again.[40]

---

[40] The tales about the Jade Dancer being a trapped or transformed human are false. So is any reference to "her" enjoying the company of a human man. Elminster says tales of the Jade Dancer leading men to the rooms are probably true. Cathalishaera used to use this method to remove troublemakers or the hopelessly drunk or to get shy men and women together, but it has become too attention-getting, and she no longer does it. Between shows, the Jade Dancer vanishes down through the kitchens and into an air shaft (disused chimney) leading to the upper floors, where she's unlikely to be found by a would-be thief. As disassembled jade, the figurine's body is worth about 9,000 gp.

Other Places of Interest in Southern Ward

Shops

Nueth's Fine Nets

This shop sells finely made ropes, nets, hammocks, ship shrouds and lines, rope bridges, window and tarp mesh, gauze, and the like. Thieves come here to buy coils of thin, waxed climbing cable at 30 gp per 120'. It is sold in one-piece multiples of that length up to four multiples (480'). A one-man throwing net for fish goes for 7 gp, and a stout tow rope for 20 gp per 100'. Tow rope is available in length multiples up to 10 (1000').

Proprietor: Thumir Aingahuth is the sarcastic, rat-faced, but ever-alert proprietor.[41]

Pelauvir's Counter

This huge, crowded former warehouse sells about everything except food and drink, from pots to lotions and carts to marbles.

Proprietor: Braum Pelauvir owns and runs Pelauvir's Counter. He's tall, beefy, and jovial.[42]

Aurora's Realms Shop Catalogue Counter

This is the South Ward outlet of Aurora's. Located next to the Red Gauntlet tavern in a crumbling tenement, this shop fronts on the Way of the Dragon. It has four guards, who work in shifts of two and two, a pretty half-elven counter clerk named Mril Juthbuck (an odd name for an elf—Juthbuck is usually a halfling surname), and a darkly handsome, arrogant service-mage named Logros Hlandarr.

Taverns

The Spouting Fish

Large, noisy ("A bit like drinking in the thick of a street brawl," one bravo told me, correctly), and popular, this brightly lit establishment succeeds largely because of its relentless street-crying advertising and its strategic location. Many folk entering the city via Southgate get to its huge, upright, spouting fish water fountain and decide they're thirsty.

Inside it's a many-leveled labyrinth of booths, benches, posts, and beams, all unpainted and very flammable. Two hired members of the Watchful Order

---

[41] Location #209 on the color map. Climbing cable is rated to take the weight of a dozen large men at once and to turn aside daggers. Since it contains twisted wire at its core, 7 hp damage must be applied to a single spot to sever it.

[42] Location #212 on the color map. Standard *Player's Handbook* prices apply. If a desired item is not listed, extrapolate from a given item—and then add some gold pieces! The shop's floor plan appears on Map 6 of the *City System* boxed set.

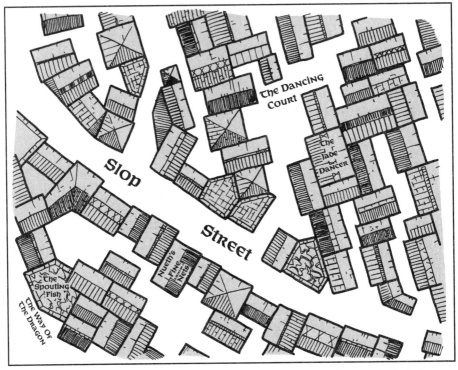

are always on duty because of the fire hazard. Zzar, wines, and beers are available, but the paltry roast fowl, bread, and sausages (1 sp/serving of each) are heavily salted to make you drink more.

Proprietress: Janess Imristar is a small, bustling, mousy woman whose loud voice and fearless demeanor belie her size.[43]

The Red Gauntlet

This old, shabbily highbrow place is dimly lit. Its booths are always full of old men remem-

bering old battles and slightly shady merchants conducting slightly shady deals in low, muttering voices. There's little food to be had beyond fried fish, way-bread, and rabbit-and-fowl stew, and little selection (house wines and house ales), but everything is cheap: 3 cp/platter of food and 2 cp/flagon or tankard. Folk are allowed to drink themselves to sleep here. Those who become noisy or feisty when taken with drink are simply slipped a little sleep syrup in their next drink. Loud snorers are taken to a back room. Others sleep where they sit, watched over against thieves

---

[43] Location #210 on the color map.

by the proprietor, Daunt Buirune, who knows what to watch for.[44]

Proprietor: Daunt Buirune, the proprietor, is a retired master thief, although that is not common knowledge.

The Swords' Rest

This quiet, little-known tavern is the warriors' drinking place, the chosen watering hole of those who swing swords for a living. It is a good place to hire out-of-work fighting men. This tavern has strong ale, zzar, and exotic drinks from the far corners of the Realms, and there's always a whole ox, boar, or deer—or all three—turning on a spit, so hearty meals (1 sp/platter) can be had at any time. Open from highsun (noon) to dawn, daily.

Proprietor: The proprietor, Beliarge "Old Boar" Maduskar, is called Bel by his friends.[45]

The Full Cup

One of the seediest drinking holes in Waterdeep, this battered place is used by bad-tempered drovers and carters. Most are too exhausted to fight when they get

---

[44] Location #211 on the color map.
[45] Location #213 on the color map.

161

here, which is for the best. It's a small, dim place dominated by a long bar with stools and an impressive, but largely dust-covered, selection of bottles behind it. There's almost always a pile of the remnants of smashed furniture outside the front door.

The Full Cup is notable for three things: the brawls that occur here with distressing regularity, the truly incredible cold winter drafts that send icy fingers stabbing into every corner of the place, and the bowls of hot buttered mushrooms (1 cp/large wooden bowl) grown in the tavern's own dung cellars. The dung is largely from the horses and oxen that crowd the streets around, and lies several feet deep in the noisome cellar.

Those who know how to discreetly ask the proprietor (and pay about 5 gp/item) can have items hidden under the dung for a month or less. After that, the hider forfeits the item. Be warned that the city watch searches here regularly for stolen items and the like and once found a buried skeleton with a dagger in its ribs. Patrons merely grunted as the bones were being carried out, "Errh. Someone who didn't pay up."

Proprietor: Gulth Djanczo is

the Full Cup's proprietor, and a nasal-voiced, coldly polite weasel of a man.[46]

Alleys

South Ward's alleys can be just as dangerous as neighboring Dock Ward's—especially for lone walkers late at night. Lantern parties tend to be a half-dozen strong or more. If you carry a light, you draw thieves, thugs, and the like to you—of course, if you don't, you can't see them coming!

Only the most interesting of these back ways appear here. For your own safety, see them by daylight.

Blacklock Alley

This long, narrow way runs parallel to the Way of the Dragon south of Brian's Street in the Tween Run area. It is named for the Blacklock, a waist-high stone obelisk about halfway down its length. The Blacklock has a hole worn in it, and youths play games that involve hurling a coconut or rag-and-rock ball through the hole to score points. Local lore says that anyone pure in heart who puts part of their body, such as an arm or leg, through the hole will be healed.[47]

---

[46] Location #221 on the color map. The *Knight of the Living Dead* gamebook gives a glimpse of this place (on the page facing entries 84A–84D).

163

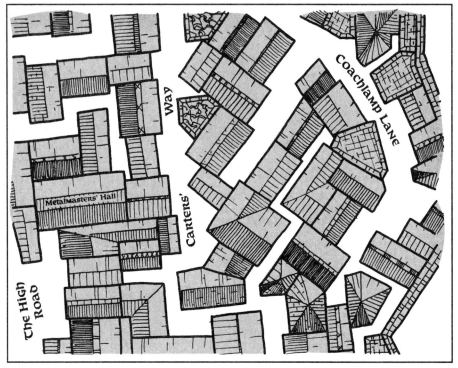

Gangs and sneak-thieves roam this alley. Anyone trying to remove, chip pieces from, or cast spells at the Blacklock will be attacked by a general rising of the neighborhood, all of whom believe the Blacklock brings them luck and wards off any tanar'ri that may roam near.

The Forcebar

This short, well-traveled passage is named for its intended defensive use. In the event that Waterdeep is invaded, huge sections of stone wall can be magically brought from the ethereal plane to block major roads in the city at strategic points, forming an inner ring of defensible walls. Just south of this alleyway, one such wall will block the High Road—and the Forcebar, along with Tilman's Lane, will form a route for defenders along the inside of this wall.

Although at least one gang has used the Forcebar to crash caravan wagons on the High Road by spurring fast carts out of it into contact with them and then launching a sudden and

---

[47] Elminster says the Blacklock is really a remnant of the altarstone of an old, now-vanished temple to Lathander. It acts as a *cure light wounds* spell on neutral good beings only, once per creature per day.

well-armed attack on the goods and wagon crew, this passage is heavily used by both the city guard and the city watch, and so is fairly safe.

Ilisar's Alley

This alley runs south from Telshambra's Street only to loop around and rejoin it again. Sometimes miscalled Illimar's Alley, this street is named for a famous local tailor who grew very rich. When he died of blacktongue fever, the bulk of his wealth was never found. Some think it's buried or walled up in one of the buildings here, because he owned the whole block.

Before Ilisar's time, this back route had a grimmer name: Grave Alley. In the days before the wizard Anacaster established *gate*-tombs in the City of the Dead, citizens of Waterdeep too poor to afford a crypt or to have a country villa to be buried at were interred here. Coffins were put in vertically under each flagstone. The eruptions of undead this caused forced abandonment of this practice very

long ago—but locals whisper that sometimes wights, ghouls, zombies, and skeletons come up from the depths of the earth here!

Mouse Alley

This very short, curving run links Blacklock Alley to Brian's Street, just west of Fishwife Alley. It is named for a famous mouse that ran along it in front of the wizard Ahghairon and turned out to be, as he suspected, a shapeshifted sorceress of great power—the goddess Mystra, in fact! It is today the haunt of one of Waterdeep's best—if that's the proper term—informants and eavesdroppers: Ruufdeidel "Roove" Ressatar, a short, imp-like little man who is perpetually smiling and has a talent for hiding, moving silently, and passing unnoticed. He can usually be found here lounging against a wall awaiting hire.[48]

The alley is said to be sacred to Mystra. Here she aids those faithful to her and punishes any who would harm her faithful taking refuge here.[49]

Of old, the wizard Thunturn,

---

[48] Roove's prices vary with the danger of the snooping task set him, rising from a base of 2 gp/day. For this, he agrees to meet with the client at least once a day at a place mutually agreed upon, but will never accept any work that involves him doing anything more active than leaving a message or sign. He's strictly an eavesdropper, not a thief, go-between, or assassin. He will always have concealed, hired allies present at such meetings to prevent an employer double-crossing him. His allies are mimics and dopplegangers!

[49] Any wizard who worships Mystra (or Midnight) fleeing into this alleyway will be instantly rendered *invisible*, and have any spells they cast since the last time they studied restored to them. In addition, they regain 1 hit point (if they have lost any), and will suddenly realize that they can *dimension door* out of the alleyway, if they wish. This benefit is lost if they leave the alleyway by other means.

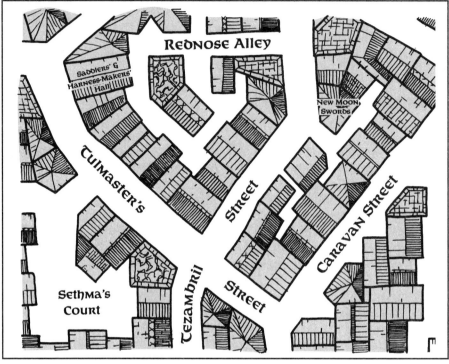

whose hair was white with age, came here in his pride and power to challenge Mystra for mastery of all magic—and she sent him away humble, stripped of all Art, his hair turned jet black from the fright of confronting Her.

Rednose Alley

This alley runs due west from Tezambril Street, just south of its junction with Robin's Way. The disused warehouses that line it house gangs of homeless youths, drifters who have come to Waterdeep seeking fortune and come up empty-handed, and fugitives from the law. They fight each other often, driven by hunger and boredom—and leap at the chance to attack or rob anyone who passes this way who looks weak enough for a half-dozen or so of them to overcome.. The alley's name comes from the many bloody noses they incur fighting with each other when they put away their daggers to avoid swift deaths.

Ruid's Stroll

This short, curving passage links Caravan Court with the nearest

Trollwall Tower (the one east of the Redbridle Stables) and is fairly safe thanks to the heavy use by the city guard and the watch. It is named for the ghost of a long-dead mage who appears on foggy nights, walking silently down it with his staff in hand and the cowl of his dark robes drawn over his head. He appears at the Court end in swirling mists and fades away again as he reaches the wall tower.

The ghost never reacts to living beings, but it is said anyone who touches or passes through it is shaken by a terrible chill,[50] but thereafter learns a truth.

Sethma's Court

Named for an old wise woman who dwelt here until her death some 30 winters ago, this cobbled courtyard is a gathering place for all sorts of birds flying over the city. They drink water from the roof cisterns all around it. No one knows why this place almost magnetically attracts them so.

---

[50] Contact with this strange phantom, which cannot be turned or dispelled, causes a loss of 1d4+1 hp which can be regained by normal healing means. By means of a note, the DM should inform the player of a character contacting the phantom that they will receive one true, full answer on something they formally request the truth about during future play. This boon works only once per character—but the hit point loss will happen each time the character contacts Ruid's phantom.

Dock Ward

erhaps the most notorious and colorful of the wards of Waterdeep, Dock Ward is known to thousands all over Faerun from travelers' tales. Most portray it as a lawless, brawling place of drunks, smugglers, roaming monsters and fell magic, where brawls are frequent.

Those tales aren't far wrong. All they leave out is the heavy city watch patrols[1] and the nonstop, day-and-night work that goes on around all that fun.

The harbor is very much a working place, full of sweating, swearing dock-wallopers loading and unloading vessels, assisted by crewmen. Carts groan hastily to and from warehouses all over the southern half of the city, carrying ship goods. Sightseers are not welcome.

Anyone who is crazy enough to want to tour the harbor can rent small boats from Albaeron Halembic of the Fishmongers' Fellowship at the Fish Warehouse.[2] The cost is 4 gp/day or 2 gp/half-day. The boat comes with oars, a small mast, two long fending poles, and a retired fisherman as skipper (who must be kept on board and in command of the vessel at all times).

Those daring or foolish enough to want to delve beneath the waters of the harbor are advised that the city guard keeps a very close watch for smugglers and items dropped for recovery by someone else later. Also, the mermen who patrol the depths do not welcome tourists, and will turn them back promptly.[3]

A further warning for those wishing to sightsee here: Unless the salty tang of rotting fish and sea life holds a special attraction for you, avoid the docks—or do not tarry overlong. I can attest to my cost that when the damp night and evening dew or morning mists are present and the clearing winds aren't strong, the stink of the harbor clings to your clothes and travels with you for almost a day.

---

[1] City watch patrols are detailed on page 17 of FR1 *Waterdeep and the North.* They pass a given point about every 20 minutes and look into a tavern or inn dining room about every half-hour.

As detailed on pages 20–22 and 23 of the *City System* boxed set booklet, the city guard also patrols Dock Ward in 12-man detachments. Typical patrol details are as given on page 23. Reinforcements will be another dozen LG hm F3s to F6s clad in chain mail and armed with maces, long swords, daggers, slings, and a pole arm appropriate to the situation.

Guard patrols pass a given street location about every half-hour. They appear in 2d4 minutes when a city watch patrol blows a warning horn in Dock Ward.

[2] On the city map in color, the Fish Warehouse is #237.

[3] Some details of underharbor features and merman patrols can be gleaned from the *Knight of the Living Dead* adventure gamebook. More is given on pages 25–26 of *Waterdeep and the North.*

Landmarks

All sailors who regularly sail into Waterdeep have their favorite taverns and lodgings, but all are familiar with Cookhouse Hall[4], the large, echoing, hammerbeam-ceilinged hall where hot meals (usually roast beef, stir-fried vegetables, and a highly peppered stew) are served to all who line up and pay 2 cp for a meal. Minted drinking water is even provided. You don't have to be a sailor to eat here. It's open from dawn to dusk, and has fed many a weary (or poor or down on his luck) traveler who doesn't mind a little coarse company and dinner conversation.

The Shipmasters' Hall, by contrast, is a private inn and dining club for captains, first mates, and ship owners and their escorts only. It's very old and elegant, with polished dark wood paneling everywhere, shining brass fittings, comfortably cushioned brocade seats, and heavy plush drapes.[5]

One of the largest privately owned buildings in Waterdeep is the shipbuilding shed of Arnagus the Shipwright, who's crafted many of the fine ships that ply the Sword Coast. Owing to the dangers of sabotage and fire, he doesn't welcome visitors, but many folk go to the docks where the slipway from his shed runs down to the harbor to peer in at the work going on. A ship launching always draws great crowds. It's the nearest thing after brawl watching to a spectator sport that Dock Ward has.[6]

The following guildhalls can all be found in this ward: the Butchers' Guildhall,[7] League Hall,[8] Mariners' Hall,[9] Watermen's Hall,[10] Seaswealth Hall,[11] Coopers' Rest,[12] Shippers' Hall,[13] Shipwrights' House,[14] and the Metal House of Wonders.[15]

The Most Diligent League of Sail-Makers and Cordwainers has as its headquarters the Full Sails tavern.[16] The Muleskull Tavern[17] serves as headquarters for the Dungsweepers' Guild.

---

[4] Location #230 on the color map.
[5] Location #243 on the color map.
[6] Location #252 on the color map. Map 7 of the *City System* boxed set has a floor plan of one of his nearby workshop buildings.
[7] Location #235 on the color map.
[8] Location #241 on the color map.
[9] Location #242 on the color map.
[10] Location #244 on the color map.
[11] Location #250 on the color map.
[12] Location #255 on the color map.
[13] Location #256 on the color map.
[14] Location #266 on the color map.
[15] Location #279 on the color map.
[16] Location #251 on the color map.
[17] Location #263 on the color map. In all cases, the guild owning the headquarters, and something of its doings, fees, and current heads, is covered in the *Waterdeep and the North* sourcebook.

The Hanging Lantern

Matchmaker & Festhall

The Lantern, an escort service known for the stunning beauty of its workers, and for the skill of its matchmakers, is famous up and down the Sword Coast.

There are many tales of clients who found a long-lost sweetheart at the Lantern or met the girl or boy of their dreams there. Merchants and the lovelorn come from up and down the Sword Coast to visit the Lantern, which is tucked into a square of shops and warehouses bounded by Shrimp Street, Pressbow Lane, Oar Alley, and Ship Street.[18]

The Place

The Lantern is a large, windowless building that rises a full six floors above the street. Thanks to flooding and old sewer tunnels, it has no cellars. It's dim inside, and hushed—except for the constant, gentle flute and harp music. Both the music and the sound-eating, I'm told, are due to magic.

The Prospect

Folk come to the Lantern for just one purpose, slipping in any of its seven doors into small, intimate rooms. In each room, a matchmaker waits.

There clients are interviewed, pay, and are ushered into one of many narrow, dark passages and stairs that leads to the room of their chosen. I'm told that not a few stabbings and stranglings occur in these dark passages when one patron lies in wait for another. Selected escorts can also meet clients by appointment. Yes, they make house calls.

The matchmakers seem expert at knowing exactly what clients want—even those who refuse to say. A wizard I met leaving the Lantern, in exchange for my promise not to name her, tells me they're not expert matchmakers, but really dopplegangers! They mind read to learn what folk like, and use their shapechanging to supply it, when their hired girls and boys can't.

The Watchful Order of Magists & Protectors knows their secret, but preserves it, along with their lives and continued operation, in exchange for their solemn promise not to slay any guests. There are rumors of occasional evil outlander wizards disappearing at the Lantern, though.

The People

No one, not even the Lantern's hired escorts, is sure how many matchmakers work at the Lantern. I'm told there are actually six dopplegangers, but they shift

---

[18] On the color city map, the Hanging Lantern is #262.

their shapes often enough to baffle any exact accounting.

The spokeswoman for the Lantern is a dignified elderly lady of rich dress and cultured manners, but it's not known if this is a real person, or a shape taken by more than one 'ganger.

The Prices

Escorts can be had for as little as 10 gp for on-the-arm service only. If acting is involved, such as playing a false part in a conversation meant to be overheard or pretending to wealth or identity in business dealings, the minimum fee is 25 gp. If more is desired, fees rise from there to a high of around 75 gp. The matchmakers have an uncanny ability to know how much a client can pay. Discretion is assured.

If a client just wants to hire bodies—a group of folk to accompany her on a stroll or tavern crawl through Dock Ward, say, as a bodyguard party, or to fool someone into thinking the client is part of a group or has lots of friends—they can be had for as little as 7 to 9 gp/head per evening. The Lantern has a call list of those down on their luck, and charges 3 gp for the trouble of sending a runner boy for them and providing suitable garb.

Travelers' Lore

The business the Lantern does forces it to deal in a little-known

sideline. It's the closest thing to a costume rental service Waterdeep has, providing fooling clothing for many occasions. Costumes are sometimes rented out, typically for 1 gp per night. Renters must pay for replacement of any damaged garments.

There are many, many tales of finding long-lost heartmates here (thanks to the shapeshifting of the 'gangers), but there are also rumors that drugged captives are kept here to await a slavers' ship or recovery by kidnap gangs. I saw no evidence of that—but I did see carried out the body of an unfortunate merchant who'd met a creditor on the stairs and been a bit too slow with his dagger.

Helmstar Warehouse

Facing the full fury of winter sea storms howling across the harbor, this warehouse stands on Dock Street, on the northeast corner of its junction with Crookedclaw Alley. [19]

The Place

This old, slightly leaning stone structure looks most impressive—in a worn, seedy way. Its carved harpies and wyverns, encrusted with white caps of bird droppings, glare down endlessly on the bustle of the docks.

The Prospect

The Helmstar Warehouse is presently run by one of the third generation of Helmstars to trade on the docks of Waterdeep: Chuldan Helmstar.

Chuldan is one of the better-known fences of Waterdeep. He buys carvings and statuary of all sorts, no matter how recognizable and hot, for 35% of the current new-made market price. No value is given for any enchantments on or magical powers of items, only on their material, size, and workmanship.

Chuldan is one of very few Waterdhavians allowed by the guilds involved to hold dual membership in guilds that are often competitors: the Fellowship of Salters, Packers, and Joiners and the Guild of Watermen. He maintains this rare position by handsome annual payments over and above his dues to both guilds. It allows him to carry on his illicit trade, which is the great majority of his business. Stolen goods find shipboard ways out of Waterdeep in a variety of ingenious packagings devised and constructed by Chuldan and his skilled, discreet staff of fourteen.

The People

Chuldan is a close-mouthed, bird-like, suspicious man with jet black eyes and hair. Always expecting double-dealing and betrayal, he is steps ahead of foes with contingency plans, escape routes, and surprises up one's sleeve—and seems satisfied when such deceits occur, as if they confirm his forethought and views on the true natures of all intelligent races.

The Prices

Chuldan deals in the handling of small cargo, from six barrels or a noble's coach to individual crates bound for friends and colleagues up and down the Sword Coast. His rates are high (2 to 6 gp per container), and he guarantees only same-season delivery. However, he has a large clientele, because he is discreet, takes extra

---

[19] On the color city map, this place is #267.

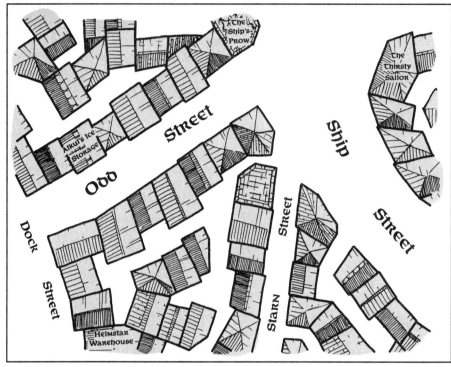

care in packing to ensure cargo safety, and undertakes to threaten, trace, check on, and otherwise persuade hired carriers to make sure cargo they take coin from him to deliver is in fact delivered to the right party as soon as possible.

Travelers' Lore

Few bother Chuldan, his goods, or his staff—word of his defenses and means of vengeance has spread. The high-vaulted, crowded warehouse is guarded by a band of margoyles whose loyalty to Chuldan seems unshakable. No one knows exactly how many of these creatures are lurking around the warehouse and Chuldan's rooftop apartments, or by what means he controls them. They hunt down any who molest him, trespass, or try to steal.

On occasions Chuldan has found it necessary to explain certain things to professionally curious men of the city watch. Usually his explanations concern a severed head, newly added to the end of a row of withered fellow trophies above Chuldan's front counter. Chuldan's words tend to reflect the view that this latest head, like the earlier ones, came in a recently unloaded cargo from far and barbarous

lands, and has something to do, he understands, with barbarian beliefs about guardian spirits that watch over goods while they travel afar. That certain of the heads seem familiar, closely resembling recently vanished rogues and ruffians of the city, is something that troubles, puzzles, and indeed mystifies Chuldan over and over again.

Chuldan invites all passersby to poke their noses into his warehouse to see the care he takes over cargo and the speed and volume of his business. He hopes (correctly) that many will be impressed—either to use his services or to refrain from trying to steal from him.

The lore of Dock Ward says the ghost of Chuldan's famous adventuring father, the bearded and brawling warrior Thalagar, drifts around the warehouse—its sewer door, in particular—in tattered splint mail, battle axe in hands, defending Helmstar territory. The ghost is said to have routed more than one thieving band who used magic to neutralize the margoyles. Thalagar especially hated lizard men, and on certain mist-shrouded nights, old sailors say, he can be seen striding silently but speedily along the length of Dock Street, storm-like of visage, axe in hand.[20]

Some of the carvings on the second floor ledge and roof of

the warehouse are crumbling away. A shattered, fallen harpy was recently found on Dock Street one morning below its customary perch. Under it was the flattened body of an unfortunate thief, still clutching the climbing line that had pulled the carving down atop her. Chuldan Helmstar had the missing rooftop carving replaced with a detailed carving that shows a crouching, terrified-looking human female in leathers holding one end of a climbing cord, and took great pleasure in pointing it out to visitors for the next few rides.

---

[20] These are always nights when lizard men have come near the harbor (as crew, captives, passengers, or visitors—perhaps disguised—to the city).

The Old Xoblob Shop

The Old Xoblob Shop is a curio shop little known outside Waterdeep, but famous in the city for its trophies of battle, adventuring bands, and exotic, faraway places. From drow sculptures to the huge, eyeless, stuffed beholder that overhangs everything, the shop is crammed with an untidy assortment of blades, treasure maps, coils of rope hundreds of feet long, statuettes of forgotten make and mysterious origin, and more. The shop is named for the beholder, killed by the proprietor in single combat long ago. *Xoblob* is all he could pronounce of its name.

This treasure trove is next door to the Purple Palace festhall, on the northwest corner of the meeting of Fillet Lane and Slut Street. Just two doors down from the Dock Ward outlet of Aurora's Realms Shop Catalogue Counter, the Old Xoblob Shop carries all the things the catalogue chain doesn't, from lizard man tribal boundary marking poles to dwarven runestones bearing treasure messages. For adventurers and con artists, it's the place to find all those necessary props

that no one else sells anywhere!

The Place

The Old Xoblob Shop is a tall, ugly old stone and timber building. Windows are few, and dust is plentiful. The street-level floor of the interior is the shop, one huge room with exposed ceiling beams supported by an irregular forest of pillars. One of the pillars, I'm told, is hollow. The jolly proprietor, Dandalus, sometimes uses it to hide shoppers on the run from the city watch or foes, keeping a display rack holding two glowing human skeletons in there the rest of the time.

A stair hidden behind the serving counter leads down to a high-ceilinged basement, containing a bucket flush jakes, which is connected to the sewers via foot-treadle trapdoor, a kitchen, and a row of huge wine casks. Dandalus does make his own wine, but one of the casks is hollow. Its front swings open to reveal a hidden room where folk on the run can hide for a fee. A kitchen cupboard has a sliding back opening into the cask, allowing a small person room to squirm out of it or food and drink to be passed in.

Dandulus sells his wine for 2 sp/glass or 1 gp/bottle. He makes a sparkling green among the best wines I've ever tasted. It's worth 10 times what he asks for it.

A broad stair leads up from the shop to a landing, where a narrow stair leads on up to the top floor. Dandalus and his wife live on the top floor in a suite of rooms connected to a roof garden. The landing also opens into a large storage loft that fills the second floor. It is windowless, has a 60-foot-high ceiling, and is usually nearly empty—a good thing, too, because a *teleport* from a certain spot on the second level of the dungeon of Undermountain brings adventurers (and sometimes monsters!) here.[21] The chamber is lit by a *driftlight (glowing globe)*, and contains an alarm-gong that rings whenever any weight is added to the room's floor.

Dandalus usually calls out cheerfully, "Come down smiling! No weapons out, please!" He also, just in case, reaches under the counter for his *wand of paralyzation.* He has standing arrangements with Khelben Arunsun and with the manager of the Three Pearls Nightclub, Xandos Waeverym, for the disposal of paralyzed monsters. Adventurers are usually relieved of their weapons, and obvious spellcasters are hand-hobbled and hooded before the paralysis wears off. If the shop is closed, Dandalus or his wife will be upstairs, the wand with them,

---

[21] The Old Xoblob Shop, the *gate* linking it to Undermountain, and the *driftlight* magic item are all detailed in the *Campaign Guide to Undermountain,* in the *Ruins of Undermountain* boxed set. See page 12 for an illustration of Dandalus and page 115 for *driftlight* details.

and will act the same. I'm told Dandalus has a backup wand that deals damage of some sort.[22]

The top floor apartments are private, but I've learned herbs are grown on the roof, that there is a little bower there for relaxing and romance on soft-starred summer nights, and that the third floor contains at least two guest bedrooms.

phies, and out-of-the-ordinary adventurers' gear in six worlds according to Khelben,[23] and the wine there is also first-rate. Dandalus cheerfully buys all sorts of bric-a-brac, paying a sixth of its worth. He is especially fond of things he can resell as spell components—or as genuine, no-guarantees magic items.

The shop is not a good place for thieves or the belligerent. The stuffed beholder is hollow, and conceals a hired wizard who can fire a *wand of paralyzation* out of its mouth to take customers by surprise. (Yes, this is a second wand of the same type. For all I know, Dandalus has a box of them under the bed upstairs!) Dandalus himself is a walking arsenal of magic, his wife has surprises of her own, and the shop bristles with concealed booby-traps to deter miscreants, including some Dandalus can trigger from afar. The shop also sports some not-so-hidden protections, such as an iron golem, Guraim the Gentle Persuader, who stands in a corner of the shop, spending most of his time as a rack for colored, scented candles.

The Prospect

The Old Xoblob Shop is perhaps the best source of curios, tro-

The People

Dandalus "Fire-Eye" Ruell is a balding, bearded, big-bellied

[22] This backup wand, Elminster reveals (he made it), is a special *wand of magic missiles*. Each triggering releases a burst of either 6 or 12 bolts (as the wielder mentally directs: half or full power). The wand is linked to three other wands hidden inside a wall of the shop and can call on their charges via a special linkage—so each missile drains a charge in the usual way, but the wand in effect has 300 extra charges to expend!

[23] Elminster agrees.

fellow who's always cheerful and sees life for the long running joke that it so often is. He makes no enemies. Those who attack or swindle him he merely charges double or more. He is always clad in breeches with bulging pockets, sometimes overlaid by an apron whose pockets are just as crammed. The pockets' contents always include a selection of lockpicks, skeleton keys, small tools, and garment pins for distressed ladies with torn garb.[24]

Arathka Ruell (lovingly called Rella by Dandalus) tends to the cleaning and cooking, but is just as charming and learned a shopkeeper as her man, if quieter. Unlike Dandalus, she doesn't dispense bad jokes and puns by the dozen. She's a priestess of some sort, but I never learned what power she serves. She's not forthcoming about it.[25]

The wizard hired by the Ruells is an ugly, one-legged, misshapen, and therefore very shy, little man who is fiercely loyal and protective of his employers.[26] His name is Hlondaglus Shrim, and he spends all the time the shop is open, from an hour after dawn to two hours after dusk, up in the beholder, eating sandwiches and whittling. He's the source of occasional showers of shavings that drift down to settle on shoppers and shop alike.

Travelers' Lore

The wares in this shop have their own lore, hundreds of little tales of dark magic, betrayal, and wild adventures. The shop itself is well-known to neighbors for the deeds of Dandalus, such as the time he wrestled a mimic to death in the street outside and the time a lich came through the *gate.* Spells in plenty burst out the windows of the shop before the undead creature was destroyed (by Arathka, the whispers say).

Dandalus refuses to go adventuring, but has been known to come to the rescue of friends and long-time customers trapped in Undermountain. He once waded into a brawl started by half-orcs in a nearby tavern, the Sleeping Wench, and laid out every combatant involved. When an arriving watch patrol mistook him for the source of the trouble, he laid them all out cold too. (Once the matter was settled, he treated the patrol to some of his wine.)

This is definitely a shop to collect such tales. Dandalus can tell you the lore or supposed lore of most of what he sells, and can recall the deeds of adventurers in and around Waterdeep for the last 30 years or so. He likes to talk. Those looking for treasure leads should pay him a visit and buy wine to talk over.

---

[24] For details of the arsenal of magic Dandalus carries on his person, see the "Folk of Waterdeep" appendix at the back of this book.

[25] The "Folk of Waterdeep" section also speaks of Arathka's faith and powers. Elminster knows all.

[26] Any attempts to *charm* Hlondaglus to do anything hostile or harmful to the Ruells will automatically break the spell and goad Hlondaglus into a killing rage.

Serpentil Books & Folios

This is one of the dustiest but most exclusive shops in Waterdeep. Some have called it the single best source of maps, charts, and books in all the Realms—and most wizards I've known agree. Located in a modest sandstone shopfront on the east side of Book Street,[27] Jannaxil Serpentil's shop is frequented by those who have come from afar in search of the rare, the unusual—and a chance to sell stolen goods.

The Place

The battered Serpentil sign hangs above an old, unkempt stone building whose wares window is boarded over, and whose black door entry is always forbiddingly closed. (When Jannaxil is open for business, a small, sliding viewing panel in the upper part of the door is left open.) Magical guardian glyphs adorn both the boards and the doors and glow faintly after dark. Few care to try their power.

Inside, the shop is very dark. It is crammed with deep-hued bookshelves, and the walls are paneled with wood. The sole light here comes from magical *glowing globes* that drift about at Serpentil's will. Powerful fire-guard spells prevent anything from igniting.

Aside from Jannaxil's desk and three chairs (two for visitors), books are the furnishings of this shop. More books are piled and shelved together here than most folk of Faerun will ever see.

The Prospect

Jannaxil handles all sorts of printed materials, from magical tomes to maps and charts of the Sword Coast waters. He likes to warn folk sagely that spellbooks give off green flames when they burn. Magical tomes and Sword Coast maps are his two specialties, but he can also find you a tome of folktales of Cormyr or the collected ballads of the long-dead bard Delshryn of Mirabar.

Jannaxil also buys printed lore, and is a cold, hard haggler. He gives 30% of the market value of all items he knows to be stolen. If any sort of literary theft occurs in Waterdeep, he typically knows about it by the next day!

The People

Most people think of Jannaxil Serpentil as just a nasty, cold-mannered old scholar, but from earlier magical researches I know him to be at least a dabbler in magic and far older than he looks. He is no doubt protected by magic, and has been known to

---

[27] On the color city map, Serpentil Books & Folios is #275.

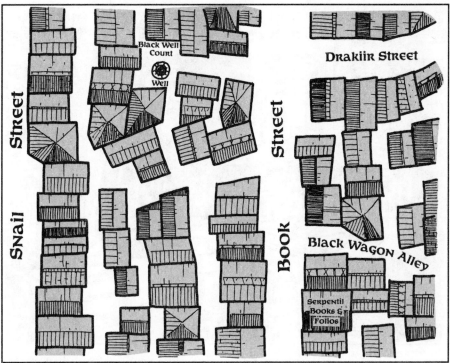

clutch a certain slim black volume to his breast when attacked in his shop. Most folk think it's just his account book—but I think it contains a tome guardian[28] monster that he uses to protect himself. There is much of the coward about him.

If Jannaxil has any family or staff, none have ever seen them. He is thought to sleep above his shop, in windowless apartments. Rumor says they include a large spellcasting chamber where Jannaxil conjures up baatezu to do his bidding.

The Prices

No deals with Jannaxil come cheap. Even the shabbiest chapbook will set you back at least 1 gp. Shoplifters are warned that Jannaxil has some way of knowing when one of his wares is leaving unpaid for, and that a binding spell prevents the guilty party from exiting. Jannaxil never confronts anyone, but simply waits for them to remove the hidden object and either pay for it or set it down and leave.

Most useful tomes, such as engineering instructions, math-

---

[28] The tome guardian monster is detailed in the sourcebook FR4 *The Magister*. Jannaxil might well have trained or allied monsters, too, such as watchspiders (detailed in FOR2 *The Drow of the Underdark* and in *The Ruins of Undermountain* boxed set) and mimics.

ematical texts, noble family histories, and detailed studies of the geography and history of a particular area, cost 15 to 50 gp.

Spellbooks are in unreliable supply, of course, and are purchased as is, with no guarantees as to the absence of curses or the efficacy of the spells within. Jannaxil typically charges a base price of 50 gp for each one plus 300 gp per spell or spell fragment contained within. Spells of the fourth or greater level command a surcharge of 1000 gp per spell. Spells of 7th level and up add 3000 gp each to the cost of a book. It is likely Jannaxil copies the useful spells from books he sells for himself, but no one has ever

found his cache of magic. Locals talk in the taverns of long crawl-tunnels where guardian monsters lurk, leading to a private study where Jannaxil keeps powerful magic.

Jannaxil does book searches for a deposit of 10 gp plus 4 gp per year thereafter. If the book is found, he charges double the usual price for it.

Papers (accounts and letters) find their way most often to Jannaxil's shop. He does a brisk business in blackmailing Water-dhavians with love letters and the like that a malicious or careless person sold to him. Jannaxil typically buys such wares for 1 to 5 copper pieces a

sheet, and sells them for 1 sp per sheet or more.

Travelers' Lore

It seems that Jannaxil's shop has always been there, but old Waterdhavians tell me it's been open some 60 years or so. During that time, Jannaxil has carried on running feuds with several scholars of the city—feuds carried on in the form of insulting gestures, gifts, and letters, or in ditties that tavern singers have been hired to perform in their taverns, for the amusement of all.

Jannaxil's cowardice has led him to pile up so many magical defenses that most folk think him to be a powerful wizard. There are many tales of thieves being blasted off his roof, or torn apart in the street outside his shop by huge black talons that appeared from thin air after they disturbed one of the boards covering his wares window.[29]

Jannaxil is said to have a special hatred of elves. He was recently wounded by Elaith "the Serpent" Craulnobur—who

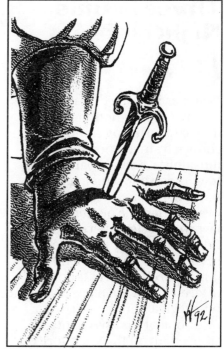

pinned one of his hands to his desk with a thrown dagger.[30]

Jannaxil loves good books. He hungers to look inside just about any book he sees or hears of, especially illuminated tomes, old maps, and well-illustrated volumes depicting female beauty. He is known to pay extremely well for such things.

---

[29] Elminster tells us the self-renewing guardian glyphs on the shop are 99 in number. A *dispel magic* will negate any one glyph (only) for 1 turn per level of its caster. Glyphs can fire once per day and are ready again 24 hours (144 turns) later.

Thirty-three of the glyphs are *spell turning* magics (enough will activate in combination to reflect back any spell 100% at the source).

Thirty-three more are *Caligarde's claw* magics (a spell detailed in the *FORGOTTEN REALMS*® *Adventures* hardcover). Some 2d4 of them will animate to attack any one being who tries to remove a board, pick the lock of Jannaxil's door, remove or harm the door, or chisel (or work magic on, including the writing of runes) any part of Jannaxil's shop walls.

The last 33 glyphs are *magic missile* spells. Any being flying up to the roof of Jannaxil's shop or forcing a magical or physical way through walls, floors, or roof will be struck by 2d12 of these missiles, and a magical alarm will awaken Jannaxil to full alertness of their activation, wherever he may be in Faerun.

[30] As related in the novel *Elfshadow*, by Elaine Cunningham.

Three Pearls Nightclub

Pearls, as it is called, is a popular evening destination for Waterdhavians, offering stand-up comics, trained animal acts, illusionists' recitals, bards, orators, and exotic dancing.[31] Its name comes from its purchase price. When the owner of the tavern that stood here (the Black Buckler) decided sourly he'd lost his last gold piece pouring ale down parched throats and offered to sell the place to anyone who'd give him the price of a meal, one of his own dancers stopped up on the stage, tore off three black pearls—nearly all she was wearing—and threw them to him, claiming the place as her own. The dancer, Halidara Urinshoon, is seldom on stage these days. She's too busy eating chocolates and drinking amberjack sherry in North Ward while her riches pile up.

Almost every evening, crowds stream up Pearl Alley to the Three Pearls, except on nights when a guild or other large group rents it for a meeting or for private entertainment. Typically it rents out at prices ranging from 50 gp for the space to 100 gp for the space and shows thrown in, cash up front.

The Place

The Three Pearls is now one huge room (plus jakes, opening off a cloak hall down one side). It has a low ceiling and is usually hot and smoky. Stout low-backed wooden benches radiate outwards from the raised central stage, which is lit from above and has a ramp entrance up into its center via trapdoor from below. The central stage has a conical raised ceiling above it, complete with a retractable circular staircase and drop ropes for dramatic entrances.

The Prospect

On the stage of the Pearl, men have raised armies, women have raised eyebrows, and everything from yeti through trolls have made jaws drop, bellies shake with helpless laughter, and hands itch to hurl things. On a typical night, comics alternate with dancers, musicians, and acting troupes—often presenting satirical ballads or sketches related to recent city events. More than once Piergeiron or Khelben has been portrayed as a buffoon, to the audience's great amusement.

The Provender

The Three Pearls offers finger food (hot sausages inside crisp-fried buns, pickles, and cream-coated fruit, all at 2 cp/serving),

---

[31] On the color city map, Three Pearls Nightclub is #273.

and drink—lots and lots of drink. Drinks are served in light clay cups that can't be thrown too far or do much damage.

A special, advertised attraction shouted out by boys at the door and on nearby streets, when available, is monster fare, such as baked stirge on toast, roast manticore, or wyvern steaks. These rarities command high prices, sometimes going for up to 7 gp/serving. Folk buy them mainly so that they can casually claim for the rest of their lives, as a conversation crusher, to have eaten such-and-such.[32]

The People

Too many performers of note have trod the stage at Pearls to list them here, from the fabled bard Mintiper to the orator Phaeros "Forktongue" of Baldur's Gate.

The owner of the Pearls seldom visits her gold mine these days, but meets daily with the manager to book acts and plan publicity.

The manager, Xandos Waeve-

---

[32] Adventurers are paid well for fresh kills, and even more for live. The more fearsome reputation a nonhumanoid monster has, the better price it fetches. Eggs fetch a lower price, and undead, poisonous, and petrifying beasts, or human-like creatures such as trolls and ogres, are not wanted at all. Recently, the Company of the Flaming Boot sold a nearly intact, dead hatchling white dragon to the Pearls for 500 gp—a price the nightclub made back several times over by selling sizzling white dragon steaks for 10 to 20 gp each, depending on size.

rym, is known as "the Dandy" around Waterdeep: a dapper, strutting little popinjay of a man, pompous and comical—but deeply committed to entertaining, and with a keen sense of humor and a reading for what the public will go for. He oversees a staff of 14 bouncers, 16 run-and-shout street boys, 12 dancers, and a house bard (currently Zalanthess-daughter-of-Zalanthar, an accomplished singer and harpist from Neverwinter).

The Prices

There is a 3 cp cover charge at the door (4 to 5 cp on some special nights), and everything inside costs extra. In addition to the food, beer goes for 1 cp/cup, house wine (very bad) for 2 cp/cup, good wine for 1 sp/tallglass, and zzar for 4 sp/tallglass.[33]

Patrons can also buy peering glasses, which are curved glass lenses that magnify things for those far from the action, for 2 gp each. Hurl birds are also for sale for 2 cp/each to throw at the stage to register disapproval or pleasure. These small hollow clay spheres are weighted with dried beans for good throwing and are covered with glued-on feather scraps gathered from nearby fowl-pluckers. They are too light to damage more than the dignity of performers.

Patrons also tend to spend coins by throwing them at the stage. There are no rooms for rent, and cloak storage is free. Outer garb is watchfully guarded while stored against thieves and pranksters, though patrons can pay—usually 1 sp/message—the guards to slip a message parchment into a particular garment in order to pass notes.

There are three private boxes. These look down through windows in the ceiling at its edge where the conical central roof peak begins to rise. These small rooms can each hold up to 10 people crammed together, and can be rented for 10 gp/evening. These have long waiting lists.

A fourth private box is reserved by the nightclub for its own use, and is often offered for free to Piergeiron or Khelben if they show up to take in an evening's fare. These two personages usually donate 25 gp or more to the club's coffers, but other dignitaries may give nothing.

Travelers' Lore

Some say the Pearls is haunted by the phantoms of a running, weeping woman pursued by a man with a drawn sword—but I couldn't find anyone who could recall any details of this rumor, or that the haunting had been seen recently.

---

[33] A tallglass is just what it sounds like: a very tall, thin glass made by sealing a bone tube at the bottom with curved, fired clay. It is hard to spill and easy to carry in the crowd—but a neighbor can easily cause a drinker to choke with skillful use of an elbow when the long glass swings up!

The Thirsty Sailor

Tavern

This infamous dive faces the Ship's Prow across the intersection of Fish and Ship Streets. It is on the east, whereas the Ship's Prow commands the west side.[34]

The Place

This ugly, poorly built tavern began as fieldstone with wooden upper levels, but many fires and wild brawls with magic as well as axes and hurled tables have changed its face. Hasty patches have been made with more vigor than skill, and little enough enthusiasm. Of scavenged, mismatched materials, they thrust like uneven buttresses from the burn-scarred, boarded-over walls. Not a window remains at street level. Those higher up look more like trapdoors than portals to admit light or air.

The Prospect

The interior of the Thirsty Sailor is no better than its battered exterior. This is the sort of place all gentler folk think every sailors' drinking hole is: one filthy, lawless, ongoing drunken brawl, where the only patrons who aren't fighting or roaring curses or bawdy songs are those who have already passed out.

It's so rough that none of Waterdeep's hard currency girls will venture into the place. Any woman one meets there is as hard-drinking a sailor or dock-walloper as the rest of the clientele, with fists to match. One has a piece of my ear as a keepsake, but that's another story.

Candles are few and soon broken. Night or day, the Thirsty Sailor is smoky and ill-lit. This would make it ideal for shady deals—if it weren't so noisy, and you weren't so apt to slip in spilled drink, or find a thief's fingers or a bored drinker's fist uncomfortably close. A fair bit of hushed business does go on among those wise enough to rent an upper room.

The Provender

The Thirsty Sailor manages to achieve its minimal rating for one reason only: If the first cause of visiting a tavern is to drink, and another is to be entertained with a brawl or two, then this tavern meets those requirements admirably. The drink here is strong, not watered (1 cp/tankard for beer; 3 cp/whisky, and 1 sp/firewine). And one never wants for brawls to watch, though it's often hard to remain a nonparticipant with the tables crowded so close together.

---

[34] This place is #269 on the color city map.

The People

The proprietor is Kaeroven "Smiles" Yuluth, a tall, rotund, unpleasant-looking man with tiny, deep-set eyes whose stare is as hard and cold as two dagger points. He has blond, curly hair and is clean-shaven, with razor scars to prove it. His nickname comes from the fact that no one has ever seen him smile save when he's dragging the latest corpse to the rear of the tavern for disposal into the sewers.[35]

Smiles wears a magical ring—a *ring of regeneration* of the vampiric sort, I believe, from what I saw happen to wounds he suffered in a brawl he waded into the midst of—and is almost always clad in a blood-smeared apron that reeks of cheap women's perfume and bears the stitched legend: "See Neverwinter by Night/Bring a Blade and Live Longer!" Why the apron smells of perfume I dared not ask him. No one else seemed to know.

Kaeroven is known to be a contact and information gatherer for the Kraken Society,[36] and to sometimes hire thieves and bravos to steal some item or

---

[35] The Sailor and much of the immediate neighborhood is on the oldest of Waterdeep's sewers, the tidal flush Smugglers' Runs: ancient, crumbling tunnels that a small pole-punt can slip through that empty right into the harbor.

[36] More about the Kraken Society is in FR5 *The Savage Frontier.*

188

rough up a citizen. He no doubt acts for someone who pays to have the deed done, but doesn't want to be connected with it.

Many in Dock Ward suspect he is linked to shadowy, unnamed smuggling concerns—and even say these provide him with most of his income. I've heard rumors of Calishite connections and even talk of the kidnapping of citizens to sell them into slavery in Calimshan! Those who cross Kaeroven openly *do* have a habit of tragically disappearing very soon.

Smiles maintains a staff of seven bouncers and six surly dwarven waiters. There are no barmaids or any women on staff and no houseboys to clean up broken glass and spills, presumably because protecting them from drunken patrons would be endless work. One bouncer is rumored to be a doppleganger who impersonates murdered patrons when the Watch calls.

Kaeroven's sidekick, errand runner, and spy is a furtive, rat-like man who goes by the grand name of Winestab. He habitually eavesdrops on most upper room conversations—from the roof above, if need be. This unsavory sneak thief's proper name is Aldaeguth. Some older citizens remember him as Oldy-gut, but his surname (if any) and origins remain obscure. Winestab has a vicious temper and long memory. Many have found him a dangerous, persistent foe. His habit of

surviving traps set for him argues that he has one or more magic items down his boot when he goes out to stalk the roofs, sewers, and alleys of the City of Splendors by night.

The Prices

An upper room rents for 1 gp per evening or any part of it, or 4 gp for the night. There are no beds nor sanitary facilities save the alley behind (via windows). Renters must bring their own lights. There are no locks, but doors can be barred from inside. The rooms are too dirty to tempt anyone sober enough to see or smell to put them to any romantic uses—or any other uses, like sleep. Most who use the rooms are lowlives plotting clumsy crimes or smuggling deals.

Travelers' Lore

A certain dark-cloaked, soft-spoken man is seen in the Sailor from time to time—a man whose features are hidden by a mask and a hood, who sometimes visibly shifts form into a female body as he leaves, and who is almost certainly a mage of some power. At least once, this one met in the tavern with other shrouded folk who must have been, by what they inadvertently revealed, mind flayers. All in all, this tavern—if not as large and noisy as, say, the Bloody Fist nearby—is a dangerous spot.

The Ship's Prow

Inn

As its name suggests, this inn juts into the broad, usually crammed, meeting of Fish Street and Ship Street like the front of a rather fat ship.[37] It's well-known among sailors up and down the Sword Coast. More than that, it's well thought of, and if my stay is to be trusted, justly so. It's best suited to folk who can stand the fishy stink of deep-sea traps and brine barrels—and the noises of dock work, drunken revelry and fighting, the night through—wafting into their rooms.

The Place

The Ship's Prow rises four floors above the street. Years of wind and weather have turned the old boards of its upper floors and outside balconies silvery. In the moonlight on a clear night, it gleams from afar down the dark dockside streets. Inside, the floors are so warped that they rise and fall in smooth curves, like the deck of a ship in the swells. The place is shabby, but feels comfortable and homelike.

The Prospect

This inn is surprisingly quiet inside, and a cozy place to sleep as such things are judged in Dock Ward. It provides an ideal haven for tired travelers newly arrived in the city and not flush enough to find beds in a better area. It's also a trysting place for masked young nobles of Waterdeep out on a lark, not wanting to be seen by their peers (I marked at least 11 such couples on my stay), and a refuge for drunken sailors looking for a bed to snore in, rather than things to smash or bodies to cuddle or punch.

The Provender

There's nothing stronger than water to be had, nor can you get anything more to eat than smoked firefin, strong cheese, and hardloaf bread, bolstered in winter only with a bowl of hot fish-head soup (for 1 sp a person, in addition to room rates). The water is brought by the barrel from wells near Amphail and laced with crushed mint. It stands in jugs in every room, and can also be had for the asking as clear, hot tea.

The People

The inn's peace and survival in the face of the ever-present danger of fire is due to the interwoven protective spells of the resident wizard and part-time cook, Shryndalla "Were-Eye" Ghaulduth. She's an ugly but cheerful old soul who pads

---

[37] On the color city map, the Ship's Prow is #268.

around in worn slippers and food-stained robes, accompanied by an entourage of cats.[38]

The master of the house is a one-eyed, scarred and silver-bearded retired sailor, Jhambrote Harkhardest. He's genial and soft-spoken, but ever alert—and never lacks a short sword and an axe at his belt. The axe is magical. I saw an eye open on its blade and swivel around to take in all present. It winked shut in an instant when it saw me watching, but I saw what I saw.

Jhambrote doesn't go out much, and has standing arrange-ments with the guilds for sup-plies. He turns away rowdy would-be guests and those deal-ing in shady goods with cold looks and grim words, and seems to have no truck with smug-glers—nor with the city watch.

The Prices

Rooms can be had for 4 sp to 1 gp per night (larger rooms and higher floors are dearer), or 3 gp to 7 gp per tenday. Most are 6 sp per night or 5 gp per tenday.

Linen is changed daily, and the fee buys a single bath per night, if one desires, stabling for a single

---

[38] Warning: Shryndalla's cats spy for her! Don't meet someone on the sly here if you don't want her to know. The cats climb along the outside walls and slip along hidden passages. You'll hear the soft thumps as they pounce on rats and mice alike at all hours.

animal, and unlimited drinking water. I, myself, would advise not availing oneself of a bath in harbor water, which smells of fish or worse. The stabling is around the back and is crowded and unheated, but feed is provided for stabled mounts.

Travelers' Lore

I'm given to understand[39] this inn is notorious among longtime inhabitants because it once housed evil beings of the infamous Cult of the Dragon. The Lords of the City are said to have given the present proprietor title to the place to keep an eye on it after the spectacular passing of his predecessor.

About 20 winters back, the inn was kept by one Halagaster Brutheen, who acquired it in mysterious circumstances from Ulcap Rhiddyn, who just disappeared one day. When the Brandished Blade, a company of adventurers, came to stay (by chance, most say), the fury of the gods reigned in the Ship's Prow—for on sight they knew Halagaster as a magically disguised red dragon on the run from them. This Halagaster-wyrm had devoured the unfortunate Rhiddyn and taken his place, aided and paid court to here by the fell folk of the Dragon Cult.

There was great battle that night, and if the Watchful Order had not been alert and plentiful, much of the ward might well have burned. In the end, the wyrm was slain, and the Dragon Cult routed through the streets. No trace was found of the wyrm's hoard. Cultists have skulked about the inn and kept a watchful eye over it ever since—seeking the dragon's hoard or something else of value they've not yet found.

Some say the dragon hollowed out a large cellar beneath the place, devouring unfortunates whose adjoining cellars he broke into. No trace of such a warren has been found, and a docker I talked with told me that in that area a large cellar would soon flood or buildings above would collapse down into it.

When I asked host Hark-hardest about this disguised dragon, he rolled a slow and cold eye around to stare levelly into my gaze, and suggested I talk to the city watch, if I was so very interested in such dangerous matters.[40]

---

[39] My source is Shabra the Beggar Queen, an old, stout, rather unwashed woman who styles herself an expert on Dock Ward. She can often be found at the Spitting Cat tavern, nursing a cup of broth-and-brandy as the hours pass. She can be induced to talk of doings and news of the area for the price of a good meal.

[40] When I tackled Shryndalla alone on the same subject, she laughed, said she'd heard about me from some of her arcane colleagues, winked, and would say no more. I suspect she was referring to the unfortunate reception that *Volo's Guide to All Things Magical* received, but I wrapped myself in dignity as if it were a fine cloak and turned our talk to lighter matters. Several times since, though, I have seen Shryndalla's cats watching me, as I walk the streets of the city.

The Blushing Mermaid

Tavern, Inn, & Festhall

The Mermaid is one of the most luxurious establishments in Dock Ward. Everything is unhurried, luxurious, and sensual, with no detail overlooked. The staff wear facemasks of black armor plate with attached black gauze veils to conceal their faces.

The Place

Fronting on Net Street within easy reach of the harbor stenches,[41] the Blushing Mermaid spans three buildings. Scents stream from amber hanging lamps. Gauzy curtains, cushions, and sound-eating carpets are everywhere. Special, extremely expensive enchantments prevent any sort of open flame from igniting them. Even fire magic is foiled. Every guest has a plush, decadent private bedroom, a private bathroom, and an office/reception room in which to entertain.

It is widely known that the Mermaid is honeycombed with secret passages, reached by sliding wall panels in every room—but few guests manage to get those panels to work.

The Prospect

The original light pleasure palace of Waterdeep, combining a place to stay with places to drink and have fun, the Mermaid has always catered to the wealthy by maintaining an atmosphere of quiet decadence. The Mermaid bends most of its attention to creating a cozy atmosphere for festhall activities—and so its food and tavern facilities suffer. True to its name, the Mermaid does offer one special drinking and dining experience: a heated, scented communal bath in which patrons soak as they eat and drink, served by mermaids, who swim in from the harbor via well-guarded secret tunnels.[42] Messy foods can simply be washed away in the lavender-tinted waters.

The Provender

Seafood—and, surprisingly, whole roast pig—are the specialties of the Mermaid's kitchens. Everything is good, if a little underseasoned, but runs expensive: 1 gp to 3 gp/person per meal. Drinks are extra, with a full wine cellar (1 gp to 22 gp/bottle, depending on your choice), plentiful zzar (the almond-flavored sherry favored by many in Waterdeep) at 1 sp/glass, and very ordinary beer at 2 cp/tankard.

---

[41] On the color city map, the Blushing Mermaid is #249.

[42] These tunnels were no doubt used for smuggling in bygone days, but they are now blocked by locked gratings with alarms, and are used by mermen and mermaids to report for shifts at the Mermaid and to dine: a special section of the Blushing Mermaid's kitchens cater to the merfolk.

The People

The Mermaid has a busy staff of over 20 very efficient, hard-working maids who frequently give personal attentions to the needs of guests. They get to keep any tips tossed their way, and also get a percentage of all the Mermaid's earnings. A seven-foot-tall, muscular blonde of northern barbarian stock named Reetha is widely known around the city, as is an agile lass from the jungles of Chult, Leilatha Subraira, who is covered from head to toes in tattoos and likes to oil her skin to keep them colorful and herself hard to grab.

The pleasant atmosphere of the Mermaid is an enforced serenity. Patrons and staff are guarded against rowdiness and violence by the watchful eye and ready spells of the proprietress, Lady Alathene Moonstar. The secret panels can only be opened by her hand—or by four magical hands fashioned of silver, enchanted by her and carried by staff members on security duty. If one goes missing, she alters the pass spells within a few hours.

Lady Alathene is old and very beautiful, her beauty kept up by magic. She glides silently around the Mermaid dressed in full formal gowns with ornate, upthrust bodices and head veils, often wearing the same sort of facemask as her staff.

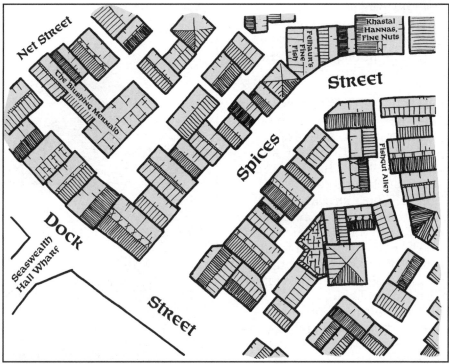

She is quick to use her magic, and fearless when facing down even drunken mages—I saw her employ disabling spells I've seen nowhere else, harmlessly confining a belligerent drunkard without injury to him or to the surroundings.

The Prices

Rooms are 3 gp to 9 gp per night (larger rooms and lower floors are dearer), or 10 gp to 50 gp per tenday. Most are 5 gp per night or 20 gp per tenday. Scents of your choice, fresh linen as needed, and unlimited, sparkling clear, scented bath water (obviously procured from elsewhere or magically cleaned) are all included in these prices.

Tipping is common. Some regular visitors give a standard 1 gp/day extra and ask that it be shared among the staff, as well as giving extras to those escorts who see to them personally.

Travelers' Lore

There are several pleasant stories, probably pure legend, about men and mermaids falling in love with each other in the pool and leaving either land or water with the help of the young man's magic, or the help of a friendly wizard, to be together.

The custom of the Hour of

Darkness provides many amusing tales and naughty pranks. In the early hours of each morning, all lights in public areas of the Mermaid are extinguished, and aside from the silver hands carried by the staff, which give off a blue-silver glow like moonlight gleaming on a sword, everyone has to find their way about by feeling. This custom causes much laughter.

In addition, there are darker whispers—of guests sometimes vanishing in the Mermaid, never to be heard of again. These tales seem to be linked to a circular staircase rising from the central mermaid pool hall to a glass-covered rooftop garden or cupola, where herbs and flowers are grown. It is adorned with bones bound to its rails and risers with fine wire.[43]

---

[43] Elminster tells us the tales of disappearing guests are true—and are due to the Lady Alathene Moonstar, an archlich whose unlife is maintained by faulty, failing enchantments. She keeps to the Mermaid because she likes to see young, lively folk having fun around her (and by magic, keeps a close watch on their activities).

Although she is seen by the Lords of the city as a force for good (sometimes sending word to Piergeiron about illicit deals and doings that she overhears in the Mermaid), she is forced to maintain her unlife by draining the life forces of living, intelligent beings (two to three a year). She must do this by direct bodily contact, and usually chooses to so use guests she dislikes or sees as evil. Their bones end up on the staircase.

Her family, the noble Moonstars of Waterdeep, knows all about her, but keeps quiet about it. In public, she ignores them and they ignore her, but privately she helps in the training of young Moonstars with magical talent and also provides safekeeping for certain treasures and incriminating items for the family. (For more details of Lady Moonstar, see the "Folk of Waterdeep" appendix at the end of this book.)

The Copper Cup

Tavern, Inn, & Festhall

The Copper Cup is one of the busiest and most famous places in Dock Ward, a must-see spot for many visitors. A large, roaring, many-leveled barn of a place, the Cup is a tavern, inn, and festhall, all in one. It opens off the South-yard, just inside the city's South Gate, and is easily reached by the High Road or the Way of the Dragon, and easily fled from down Smugglers' Run alleyway.[44] Travelers overwhelmed by the size and bustle of the City of Splendors can easily find the Cup, get much Waterdeep offers without ever leaving it, and boast when they get home of having stayed at one of the wildest places in the notorious Dock Ward!

The Place

The Cup goes several cellars deep as well as four—in some places five—floors up. It is actually three linked old, converted warehouses built tall and massive of dressed stone with outside catwalks and back alley ladders.

The cellars are prone to flooding, and reek of mildew. Except for dumping carrion and garbage, they are little used. All of the floors above, though, are used the day and night round—so much that the old floorboards often shake from all the bustling.

The Prospect

As an inn, the Cup is pretty poor. A patron's stay is ruled by constant noise. The Cup is always busy, with festhall traffic in the halls and vacant rooms at all hours. It's a lousy place to try to get some sleep.

The Cup is rescued by its services. Everything is available for a price, from having boots mended to mating riding stallions. If the staff people personally don't provide it, they have standing arrangements with someone who will.

As a tavern, the Cup has an ever-changing clientele, and no quiet places for intimate talk, haggling, or involved planning unless you rent a room. It does have cheap, plentiful, and fairly bad (watered down) ale, as well as good (but expensive!) wine, sold by the bottle.

As a festhall, the Cup is one long, ongoing party. It's not a place to visit and remain unseen or to relax and stretch—it's where one goes to romp. The dancers are acrobatic and expert contortionists. Their common costume is little more than a sheen of sweat!

The Provender

Most food at the Cup is order in. It is brought up to your room

---

[44] On the color city map, the Copper Cup is #232.

ably, and know how to have a good time.

The People

Few know that the Cup is owned and run by six of its dancers: Vivaelia Sunder, Evethe Untusk, Yululee Lantannar, and Jhandril Neth (the females), and Ilintar Belereth and Tiirlon Windstar (the males).

They take turns dancing, renting out as escorts, and tending bar with their large staff, and seem to love the life they've built.

The Prices

Rooms can be had for 1 gp to 7 gp per night (larger rooms and lower floors are dearer) or 10 gp to 40 gp per tenday. Most are 2 gp per night or 15 gp per tenday.

Linen is changed daily, and the fee buys a single scented-water bath per night, if one desires., unlimited drinking water, and stabling for one or two animals in a covered and constantly attended stable. Additional beasts are 1 gp/night each.

Travelers' Lore

Every visitor to this ongoing party has their own favorite tale of goings-on at the Cup, whether it's leaping from table to table or wilder pursuits, but this place has no hidden plots or deeds (or does it? I did see a lot of folk slipping down towards the cellars . . .).

from other places in the city at their prices plus 1 cp per dish for the runners of the Cup to bring it to you, hot, through the streets.

Ale costs 1 cp/tankard. Dark ale (the good stuff) is double that. Wine goes for 2 sp to 3 gp/bottle, depending on quality and scarcity. Good vintages are about 1 gp/bottle.

The Cup's kitchens are famous for two things: hot fish chowder, that tastes mainly of pepper and old beer (2 sp for a large wooden bowl), and cinnamon butter toast (1 cp/plate of six hot, dripping slices). The cinnamon butter toast is much favored by everyone who samples it for after the fest light dining.

The company of the Cup's beauteous and well-trained companions (of either gender) costs 10 gp per evening or any part of it. These escorts know the City well, can play most games

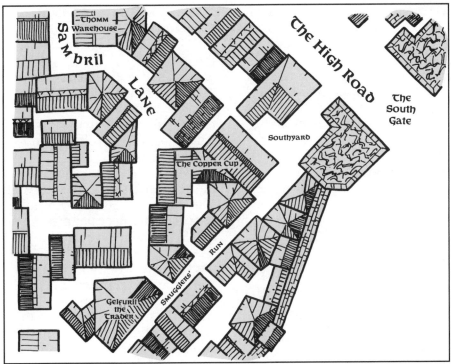

Other Places of Interest in Dock Ward

Shops

Red Sails Warehouse

This warehouse offers rental space to all, no questions asked. Material to be stored can't be alive or flammable. Space is 1 cp/day per longbox. The longboxes are more or less coffin sized.

Empty cubicles of up to two longboxes deep and eight high are available—multiply the fee accordingly. If cooling is needed, ice and watching costs an extra 2 cp/day per longbox.

Proprietor: The proprietor, Orblaer Thrommox, is fat, bearded, and very strong.[45]

Gelfuril the Trader

Gelfuril, who runs this crammed shop, will sell or trade just about anything. He deals in barter (but does *not* run a pawnshop) as well

---

[45] Location #265 on the color city map. Used by a known fence, One-Eyed Jukk (see Chapter 4 of *Waterdeep and the North*).

as coinage. Much of his wares are old or heavily used, but his prices are very reasonable. Gelfuril is more than he appears. As locals will tell, he once felled a fleeing thief with a *flame strike*.[46]

Proprietor: Gelfuril the Trader, the proprietor, is a soft-spoken, stout little man.

The House of Pride

This well-stocked perfume shop carries exotic scents from all over Faerun—from ashes of burnt snowsnake to the musk of the female giant slug. The shop is run by two sisters and is guarded by trained hunting dogs of compact build and extremely loyal temperament.

The House of Pride is crammed with a forest of glass bottles of all sizes, shapes, and hues. It is protected by a special enchantment that prevents glass from breaking. The glass here can still be vaporized or melted, but will not shatter or fall apart.[47]

Proprietresses: The two sisters who run the House of Pride, Arleeth and Ilitel Harmeth, have whimsical senses of humor. The two of them always model several of their wares on various locations on their bodies.

Aurora's Realms Shop Catalogue Counter

This is the Dock Ward outlet of the famous Faerun-wide all goods retail chain. Located in a nondescript tenement building next door (to the north across a narrow side alley) to the Purple Palace festhall, this shop fronts on Slut Street.

I was unable to learn just who the mage on staff at this shop was. The flint-eyed order clerk would not even volunteer her own name, and as she stood seven feet tall and was more than twice as wide as me, I did not press her for details. She is flanked at the counter by two burly men-at-arms at all times when the shop is open (dawn to dusk), but she overtops even them, and hardly seems to need the bodyguards.[48]

Taverns

The Blue Mermaid

A clean, well-appointed but worn place, frequented by safe folk. Good ale, bad wine, and an utterly safe, boring atmosphere.

Proprietress: Mother Jalyth Hlommorath, a pleasant, well-meaning, maternal sort, runs the Blue Mermaid.[49]

---

[46] Location #231 on the color map. For a shop floor plan, see Map 6 of the *City System* boxed set.
[47] Location #259 on the color map.
[48] Elminster reveals that the beefy order clerk is one Aglatha Shrey (her size is due to half-ogre blood), and the mage who *teleports* goods into the shop is one Beradyx Halfwinter, a fat and lazy lackspell (weak) wizard.
[49] Location #257 on the color map.

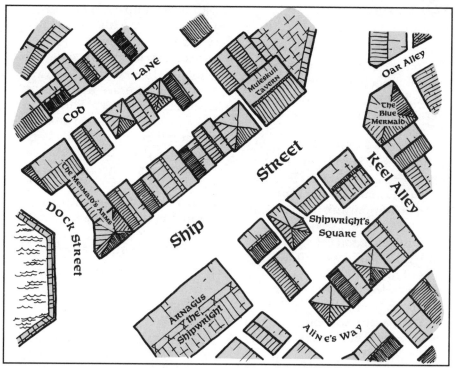

The Friendly Flounder

This small, unassuming local tavern stands on the west side of Book Street, just across from the mouth of Candle Lane. It serves both good and bad beer, and patrons can get hot buttered blackbread and fried fish with their drinks.

Prices are 1 cp/tankard for flounder beer (the bad stuff, called teethrinse by everyone), 2 cp/tankard for best and bold ale, and 1 sp for all-one-patron-can-eat of fish, with bread 1 cp/loaf extra. The food is hearty and not over spiced. The few bottles of wine in its cellar are far more pricey—but many Waterdhavians thrive on an affordable daily meal of fry at this drinking spot.

The Friendly Flounder's unspectacular fare and modest structure keep it unknown to most visitors to Waterdeep, but it is a real find for no-bother eating.

Proprietor: Eaengul Skull-crown , who owns and runs the Friendly Flounder, is a gentle, balding giant of a man. He's reputed to have a natural talent for seeing the auras of magical items and enchantments.[50]

---

[50] Elminster has brought us blackbread. It's something like pumpernickel (molasses gives it the hue).

The Hanged Man

The Hanged Man is a gathering place for poets, scriveners, writers, calligraphers, and other literary folk, and is a good place to hear a tale. The patrons tend to smoke pipes, snore a lot, and to be hopelessly behind on everyday news. They also tend to be rude and opinionated, but not of the build or temperament to actually engage in physical disputes. A surprisingly good selection of wine is available, as well as all sorts of ales.

Proprietor: Auldenuth Orbrymm is the proprietor. Patrons who come up short on a bar tab are occasionally allowed to work it off by him by beating two of the regulars at a tall tales contest (if they lose, they do dishes).[51]

The Sleeping Snake

This rowdy place is roughly furnished in hastily mended furniture. The dockhands who drink here spend a lot of time breaking it over each others' heads. There are rumors that a fence of stolen goods can be contacted here—if you can do any business amid the howls and hoots that ring out as human,

half-elven, and even half-orc wenches dance on the tables. (Some even try to sing!) There is a fine of 1 sp for hitting a dancer with any hurled object. Dancers willing to do more than dance negotiate other fees. The standing joke goes that any snake able to sleep through all this must be very, very dead.

Proprietor: Alard Belaerl, the proprietor, is a tall, gaunt, hatchet-nosed man with an annoying nasal voice.[52]

The Sleeping Wench

This tavern is a quieter, cheaper alternative to the Sleeping Snake (see above). There's still dancing on the tables and the cheaper sort of drink, but this place has a better class of clientele and background music (of the lutes and toots variety).

I still can't picture anyone sleeping in here unless he were deaf, but it's quiet enough that you can overhear conversations at nearby tables—usually talk of merchant feuds, city gossip, and the worsening state of the Realms in general.[53]

Proprietor: Peldan Thrael, who owns and runs the Sleeping Wench, is middle-aged, of middling height, nondescript, and

---

[51] Location #258 on the color map.
[52] Location #245 on the color map. The fence rumor is false, but allows a dockhand agent of the Red Sashes to observe a stream of folk engaged in shady business. See page 35 of *Waterdeep and the North.*
[53] Location #261 on the color map.

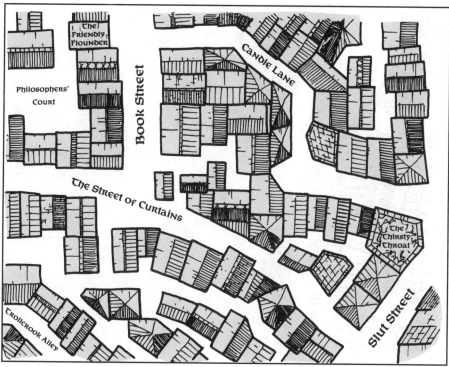

mustachioed. Overall, the type who blends well into crowds.

The Thirsty Throat

This tavern is as ramshackle an establishment as its name implies. A merchant described it to me as "a pile of wood taking its own lazy time about falling into the street," and he got it right. All the furniture is crowded together and bolted down.

"Crowded, dark, and smells of stale beer," I wrote, years ago, on my first visit—and it hasn't changed a bit. What it does have to offer is mediocre beer at low prices. A tankard as big as a man's head costs 1 copper piece. Those who like to laugh and brawl tend to go elsewhere. This place is full of quiet men drinking themselves into slumber with a handful of coppers.

The washrooms are interesting. You climb down a ladder into a little antechamber opening right into a harborbound sewer channel. Men climb down one ladder, and ladies down another—and end up facing each other in the same room, about an arm's stretch apart. It's an ideal place for exchanging items on the sly, dumping incriminating things into the sewer, or even for

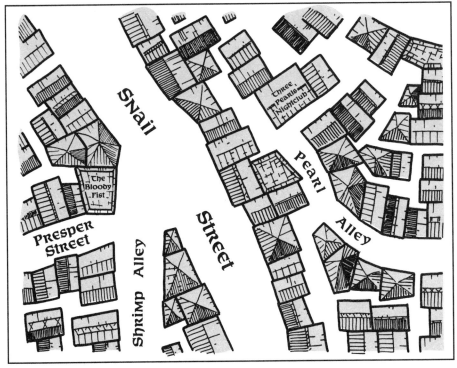

easily getting into Waterdeep's sewer network.[54]

Proprietor: Bulaedo "Fists" Ledgileer, a monstrously fat, toadlike man with forearms as big as the larger hams you'll see for sale down the street, runs the Thirsty Throat. His nickname comes from his habit of knocking men cold with one punch.

The Bloody Fist

I suppose this notorious dive is a good example of just how bad a tavern can possibly be. Repeated furniture breakage has resulted in only wall benches and a stand-up elbow bar in the center of the room being left. Wooden mugs have replaced metal, ceramic, and glass vessels, and the beer barrels are chained down to prevent their easy use as missiles.

Drinkers stand herded together like rothe in a pen, snarling and belching, and fights are almost constant. Bullies and angry people come here to pick fights, and a room upstairs is retained for a succession of novice priests of Tempus, who dress broken bones and perform minor healing magics in return

---

[54] Location #274 on the color map.

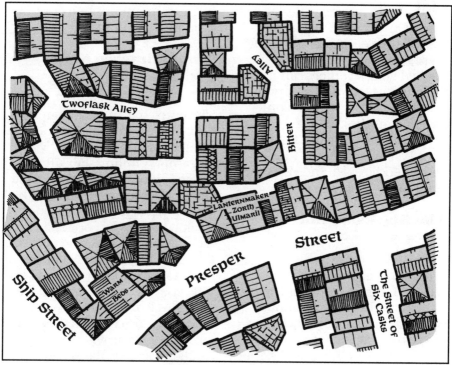

for donations to the war god.

One local bard, Talashamber of the Flame Tabard, even dubbed this place the Watching Wargod in a sarcastic ditty about the two-fisted heroes of Waterdeep, and the nickname has passed into general usage, as in: "Let's drain a few at the Wargod." Men down on their luck can be hired here, but there is little else of interest.[55]

Proprietor: Uglukh Vorl is a half-orc who has been known to yawn in the midst of a full-scale swordfight. He defends himself with a sleep-poisoned, double-bladed battle axe whose central shaft ends in a spear blade.

Inns

Warm Beds

This establishment delivers just what it promises—and little more. Each bed is warmed by three heated stones placed in it before the renter retires. There is hot water available for washing, heated by the bucket beside the same giant hearth that warms the bedstones. Rooms with one to four single beds are available.

This inn has no stabling (most patrons sell their mounts or stable them at a caravan stable in

---

[55] Location #272 on the color map.

South Ward), and provides no food of any kind. Quiet is expected after dark, but as long as there's no noise above low-pitched voices, renters can use their rooms for whatever purpose they please (such as conferences or meetings).[56]

Proprietress: Shalath Lythryn runs Warm Beds. She is kindly, plain, middle-aged, and very, very observant.

The Blackstar Inn

This dignified, even haughty inn is like a fortress on the outside, with barred windows, stone walls, and a slate roof. Its lobby has two armed guards, and the four hostlers in the locked stables are also armed.

Fees are high (typically 1 gp per head per night, plus 1 sp per animal stabled), but in return, guests get almost soundproof rooms (a rarity). Each room has a hip-bath, a double bed, water and wine provided for drinking, and various pamphlets and chapbooks provided for light reading. Each room also has its own fireplace, albeit with a miserly supply of firewood, and the patrons tend to keep to themselves. A good place to get a long, sound sleep.[57]

Proprietress: Asiyra Bold-winter is the proprietress of this inn. Her manner is one of upper-crust, noble dignity.

The Splintered Stair

The entry hall of this room rises up three floors, overlooked by interior balconies linked by elegantly spiraling stairs. Its name comes from a memorable fight between adventurers, 20 winters ago, in which the fury of wielded blades left one stair damaged almost beyond repair. I love the opulent entry hall, but . . .

The stair has been replaced, but little else has been done to make guests welcome. The large, luxurious rooms are cold and dark, and chamber pots provide the only sanitary facilities. Rates are 1 gp/ night for a person and mount or 5 sp/night for a person only. Extra animals, and extra persons sharing the same room, are 4 sp each.[58]

Proprietress: Shalanna Duthmere is a pale, worn-looking lady from Daggerford who directs her six daughters in running the inn. She is a widow and is very tight with money.

The Rearing Hippocampus

This is probably the classiest inn in Dock Ward, and is favored by

---

[56] Location #270 on the color map.
[57] Location #276 on the color map.
[58] Location #277 on the color map.

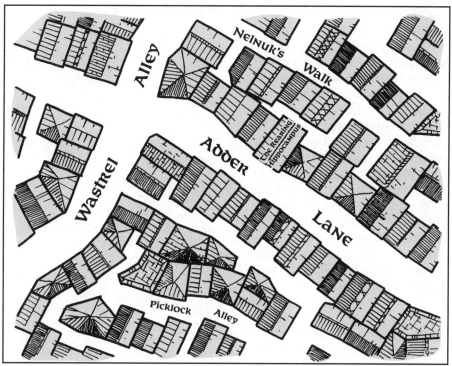

many caravan masters and by merchants who want a good, secure place to sleep without announcing their arrival to observant eyes in better wards.

Adorned with a life-sized carved wooden hippocampus out front, this inn offers broth and toast at all hours, private rooms with canopied beds (warmer than most accommodations in Dock Ward, especially in winter) and carpeted floors. It is favored by many regular visitors to the city who have business near the harbor. It recently became a dangerous tavern known as the Hidden Blade for a short time, but has reverted to its former owner and favored reputation.[59]

Proprietor: Barl Shardrin, the proprietor, is a quiet, attentive, polite man.

Festhalls

The Mermaid's Arms
Inn, Tavern & Festhall

This large, fairly new establishment is adorned with rich sea-blue draperies and takes the form of a series of elegant dining

---

[59] Location #278 on the color map. Its brief career as the Hidden Blade is mentioned in the Harpers novel *Elfshadow*, by Elaine Cunningham.

lounges, in which one dines or just drinks with an attractive host or hostess (or alone). One can take rooms for the night alone, or with someone else. Increasingly, the Arms (having acquired a safe reputation) is being used by single gentlefolk on the prowl for a night of love. In other words, patrons are going there to meet each other, not to hire a host or hostess for the night.

The Arms is large, well-lit, always busy, and can be quite expensive for the works (stabling, a room, meals, drinks, and companionship are all billed separately). Its nature makes it ideal for visitors intending to use it for some purposes. A merchant could take a room there, meet a business colleague there and eat dinner (perhaps with attractive house escorts), then go elsewhere for drinks and a play or show. The merchant could then stagger home late, knowing a comfortable room awaits.

This is an interesting trend. The only thing I regret about the Arms is that I'm far too apt to meet friends or business partners in its lounges when I want to slip up to my room unseen—or slip out unobserved.[60]

Proprietress: The Arms is run by Calathia Frost, a handsome and winning lady with a gorgeous, throaty voice. She keeps to herself and does her job.

The Purple Palace

This is the closest thing Waterdeep has to a Calishite silks-boudoir. Its lavender silk draperies and gauzy hangings are heavily perfumed. Everything is cushions, soft carpets, music, and purple-tinted, spiced wine.

Companionship is expensive and (reputedly) very good. Some of the most famous are Naneethil of the Sword Tattoo and Dessra of the Dark Desires.[61]

Proprietress: The proprietress, Tathla "Flamehair" Nightstar, was famous as a courtesan in Calimport 30 years ago, and is still a great beauty. Her blood-red hair surrounds her like a cloak, and is so long that it trails behind her on the ground!

Alleys

Dock Ward boasts the most colorful and dangerous alleyways and courtyards in the City of Splendors. Tourists are advised to be very sure of their personal defenses before walking any of these by night, even if not alone.

Arun's Alley

Running east off Ward's Way between Lackpurse Lane and Belnimbra's Street, this wide

---

[60]Location #264 on the color map.
[61]Location #260 on the color map.

carters' way services many warehouses and businesses along its short length. It can be a fascinating place to watch skilled loaders and unloaders, who can throw and catch heavy barrels and crates with speed and accuracy.

Except for those who look threatening and have weapons at the ready, this is as safe as an alley gets. Private guards belonging to the businesses and to the Fellowship of Carters and Coachmen guild are everywhere, vigilant and armed with crossbows, clubs, and short swords.

Black Wagon Alley

Running east off Book Street to the north of Candle Lane, this narrow way leads to a warren of houses of the poor, including some thieves. City watch patrols are often busy cutting away tripwires and stranglewires from its more easterly stretches. It is named for the ghostly apparition of a black plague wagon that is sometimes seen slowly and silently moving up the alley, without horses or a driver!

Black Well Court

Opening west off Book Street, across from the end of Drakiir Street, this cramped courtyard is known for its long-polluted well (the water *is* black!) and as the

meeting place of many gangs of street ruffians, thugs, and cultists over the years. As such, it is regularly patrolled by the city guard and the watch—but they often encounter thugs, Dragon Cultists, or worshippers of Loviatar "ministering" to some poor victim kidnapped from somewhere nearby.

There are also rumors of *something* living under the black water in the well that comes out at night to snatch and feed on passersby.

Candle Lane

Sometimes called Candle Alley, this winding way links Book Street and the Way of the Dragon. Its name comes from its extreme gloominess (it's overhung by tall houses), which made bookish sorts lit targets for thieves. It is now heavily patrolled. The Thirsty Throat tavern stands at its eastern end.

Caedermon's Walk

Linking Shipmasters' Hall with Wharf Street, this route is named for the ghostly ship captain who often walks up it, wooden clogs echoing in the mist, leaving wet footprints in his wake.

Caerdermon was drowned in the harbor by his mate, and rose as a revenant to follow his killer

to Shipmasters' Hall. A fearful wizard there blasted him to dust before he could slay the mate—and ever since, Caerdermon's phantom has walked this alley. There are whispers that the sea captain's ghost can slay or harm those who block his path.

By day, this route is busy with carts serving the businesses all around. It is one of the alleys dominated by muscular men moving heavy barrels with one-man push-dollies.

Fishnet Alley

Linking Spice Street and Dock Street in a dogleg west of Wharf Street, this narrow, crowded alley gets its name from the drying nets that are hung across it at various levels from wall hooks by night or for repair by day.

Down the years, these nets have broken the fall of many thieves and lovers leaping from windows, or have been dropped from above by thugs to entrap people passing along the alley. Although it looks like the web-choked lair of some giant spider, this alley is usually quite safe. However...

Manysteps Alley

Running parallel to and between Slut Street and the Way of the Dragon, this long, winding back way is home to many soothsayers, shady moneylenders, message runners, and fix-it-for-you thug bands. Avoid it if well-dressed or carrying obvious wealth. Thieves are never far off.

Melinter's Court

Behind (east of) the Hanged Man tavern, this dark courtyard is often full of pipe smoke, as philosophers spill out of the tavern, tankards in hand, to continue debates begun inside. Named for the evil mage who, a decade or so ago, formed a gang of thieves that met here to plan their villainy, this courtyard continues to be used from time to time by the evil mages who were once Melinter's apprentices.

Melinter is dead, but at times mages arrive at night, *sleep* any patrons in the courtyard, and meet to plan dark deeds. I couldn't find anyone willing to tell me very much about these wizards, but I did hear the names Azibar of the Seven Skulls, Felibarr Blacklance, and Onshall Goldcloak mentioned.

Philosopher's Court

Better known to locals by its derisive name, the Foolsquare, this sunny court has always been where old men, drunkards, young thinkers, and the more

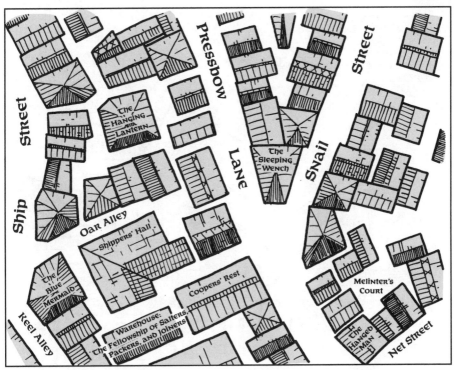

The Hanging Lantern

Street

Pressbow

Street

The Sleeping Wench

Lane

SNail

Ship Street

Oar Alley

Shippers' Hall

Coopers' Rest

Melinter's Court

The Blue Mermaid

Keel Alley

Warehouse: The Fellowship of Salters, Packers, and Joiners

The Hanged Man

Net Street

daring of the city's wealthy intellectuals have gathered when the weather is good to argue, flapping their jaws on a raised dais and weathered chairs. Drunks sleep under both the dais and the chairs by night.

Certain nameless nobles pay for torches and a standing city watch patrol to keep proceedings from being interrupted by thieves, ruffians, critics, or nightfall. Some whisper that Piergeiron or Khelben Arunsun or Mirt pay for the arrangements, but many nobles have been heard to say that "an afternoon stroll to hear the fools is better mirth than most shows thrice the price."

Round Again Alley

Paralleling Wastrel Alley on the west, from north of Adder Lane to Belnimbra's Street, this narrow alley doubles back on itself (hence its name), and is the favored testing ground of someone who can create magical illusions of beholders.

Many Waterdhavians have seen silent, menacing eye tyrants gliding along the alley, eyestalks writhing—only to fade away at the touch of hurled objects, or upon reaching the end of the way. What this means, and if it is dangerous, is not yet known.

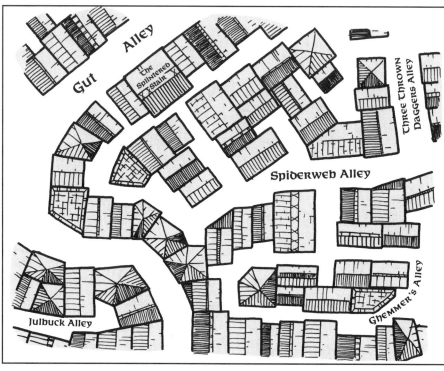

Gut Alley

The Splintered Stair

Three Thrown Daggers Alley

Spiderweb Alley

Ghemmer's Alley

Julbuck Alley

Thelten's Alley

Running northwest off Watchrun Alley, across from the end of Drawn Sword Alley, this short way is named for the crazed wizard who dwelt here. Through some arcane magic, he survives as a wizshade,[62] and can still be encountered here or in Thelten's Court, which opens off this alley to the north.

This sometimes-seen magical apparition may whimsically ignore or aid folk, but more often attacks. The Watchful Order's best efforts have not yet succeeded in destroying Thelten's strange remnants.

Three Thrown Daggers Alley

Linking Blackstar Lane and Spiderweb Alley, this winding way is famous for the curse cast here by the mage Arundoom. Struck in the back by three daggers hurled by a treacherous apprentice, he survived to take revenge. Once for each of his eight years of apprenticeship, the apprentice was driven by magi-

---

[62] Detailed in Volume 7 of the *Monstrous Compendium* (the first SPELLJAMMER® Appendix).

cal *fear* to flee up the alley and there face three animated daggers that swooped out of thin air at random points up and down the alley.

The spell survives, despite the efforts of later wizards to eradicate it. Because of this, anyone using the alley must beware three random attacks.[63]

Thugs sometimes lure or chase intended victims into the alley to get them injured. This route is sometimes called just Thrown Dagger Alley.

Trollcrook Alley

Linking Snail Street and Slut Street, this relatively open, safe passage is today much used by carters—rushing wagons are its chief danger. Of old, it was frequented at night by a vicious gang of trolls dwelling in the city's sewers. They slew many citizens before being hunted down. Some sages misname this alley Troll*crush* Alley.

Twoflask Alley

Running due west from the midpoint of Bitter Alley, this way turns south and then loops back north across itself to reach the broad way of Fish Street. The back way into the Thirsty Sailor, this still-dangerous passage is a haunt of thieves, thugs, and ladies of the evening who defend themselves or fell would-be customers with sleep-poisoned rings or long nailsheaths. Its name comes from an old joke about needing to drink two flasks of wine to have the courage to walk down it.

Watchrun Alley

This northeast/southwest route links Nelnuk's Walk with Redcloak Lane and Gut Alley, and gets its name from its frequent use by the city watch and the city guard to hurry across this part of Dock Ward. Being in the path of a running (or mounted, and charging!) patrol is itself a danger—and carters at times race each other along this route.

Thieves and cruel pranksters have been known to stretch tripwires and stranglewires across this alley by night. It is common knowledge in the ward that major gangs in this area have hired eyes watching this route to keep track of the city guard and the city watch.[64]

---

[63] Make three Dexterity checks. Success means a gleaming dagger flashes out of nowhere, passing close by, and vanishes again. Failure means it strikes the victim, hilt-deep, for a chilling 4 hp of damage, and then fades away.

[64] Persistent rumors tell of crossbows waiting behind sliding wall panels along this route—large tripod-mounted weapons firing spear-sized quarrels (one per 3 rounds, range: S5, M10, L15; damage: 2d6 vs. S- or M-sized target, 1d8 vs. L-sized target).

Appendix 1:
Folk of Waterdeep

s has been said before, the people of Waterdeep *are* Waterdeep. No guide to the city is complete without a mention of the more colorful and influential folk who live there and shape Waterdeep into what the city is.

With Elminster's help, we've included a "best guesses" list here of the probable classes, levels, and alignments of some of the Waterdhavians Volo mentions. Adventurers be warned: Much of what is said here may be wrong!

This list is alphabetical by first name (or only known alias) because so many citizens of Waterdeep lack surnames. Only ability scores of 16 or greater are listed, and the standard Realms character statistic abbreviations are used.

AGLATHA SHREY (LN half-ogre female F5; ST 18/74). Aglatha is an order clerk for the Aurora's Shop in Dock Ward, and enjoys participating in tavern brawls—her specialty is throwing men bodily through doors, windows, or tables.

ALARD BELAERL (NE hm F3/T4). A tall, gaunt, hatchet-nosed man with a nasal voice, Alard uses his dancers as spies, selling information about rich visitors to thieves.

LADY ALATHENE MOONSTAR (CG hf W19; an archlich—detailed in SJR1 *Lost Ships*—whose unlife enchantments are flawed). Lady Alathene can turn her undead attacks and powers on and off at will, can't be turned, can use all magic and learn new spells, and maintains her unlife by slaying two to three living, sentient beings a year through *energy drain* spells. She has few friends and always seeks someone she can trust.

ALBAERON HALEMBIC (LN hm F3). Although Albaeron is grizzled and elderly, he is a skilled helmsman and navigator.

ALDAEGUTH. See Winestab.

ALEENA PALADINSTAR (LG hf W9; DEX 16, INT 18, WIS 16, CHA 16) Aleena is the daughter of Piergeiron, and secretly apprenticed to Khelben "Blackstaff" Arunsun. She dwells in the palace. She is grave, reclusive, and

Aleena Paladinstar

tall—enough so that she once wore her father's armor and deceived people into thinking him present by aping his stride and movements.

ALLET TZUNTZIN (CG half-elf f W9; DEX 18, IN 18, CHA 17). Allet is a half-owner of the Misty Beard tavern in North Ward. She is slim, lithe, and dark-eyed, and has many suitors. Her will of steel is hidden under soft speech. She is firmly loyal to her sister, Vindara. She plans to marry into a noble house or found her own clan of magic-wielding half-elves, someday. Allet owns and wields many wands (see Misty Beard footnotes for a partial selection).

AMARATHA RUENDARR (NG hf F4; ST 16, INT 16, WIS 16, CHA 16). Amaratha is the charming and beautiful proprietress of the Jade Jug inn in Castle Ward. An adventuress who retired when a lich's curse destroyed her right arm (her swordarm) and prevented any known magic, thus far, from regenerating it, she has put her money into running Waterdeep's most luxurious inn. Amaratha runs the Jade Jug as the sort of place she'd like to stay in—and does, as a guest, when it's not full. She has a perfect memory, and makes a point of learning the names and details that guests want to give her, so that she can take an interest in their doings and make them feel important on their next visit. This ability has made her very useful to the city watch on many occasions. Although her profit margin is small, she grows steadily wealthier, as word of mouth makes the Jug a more popular place, despite its prices, year after year. The Jade Jug is already *the* place for visiting nobility to stay, or for Waterdhavian

Amasanna Vumendir

nobles to stay while their villas are being rebuilt, repaired, or simply cleaned up after a particularly successful party.

AMASANNA VUMENDIR (NG hf F0; DEX 18, INT 18, WIS 17). Amasanna is the proprietress of Dacer's Inn in Sea Ward. She was born to slave parents from Chult, who escaped from Calishite slavery. This is why she has dusky skin and a hatred of Calishites and slavers. She is agile and energetic, speaks seldom, but sees and knows all. She uses hand gestures with her well-trained staff, who love her and are utterly loyal to her.

ANSILVER THE LOCKSMITH (LG hm P5 of Gond; DEX 18, INT 18, WIS 17). Ansilver keeps his status as a priest of Gond secret even from other clergy of Gond. He is the proprietor of the Golden Key shop in Castle Ward. Although elderly, Ansilver remains alert. He wears thick spectacles, and has a sharp-beaked nose and a habit of always humming to himself. Ansilver is a wealthy

landowner, and has many holdings in South Ward and in the farmland east of Waterdeep.

ARATHKA "RELLA" RUELL (CG hf P14 of Selune; DEX 16, INT 16, WIS 18). Arathka Ruell is the wife of Dandalus Ruell, co-owner of The Old Xoblob Shop. She worships from her rooftop bower and is the secret hand of the lady in Waterdeep (as opposed to the well-known priestesses of the House of the Moon). She sponsors and aids many adventurers, and has acted as den mother to such famous bands as the Company of the Caltrop and the Flamehurling Five.

ARLEETH HARMETH (NG hf F1; DEX 17, CHA 17).

ARNAGUS THE SHIPWRIGHT (LG hm F7; ST 17, DEX 16, CON 17, INT 17, WIS 17, CHA 16). The wealthiest, and probably the most skilled, shipbuilder in Waterdeep, Arnagus is a very influential member of not only his guild but of trade matters throughout the city. He is friendly to all, but says little, and keeps out of the public eye as much as possible. His sharp gaze misses little, and he has been known to report thieves, smugglers, murderers, and the like to the city watch. (For shipbuilding fees and times, see *Waterdeep and the North.*)

ASIYRA BOLDWINTER (LE hf P3 of Loviatar). Asiyra eyes all guests for possible converts/targets/fellow devotees, but otherwise keeps her faith secret (though some have heard her whip in the cellars, late at night). Her outward manner is one of upper-crust, noble dignity, but like many devotees of the Mistress of Pain, she wears a blood-burrs belt under her gowns that sometimes betrays her devotion.

AULDENUTH ORBRYMM (NG hm F5 [retired]) Auldemuth is a master forger, but is retired.

AZIBAR OF THE SEVEN SKULLS (NE hm W9) Azibar is known for the enchanted flying skulls that are always with him, darting and hovering—and spitting spells at his foes.

BALAGHAST BRIGHTLINGAR (NG hm F8; ST 17, WIS 16, CON 16). The proprietor of the Pilgrims' Rest inn in Sea Ward, Balaghast is a gruff, hard-working retired mercenary. His manner conceals kindness and willingness to help those in need.

BALARG "TWOFISTS" DATHEN (CN hm F5; ST 17, DEX 16, CON 16). Twofists, the proprietor of the Red-Eyed Owl tavern in Castle Ward, is prone to brawling and wenching with equal vigor and noise. He is bluff and bristle-bearded, with long, unkempt red hair. His rough voice is often heard calling out coarse jests to tavern patrons, and his arm has a deadly aim with hurled platters or tankards. He is always willing to pitch in to a fight.

BALTHORR "THE BOLD" OLASKOS (NE hm T8; ST 16, DEX 17, WIS 16, CHA 16). Balthorr is the loud-voiced and friendly proprietor of Balthorr's Rare and Wonderful Treasures in Castle Ward. His "hail-fellow, well-met," sincere attitudes are belied by the fact that he secretly fences stolen goods and is sympathetic to the Shadow Thieves (the outlawed Thieves' Guild).

BARL SHARDRIN (CN hm F3). Barl is a quiet, attentive, polite man who can reveal much about Waterdeep to anyone who bothers to sit and talk with him.

BELIARGE "OLD BOAR" MADUSKAR (LN hm F8; ST 17, CON 16) Beliarge, known as "Bel" to his friends, is the proprietor of the Swords' Rest tavern. This wary old warrior is grizzled and stout, but still capable.

BERADYX HALFWINTER (LN hm W9) A fat and lazy wizard who enjoys good wine, ale, and cheese, Beradyx pursues "spellhurling for hire" in the safe confines of a city. He hires out for only noncombat and legal situations. His spells are few and his Art weak, earning him the contempt of mages like Elminster. He works as the transportation mage for Aurora's Shop in Dock Ward.

BLAZIDON "ONE-EYE" (CN hm F6 [now]; ST 16). This veteran warrior comes out of retirement from time to time, but spends most of his days uniting—for a small fee—hireswords with caravan masters and others wishing to hire them. By day, he's usually to be found sitting on a stool in Virgin's Square, where the fighting men have learned to gather. By night, he's busy in one of the private rooms of the Bowels of the Earth tavern in Trades Ward—which he owns, although few in the city know that—or making the rounds of other taverns and inns, looking for warriors who need work. One-Eye is grizzled, hairy, and stout with thickly muscled forearms that brand him as a fighter from far off. He always wears a *ring of the ram* and a *vampiric regeneration ring*, and carries at least one *potion of super-heroism* and one of *extra-healing*.

BRATHAN ZILMER (LG hm F5; ST 16, INT 16, WIS 16, CHA 16). Brathan, Guildmaster of the Fellowship of Innkeepers and proprietor of the Pampered Traveler inn in Castle Ward, is solemn, wary, and darkly handsome. Brathan is the last survivor of an adventuring band slaughtered by a mage it attacked in a northern ruin. The mage, a horned man in purple robes who called himself Zulorr Thaeran, swore he'd slay every last one of them slowly and painfully (though that was two decades ago). Brathan is always alert for some sign that the mage has found him at last and is coming to torment and slay him.

BRAUM PELAUVIR (LG hm F6; ST 17, DEX 16). Braum is proprietor of Pelauvir's Counter store in South Ward. Braum, who is tall, beefy and jovial, has a memory decades-long and sharp with detail. He has largely retired from battle.

BRAZAUN OF BALDUR'S GATE (CN hm F0; DEX 18, INT 18, CHA 16) Brazaun, a feast cook for hire of brilliant skill, is noted for his savory pastries and wine-flavored ices. His lowest fee is 100 gp/night, payable in advance—plus, of course, the cost of the ingredients he requires. These ingredients typically cost about 10 gp/guest, and must be laid in by his client, not by the quick-tempered, dashingly handsome Brazaun himself. Brazaun is given to dancing and singing as he works in the kitchen. He's a lady-chaser and tippler of legendary capacity.

BULAEDO "FISTS" LEDGILEER (NE hm F5; ST 18/12, CON 18; 70 hp—the maximum number possible). During Bulaedo's career as a warrior, he was poisoned many times, so is 40% likely to be immune to any poison used on him.

CALATHIA FROST (CG hf F9; DEX 16, CHA 17). The Mermaid's Arms is run by Calathia Frost, a handsome and winning lady with a gorgeous, throaty voice. She usually keeps to herself and does her job, but will not condone any activities that she considers evil going on in the inn. She keeps her favorite long sword (a *long sword +2)* and a suit of chain mail in a cedar chest at the foot of her bed, underneath some blankets.

CALLANTER ROLLINGSHOULDER (NE hm F1; ST 16, CON 17). Callanter is the proprietor of the Sleepy Sylph tavern in Castle Ward. He is tall, fat, and dresses in Calishite silken finery, with gold bells on the ends of his *huge* mustache.

CATHAL SUNSPEAR (LN hf F0; INT 17, WIS 16). This cultured, middle-aged counter clerk of the Castle Ward outlet of the Aurora's retail chain was born to a wealthy family of Tethyr. Cathal is now an investor deeply interested in the behind-the-scenes deals of guilds and noble families.

CATHALISHAERA (CN hf W10; DEX 17, INT 18). Cathalishaera, the reclusive, shy owner of the Jade Dancer, loves to animate the famous dancing statue for which her establishment is named, but would never dare to dance in public herself. She is a one-time apprentice of Kappiyan Flurmastyr who once sought adventure but withdrew in terror from the dark magic of baatezu to a life of hiding and using her magic for small things. She secretly dreams of meeting a brave, loving, young wizard to protect her and to taste adventure with him again.

CHETH THANION (LN hm F4; ST 16, INT 16, WIS 16). Cheth, proprietor of the Wandering Wemic inn in Sea Ward, devotes his life to building his inn into a special place. He is big and burly, with blond hair and broad shoulders. Although he conveys an easygoing nature, he is far more alert than he seems, and never forgets a face or any debts or cheating.

CHULDAN HELMSTAR (CN hm T4). Chuldan is a sly man of many secrets. He reminds some of a fox or a weasel.

DANDALUS "FIRE-EYE" RUELL (CG hm F14; ST 18/02, DEX 17, INT 16, WIS 17, CON 16, CHA 16).This fat, jolly, balding, bearded proprietor of the Old Xoblob Shop always has bulging pockets and always carries on his person the following magic: a *ring of free action,* a *ring of spell turning,* a *greenstone amulet,* 2 *potions of extra-healing,* an *elixir of health,* 2 *iron bands of Bilarro* spheres, and 6 *beads of force.* He may well carry more magic and definitely has an *invisible broad sword +3* somewhere near at hand.

DARION SULMEST (LN hm F0; DEX 18, INT 17, WIS 17). While he is spokes-man for the Order of Cobblers & Corvisers, Darion is also the propri-etor of his own very expensive, but top-quality, shop in North Ward. Darion is sometimes sarcastic, extremely wealthy, and handsome. He is rumored to have several noble ladies as intimate companions and to hold the ear of the Lords of Water-deep. Darion is secretly a wistful would-be adventurer who always likes to hear tales of danger. He sometimes sponsors adventuring bands.

DAUNT **B**UIRUNE (CN hm T13, ST 16, DEX 18, INT 16). Daunt Buirune is retired from thieving and is now the proprietor of the Red Gauntlet tavern. He is silent, watchful, and always pleasantly wary.

DELBORGGAN THE **B**LADE (CG hm F9; ST 17, WIS 17, CON 17). Delborggan is a grizzled, one-eyed ex-adventurer. Formerly, he was a famous hero of northern exploration who led the men of Lith through many monsters and icy perils to reach isolated Snowkeep. He is a man driven to adventuring by grief (as he says, "For it is an ill thing—a heavy thing—for a boy to be not loved by his father"), who now views the world with buoyant, if cynical, good humor. As the proprietor of the Riven Shield Shop in Trades Ward, he's always armed with magic items, including (under his eyepatch) a waiting magical eyecusp that can spout beams of fire when he desires (details of this item left to the DM).

DESSRA OF THE **D**ARK **D**ESIRES (CN hf F2; DEX 16, CHA 16).

DHAUNRYL **Z**ALIMBAR (NG hm W10; INT 18). Dhaunryl Zalimbar is the tall, kindly, gangling and rather shy service-mage of the Trades Ward outlet of the Aurora's retail chain. A studious sort with little taste for danger or adventure, Dhaunryl is a collector and student of heraldic devices. He sketches all badges, crests, and escutcheons he sees in Waterdeep, as well as noting down and memorizing most of the mottoes he encounters.

DLARNA **S**UONE (LN hf F2; ST 16, INT 17). Dlarna Suone is the chief guild buyer and seller for the Vintners' (et al.) Guild. She resides at their headquarters, the House of Good Spirits. Sharp-tempered and sharp-witted, she is quick to size up a person and to smell deceit. Her hobbies are breeding cats and racing horses. (She likes to be in the saddle.)

DOBLIN **G**OUNAR (CN hm T3; DEX 16, IN 16). Doblin, proprietor of Gounar's Tavern in Sea Ward, is a cold, self-important, cruel and arrogant man of cutting manners and an open lack of caring for others.

EAENGUL **S**KULLCROWN (NG hm F4; ST 17, CON 18). A gentle, balding giant of a man, Eaengul Skullcrown is descended from a now-fallen noble family of Amn. He is now the proprietor of the Friendly Flounder in Dock Ward. He's reputed to have a natural talent for seeing the auras of magical items and enchantments.

EIRAKLON **M**ARIMMATAR (LN hm F9; ST 17, DEX 17). As housemaster (security chief) of the Gentle Mermaid in North Ward, Eiraklon oversees the daily running of the place, but is seldom seen by patrons. He suspects that shady money backs the Mermaid, but dares not try to investigate. His suspicions have arisen because there's so much money passing through the Mermaid, and its spending is never questioned by anyone. Eiraklon also has the constant feeling of being watched. Xanathar (the beholder crime lord of Waterdeep) wants an unwitting, respectable agent doing his best for the Mermaid, and so Eiraklon has a free hand in hiring and managing in order to make the Mermaid the best possible place of its kind. His efforts make the Mermaid

profitable in its own right and a means of attracting into the city wealthy folk who can then be fleeced.

ELGUTH IRAMBLIN (CG hm F1). Elguth is the stableboy at the House of Good Spirits, and an expert guide to the gambling houses and festhalls of Waterdeep. He is a member of the Vintners' (et al.) Guild.

EVETHE UNTUSK (CG half-elf f F4; DEX 18, CHA 17). Evethe is a dancer, bartender, escort, and part-owner of the Copper Cup. She is known for her love of music, especially elven songs and human ballads about elves.

FELDYN GOADOLFYN (NE hm T8; DEX 17, INT 17). Feldyn is the nondescript-looking, cold strategist who is the owner of the Old Monster Shop. He has been described as a dangerous, patient enemy.

FELIBARR BLACKLANCE (CE hm W12). Felibarr Blacklance is the developer of the *blacklance* "blast beam" spell. He is a cruel killer.

FELSTAN SPINDRIVVER (CG hm F4; ST 16, INT 16). Felstan is the amiable keeper of the Cliffwatch Inn in North Ward. He is quick to help-adventurers and a great fund of free lore to lodgers on the talk of the city and adventuring deeds.

FELZOUN THAR (CN dwarf m F6; ST 17, WIS 17, CON 18). Felzoun is the proprietor of Felzoun's Folly tavern in Trades Ward. He is a loud-voiced, incredibly energetic host who is always bustling about. He fears no one and always carries two throwing axes under his apron. Felzoun is bristle-bearded and balding, with a

red face and red beard.

FILIARE (LN hm F5 [now]; ST 16, INT 16, CHA 16). Filiare, a jovial ex-mercenary, is the proprietor of the Inn of the Dripping Dagger in Trades Ward. He has been known to show kindness to adventurers and mercenaries down on their luck. He is also the father confessor to, and sometime intimate friend of, many unhappy noblewomen of Waterdeep.

LADY GALINDA RAVENTREE (CN hf F0; DEX 16, INT 16, CHA 16). This catty young noble is devoted to festive frivolity, fighting with her social rivals, and sampling as many young men as she can entice into her reach. Lady Galinda can briefly be seen at this work in the novel *Elfshadow*.

GELFURIL THE TRADER (CG hm P6 of Tymora). Gelfuril is a retired priest.

GORDRYM ZHAVALL (LN hm F4; ST 16, DEX 16, WIS 16). Gordrym is a calm, expressionless man who is second guild buyer (after Dlarna Suone) for the Vintners' (et al.) Guild. He resides at their headquarters, The House of Good Spirits. He is secretly a gambler and heavily in debt. Gordrym is a known master blender of wines.

GOTHMORGAN ILIBULD (CG hm F2; INT 18). Gothmorgan is the proprietor of the Singing Sword tavern in Castle Ward. He is a likable former adventurer who retired when he found the sword (of the tavern's name) in a monster-haunted ruin. Gothmorgan is tall and polite. While he is always watchful, he is known primarily for his dry humor. His wealth increases daily.

GULTH DJANCZO (NE hm T7; DEX 17). Gulth is the proprietor of the Full

Cup tavern. A nasal-voiced, coldly polite weasel of a man, he probably has hidden magic items on his person for defense.

GUTHLAKH "HANDS" IMYIIR (LN hm F7; ST 18/00, CON 16). Guthlakh stands more than six-and-a-half feet tall, with corded muscles and a battered, sword-scarred face. He is the proprietor of the Sailors' Own, a dockside tavern in Castle Ward. His demeanor is slow and deliberate, and he seldom smiles.

HAHSTOZ BAERHULD (NE hm T6 [now]; DEX 18). Hahstoz is the crooked proprietor of the Golden Horn Gambling House in Trades Ward. A dark-haired and complexioned, habitually expressionless man, he moves with a silent grace.

HALA MYRT (NE hm F5; ST 16). Hala Myrt, a fat, resentful man, spends most of his days sitting on a barstool at the Grinning Lion tavern, as a contact for the fence Orlpar Husteem. He is a wary man and carries a capsule of dream sauce in his hair. If he bites it, he'll fall instantly into a slumber of wild, swirling dreams from which he can't be roused for 1d6 days. During this time, even magical means won't arouse him or enable others to learn things by compelled questioning or mind-reading.

HALIDARA URINSHOON (LN hf F1; DEX 16, CHA 15). Halidara, who is the owner of the Three Pearls Nightclub, an exotic dancer and a shrewd investor, lives a life of luxury and party-going in the city's North Ward and partakes often and heavily of chocolates and amberjack sherry.

Hilmer

HILMER (LN hm F9; ST 18/00, DEX 18, INT 17, CON 16, CHA 16). Hilmer is a master armorer and proprietor of his own shop in Castle Ward. Although he is now retired, as an adventurer he was known to have explored Myth Drannor and much of Undermountain. He is tall with broad shoulders. He is known to be just, honest, and soft-spoken. He is a close friend of suspected Lords Durnan and Laeral.

HLONDAGLUS SHRIM (NG hm W9; INT 18, WIS 18). Hlondaglus is a short, shy, ugly little man with misshapen features and one wooden leg. He is fiercely loyal to the Ruells (Arathka and Dandalus).

ILDAR ORSABBAS (CE hm F0). Ildar, the stout, fun-loving, slightly pompous proprietor of Orsabbas's Fine Imports in Trades Ward, is nicknamed the "Duke of Darkness" for the masked, sinister guise he wears to nobles' feasts. While he is wearing this costume, he loves to threaten,

dance, and seduce. He goes to such feasts partly to sample the tapestries, wines, and perfumes that he has been known to fence—a trade that has earned him his other nickname: Fingers.

ILINTAR BELERETH (CG half-elf m F6; ST 17, DEX 17, CHA 16). Ilintar is a dancer, escort, bartender, and part-owner of the Copper Cup. He sees all but says little.

ILITEL HARMETH (CG hf F1; DEX 18, CHA 16).

ILMAIREN ARNSKULL (LN dwarf m F6; ST 17, CON 17). Ilmairen, a fat, dark-eyed dwarf, acts as a contact with his friend Jaerloon for dwarves visiting Waterdeep. He works from the dining room of the Raging Lion inn in North Ward. He is a skilled whittler and mimic, and has often been known to sing as sweetly as any human soprano as he parodies a singer's performance.

IMMITHAR "THE GLOVE" (CN hm T6; DEX 17, INT 17, CHA 16). Immithar owns and runs the Blue Jack tavern in Castle Ward. He is a fast-moving and quick-witted fellow who is known as a joker, a good strategist, and a good judge of character and consequences. He is also an expert mimic. He retired from thieving, and now invests in shipping and rental rooms.

JAERLOON BUCKLEBAR (LG dwarf m F7; ST 16, DEX 16, CHA 16). Jaerloon, with his friend, Ilmairen, acts as a contact for dwarves in Waterdeep from a base in the dining room of the Raging Lion inn in North Ward. He is a white-bearded, weather-faced but kingly dwarf, who is a skilled

Jathaliira Thindrel

whittler and wrestler. Jaerloon is uncannily adept at striking missiles out of the air or catching them (consider his DEX to be 21 when dealing with missiles).

JATHALIIRA THINDREL (CN hf F0; DEX 18, INT 17, CHA 16). Jathaliira is the petite, pert, and always-bustling proprietress of the House of Purple Silks festhall in Sea Ward. She is sharp-tempered but passionate, middle-aged, and wealthy. She has built up a large fortune (almost a million gp in ready cash) by shrewd investments in Waterdhavian companies and by carefully purchasing valuable city real estate. (The real estate's value is close to another four million gp.) She has arrangements with the Watchful Order to rescue her in the case of kidnapping and ransom, when she calls them by means of a certain magical bell that she wears in her hair. Each use of the bell costs her 40,000 gp, but she's only had to use it twice. Each time she seized more than the fee from her would-be captor. Jathaliira can also

call on her bouncers and her friend, Khelben Arunsun, for support and protection.

"MOTHER" JALYTH HLOMMORATH (NG hf F1). Mother Hlommorath is fat, bustling, and gossipy. Any secret told to her is all over the city within the day.

JANESS IMRISTAR (CN hf F3; INT 16). Janess Imristar owns and runs the Spouting Fish tavern. She is a short, mousy, loud-voiced woman who is always bustling. She is quite fearless.

JANNAXIL SERPENTIL (NE hm W14; INT 18). This cold, much-hated bookseller and fence is a coward born long ago in rural Amn who early on discovered how to make *potions of longevity*—and then killed the man he learned that lore from. He's gathered much magical lore over the years, and has summoned baatezu, trained and magically bound various guardian creatures, and collected the following magical items that he carries on his person or keeps near at hand in his office: a *wand of paralyzation*, a *brooch of shielding*, a bag of *dust of tracelessness*, a pair of *eyes of minute seeing* lenses, a pair of *gauntlets of ogre power*, a pair of *gauntlets of swimming and climbing*, a *hat of disguise*, several jars of *Keoghtom's ointment*, a *necklace of adaptation*, a *periapt of proof against poison*, and a collection of an unknown number of *Quaal's feather tokens*. Jannaxil also possesses an unknown number of spellbooks and other magical items, hidden in a cache somewhere underground in Waterdeep.

JHAMBROTE HARKHARDEST (LN hm W9).

JHANDRIL NETH (NG hf F2; DEX 17, CHA 14). Jandril is a dancer, escort, bartender, and part-owner of the Copper Cup. She is known for her frequent changes in her (rather impassioned) relationships with her intimate friends, which usually end in tempestuous fights in which many things get broken.

JHANT DAXER (LE hm T9; DEX 18, INT 17, CHA 16). Jhant, a wary, sharp-featured, fox-like, unpleasant and ruthless man, is officially owner of the Gentle Mermaid in North Ward. He is actually a front man for the beholder crime lord Xanathar. Before becoming Xanathar's agent, Jhant was a caravan owner and money-lender operating out of Baldur's Gate, although it is not a well-known fact in Waterdeep. Jhant runs smuggling, money drop, kidnapping, and goods reallocation errands for Xanathar, and is seldom at the Mermaid.

KAEROVEN "SMILES" YULUTH (NE hm F8).

KAPPIYAN FLURMASTYR (NG hm W11; INT 18, CHA 16). At over 90 years of age, Kappiyan is tall, thin, and distinguished. He is known as Waterdeep's "potion wizard" and is the kindly tutor to a succession of female apprentices. A noted maker of potions and periapts, Kappiyan is also always researching the better spellcasting of low-level magics. He is moved to anger by the misuse of magic. He always wears robes, with a *wand of paralyzation* up one sleeve, a *wand of magic missiles* up the other (in forearm sheaths), and a *wand of negation* down one boot. At his belt he carries a plain, non-magical dagger, a light purse, and at least three *potions of healing*.

KATHLIIRA SALARTH (CG hf T4; DEX 17, INT 18, CHA 16). Kathliira is a famous hire cook who goes to a client's kitchen and whips up the food for a feast with ingredients already laid in. Her sweets are legendary up and down the Sword Coast, but Elminster and Khelben "Blackstaff" Arunsun both agree her soups are her true masterpieces. They're the best they've ever had on any world! Kathliira's fee is always 200 gp/night. Often common folk join purses together to hire her for a house party, whereas most hire cooks only cater to the wealthy and noble.

KHALOU MAZESTAR (CG hf F3; ST 16, INT 16). Khalou is the fat, talkative, wise-cracking lady bartender of the Jade Dancer. She loves to talk to guests, and is known as a great source of jokes, information on current fads and interests among the young, and gossip about Waterdeep's rich and noble folk—especially envious talk of gems and extravagance.

KRIIOS HALAMBAR (LN hm F0; DEX 18, INT 18). Kriios, guildmaster of the Council of Musicians, Instrument-Makers, and Choristers, is a matchless lutemaker and a skilled harpmaker. He is the proprietor of Halambar Lutes & Harps in Castle Ward. Kriios is habitually expressionless and has unusual, large, black-pupiled eyes. He is a very wealthy snob and a severe critic of musicians. He holds himself as too exalted to arrange music for a noble's feast, but is a supplier of instruments to many musicians who must play at such feasts to make a living.

Loene

LEILATHA SUBRAIRA (CN hf T6; DEX 17, CHA 15). Leilatha is an escaped slave from Chult who gave her Calishite masters the slip in Waterdeep long ago and killed them when they came looking for her. Her entire body is covered in tattoos. She keeps her skin oiled except when creeping around rooftops at night to go thieving.

LHAERHLIN MASRAM (LN hm F8; ST 16). Lhaerhlin is the affable but stone-faced proprietor of the Raging Lion inn in North Ward. A tall, stout man of many secrets, he always wears a *ring of spell turning* and a *ring of lightning* (equal to a *wand of lightning*).

LOENE (CG hf F9 [now]; ST16, DEX 17, CHA 16). Loene, a graceful, sensuous former pleasure girl, was rescued from slavery by the Company of Crazed Venturers. She won a place in their ranks, and later became a gambler, adventuress for hire, and the lady love of Mirt. Today she is a rich landlord in the city. She still

trains warriors and can be hired as an adventuress for 2 gp/day. She wears a *ring of spell storing* holding *dispel magic, fly, sending,* and *wall of force.* She has large hazel eyes, a magnificent tawny body, and dark blonde hair. She will use the *sending* to call on the [now 14th level] mage Nain Keenwhistler for aid when her life is in peril.

LOGROS HLANDARR (LN hm W9; DEX 16, INT 18, CHA 16). Logros is service-mage to the South Ward Aurora's outlet. Arrogant and given to acting important and mysterious, he desperately wants to be part of real intrigue—with a minimum of danger.

THE MASKED MINSTREL (CG hf B4; DEX 17, INT 16, CHA 17). None know the true name of this mysterious lady of the evening who frequents Jesters' Court in Castle Ward. She can be found there on warmer evenings, playing a harp, lyre, or lute. She has a pleasant singing voice, and always appears masked. She entertains clients nearby on the wooded slopes of Mount Waterdeep. Some say she's a Harper agent, others that she's demented or some sort of spy for a foreign realm. Her true origins, aims, and past remain obscure.

MHAIR SZELTUNE (NG hf W17; DEX 17, INT 18, CHA 16). Lady Master of the Order Mhair Szeltune is head of the Watchful Order of Magists & Protectors. A serene, efficient, petite lady of iron will, she is an uncommonly good judge of character. She is friend to Khelben "Blackstaff" Arunsun, has long, glossy black hair, and very, very blue eyes. She usually carries a staff when in public—

Mhair Szeltune

reputed (correctly, Elminster says) to be a *staff of the magi.* Mhair often wanders the city in the magical guise of an old crone leaning on her stick (the staff) in order to see what treatment she'll get and what's going on when there's no one important to see. She has been known to teach adventurers who tease or torment the ugly old lady a sharp lesson. However, Mhair can be a kind, loyal friend.

MORATHIN "HOOKS" BELMONDER (LN hm F0; ST 17, DEX 17). Morathin is a burly, hearty man skilled at butchery. He is an expert, strong-stomached judge of musculature, and the type, age, and condition of meat. (He can tell diseased meat with 88% accuracy and tainted/poisoned meat 94% of the time.) Morathin is Second Knife of, and public contact for, the Guild of Butchers. He makes over 400 gp clear profit on a typical business day, and is considered a very rich man.

MRIL JUTHBUCK (CG half-elf f F4; INT 16, CHA 16). Mril is the counter clerk

at the South Ward Aurora's outlet. She loves drinks, jokes, and dancing, and is friendly to all.

MRORN "BLACK BRACERS" HALDUTH (LN hm F6; ST 17, DEX 17, CON 17). Mrorn's nickname comes from the bracers he never removes, which are black-hued *bracers of defense AC2*. He leads the seven bouncers at the House of Good Spirits, and is a calm, no-nonsense, untalkative man of quiet voice and iron strength.

MUNZRIM MARLPAR (LN lizard man m F6; ST 16, IN 16). Rare among his kind for his intellect and nine foot height, this dignified, fearless individual tends bar at the Misty Beard tavern in North Ward. Munzrim is sensitive and caring. He's a keen study of human life, and is great friends with a spectator named Thoim Zalamm. Human females have begun to interest him—and he has befriended not only his employers, but several regular patrons.

MYRMITH SPLENDON (LN hm F9 [now]; ST 18/04, WIS 16). This noted weapons tutor makes a good living training all who pay his fees in the expert use of weapons. Myrmith is always alert, and it is said he never sleeps and can see behind him. Myrmith, who is a very strong man, is an ex-adventurer and mercenary who accumulated quite a few magic items and gold pieces before settling down in Waterdeep. He also picked up many powerful wizards up and down the Sword Coast North as friends.

NANEETHIL OF THE SWORD TATTOO (NG hf T3; DEX 16, CHA 16). Naneethil is famous for the tattoo of a vertical sword, hilt uppermost, that runs down her front from throat to crotch. It is not actually a tatoo, but a brand, forcibly bestowed on her by orc slavers intending to sell her to Thayan buyers. She escaped them years ago.

NARTHINDLAR OF THE NINE SPELLS (LN hm W12; INT 18, WIS 16, CON 16). Narthindlar is a wizard who loves magic concerned with growing things and has a fondness for lemons. He installed the lemon trees in Lemontree Alley and magically nurtures them. A shy, retiring, rather paranoid fellow, he is known as Narthindlar of the Nine Spells because he worked with a priest of Silvanus to develop a special *contingency* spell that triggers nine precast first level priest spells upon his person when he is brought to 4 hp or less or when he speaks a secret activation word. These spells are *bless, cure light wounds* ×, *pass without trace, protection from evil,* and *sanctuary.* He has used this spell twice—once when beset by raiding orcs in the wilds and once when attacked by brigands in an alley in Waterdeep—so most of the city folk have heard of it.

NLEERA TARANNATH (CG hf W10; DEX 18, INT 18, CHA 16). Nleera is a Harper mage who has recently begun to act as a contact for Those Who Harp by impersonating one of the Tesper family ghosts—with the aid of the ghosts themselves—during public parties at the Tespergates villa in Sea Ward. She is demure, cautious, and well armed with magic items and spells, including one that will summon the city guard at full speed should she need them.

OLHIN SHALUT (LN hm F4; ST 16, WIS 17). Olhin Shalut, a wealthy investor and retired adventurer, is the proprietor of the Ship's Wheel tavern in Sea Ward. He is old, affable, and pompous. He always wears or carries a *ring of blinking*, a *ring of protection +3*, a *rod of lordly might*, an *iron bands of Bilarro* sphere, and a *short sword of quickness (+2)*. He also owns other magic items, which he will use when expecting trouble.

ONGAMAR TATHLOON (LN hm F9; ST 18/00, CON 17). Ongamar tends bar in the Bowels of the Earth tavern and is the friend and confidant of the owner, Blazidon One-Eye. He is even-tempered, bald, and incredibly muscular. He wears two gold earrings—an *earring of spell turning*, which functions as the magical ring of the same name, and an *earring of protection +3*, which also functions as the ring of the same name.

ONSHALL GOLDCLOAK (LE hm W11). Onshall works with tanar'ri. He is known for always working revenge on those who deal him even the slightest of setbacks.

ORBLAER THROMMOX (NE hm F6; ST 18/04). Orblaer is fat and wears a full beard.

ORGULA SAMSHROON (LG hf F0; INT 17, WIS 17). Orgula is the counter clerk of the Trades Ward outlet of the Aurora's Realms Shop catalogue retail chain. She is a stout, middle-aged motherly sort, whose easy manner and encyclopedic knowledge of the Realms—and of Aurora's stock—have made her famous among patrons. She never forgets a face and has a perfect memory for details of dress and description. She serves as a

Orlpiir Hammerstar

Harper contact and one of many sets of eyes for Piergeiron.

ORLOTH THELDARIN (NG hm F0; DEX 17, INT 17, CHA 17). Orloth is the counter clerk for the Sea Ward outlet of the Aurora's retail chain. He is a man of effeminate manners (tempered with tact and courtesy) who has superb taste and the knack of recalling colors precisely, even when seen only once and long ago.

ORLPAR HUSTEEM (CE hm T4; DEX 17, INT 17). Orlpar is the bored, thrill-seeking, cunning younger brother of Orbos, head of the Husteem noble family. From his house on Golden Serpent Street, he operates as a fence, dealing largely in spices, scents, wines, and various potions, but occasionally in large and unique thefts. Unbeknownst to almost everyone in Waterdeep, Orlpar has connections to the beholder Xanathar, who has given him a small death tyrant (an undead beholder, missing several of its eyes) to defend his vaults, which have sewer tunnel

connections to areas used by Xanathar's organization. Orlpar probably also has a hired mage and magic items to defend himself with.

ORLPIIR HAMMERSTAR (LG hm F2). A onetime city guardsman, Orlpiir is now proprietor of the Grey Serpent inn in Trades Ward. Orlpiir is a man with dwarven blood in his remote past (hence the family name), but he himself is almost seven feet tall. He is thin and austere, with a cultured voice and a beaky nose. Orlpiir is very rich. He always wears a *ring of spell turning*, which is his only magical treasure.

OSBRIN SELCHOUN (LN hm F3; ST 16, WIS 16). Osbrin is the fat, very short, red-faced proprietor of Selchoun's Sundries Shop in Sea Ward. He always seems out of breath, but has a rolling gait and an energetic, cheerful nature.

PELDAN THRAEL (LN hm F2). Peldan is middle-aged, of middling height, nondescript, and mustachioed. Overall, he is the type who blends well into crowds.

PERENDEL WINTAMER (NG hm W6; DEX 16, INT 18). Perendel is the proprietor of the Smiling Siren theater and nightclub in Castle Ward. He is a slim, young, intense lover of the arts, and the bearer of a dapper thin mustache. Perendel dreams of meeting and marrying a beautiful female bard. He is hopelessly smitten with the Simbul, whom he saw once from afar. She was using spells to blast a band of orcs to so much smoking meat.

PHALANTAR ORIVAN (NE hm T7; DEX 18, INT 16). Phalantar is a rich man who sponsors adventurers and

mercenaries, and guards himself with magical dusts and poisonous gases. He has become partially or wholly immune to many. He is the proprietor of Phalantar's Philtres & Components shop in Castle Ward. Phalantar always smiles gently and moves smoothly and quietly.

PHANDALUE TARINTHIL (NG hf F0; CHA 17). Phandalue is the breathtakingly beautiful counter clerk of the North Ward Aurora's outlet. Despite her sharp tongue and short tolerance for fools, she is constantly pursued by half the young noble males of Waterdeep.

QUENDEVER ILISTRYM (LN hm F0; CHA 16). Quendever Ilistrym owns and operates the Unicorn's Horn inn in Trades Ward. A haughty, effete, very rich man of Amnian descent and noble airs, he likes to gamble and puts on disguises to go tavern crawling in Dock Ward for excitement. He is indolent and unskilled, but exceedingly handsome and well-mannered.

QUIRTAN ONDEVER (CN hm W10; INT 18). Quirtan is the service-mage of the North Ward Aurora's outlet. He is secretly a timid fan of adventurers and high-living nobles, and he always acts mysterious and sinister, as if at the heart of all intrigue in Waterdeep. This manner amuses many, but also gets him invited to a lot of parties. To an adventurer, Quirtan is useful only as a source of information overheard at such feasts.

REETHA (CG hf F9; ST 18/04, CON 16). A barbarian of gentle humor with an impish derision for cultured ways and snobbery, Reetha has a love of wrestling with men as large and as

strong as herself, particularly adventurers.

RELCHOZ HRIIAT (CN hm F1; INT 17, WIS 16, CHA 16). Relchoz is the short, jolly, gluttonous proprietor of Hriiat Fine Pastries in North Ward. He is the public contact for the Bakers' Guild and—though most Waterdhavians would be astonished to learn it—one of the wealthiest investors in the city, who has a share in almost a fifth of all current nonguild-exclusive business concerns.

RUUFDEIDEL "ROOVE" RESSATAR (CE hm T6; DEX 17, WIS 17). Ruufdeidel is a short, imp-like man who is always smiling and is good at hiding, moving silently, and passing unnoticed. Roove is one of the best eavesdroppers in Waterdeep, and can usually be found for hire in Mouse Alley.

SABBAR (CE hm W17?). Elminster has no idea if this infamous wizard is still alive or not. He had learned the means to travel the planes when he disappeared, and his sanity was not then what most folk would call stable, either. He is probably dead, but may yet reappear.

SAERGHON "THE MAGNIFICENT" ALIR (LN hm W10). Saerghon the Magnificent is the service-mage for the Sea Ward outlet of Aurora's. A pompous man of airs and flourishes, Saerghon hasn't mastered half the magic he owns, and depends for his safety on the *rings of spell turning* and *spell storing* that he wears. (The *ring of spell storing* contains: *invisibility*, *fly*, *Evard's black tentacles*, *wizard eye*, and *feeblemind*). Along with these two rings, Saerghon wears many other sparkling begemmed rings, so that every finger is adorned.

SELCHAROON NRIM (LN hm W6, INT 17). Selcharron is the bouncer at the Jade Dancer. An alert, grimly serious man who has gone bald young, but retains a ratty red beard, Secharoon is proud of his large, ornate (and enchanted—just what they do, he keeps secret) golden earrings. When on duty, he wears a *ring of invisibility* and a *ring of jumping*, and wields a *wand of paralyzation*.

SHABRA THE BEGGAR QUEEN (CG hf P7). Shabra was once a priestess of Tymora—until she grew too cautious. She's still a 7th-level priestess because Tymora still remembers her youthful adventuring exploits fondly. Shabra will fight or attempt anything dangerous only in an emergency, and has now 54 winters. The disarrangement that a specially enchanted *invisible mace +4* hanging at her belt causes is concealed by a ragged half-cloak.

SHALANNA DUTHMERE (LN hf F1). Shalanna Duthmere is a pale, worn-looking lady from Daggerford who directs her six daughters in running the inn. She is a widow and is very tight with money. She secretly dreams that a dashing, handsome adventurer will ride in someday, and make her happy for the rest of her days. The beauty of her teen-aged daughters makes it more likely that any dashing heroes will go for them instead.

SHALARA MALARKKIN (CG hf W2; DEX 16, INT 18, CHA 16). Shalar is the 16-year-old current apprentice of Kappiyan Flurmastyr. She is an earnest and emotional lass who keeps house for Kappiyan and wears breeches, boots, tunic, and a *periapt*

Shyrrhr

of protection +1 (equal in effects to a magical *ring of protection*).

Shalath Lythryn (LN hf F1). Shalath is kindly, plain, middle-aged, and very, very observant.

Shalrin Meraedos (LN hm F6 [now]; ST 16, INT 18, WIS 16). Shalrin, Gentleman Keeper of the Solemn Order of Recognized Furriers & Woolmen, is the careful, observant, soft-spoken proprietor of Maerados Fine Furs. The fur half-cloak he always wears conceals twin shoulder-sheathed *swords of dancing* that fly back to him when he calls them. He is known to use other protective magics and is rumored to have recently begun a stellar adventuring career in Undermountain and the Realms Below. He will not speak of such matters.

Sharra of the Invisible Dragon (CG hf W21?). This wizardess dwells somewhere in the North, but is rumored to have an abode in Water-

deep to which she comes only in magical disguise. Her nickname comes from spells she's developed that allow her to duplicate many dragon powers, so that lesser mages have sworn she had an invisible dragon present to aid her. Elminster doesn't know what she's up to these days. She has been known to send warnings and information to local Harpers from time to time.

Shryndalla "Were-Eye" Ghaulduth (CG hf W16).

Shulmeira Gondalim (CG hf F0; DEX 17, INT 17). Shulmeira Gondalim is the proprietress of Gondalim's inn in Trades Ward, and the granddaughter of its founder. She is young, short, slim, and plain, but charming. She runs the inn with quiet expertise.

Shyrrhr (NG hf F0; DEX 16, CHA 16). Shyrrhr is a lady of the court who works for Piergeiron chaperoning—and spying on—diplomats and other important visitors. She was born in Deepingdale, but is now ranked as a noble in Waterdeep. A tall, perceptive woman with green eyes and long, straight bronze-hued hair, Shyrrhr is elegant, kind, soft-spoken, and can drink great amounts without becoming intoxicated. She is also very learned about elven customs.

Simon Thrithyn (NG hm F3, ST 17, CON 16). The stolid innkeeper of the House of Good Spirits, Simon is a member of the Vintners' (et al.) Guild, and a timid, but capable, fighter.

Smiles. See Kaeroven.

Stromquil Halazar (CE hm W6 [now]: Illusionist; DEX 18, INT 18). This tall, aristocratic, and sneering man is a master jeweler, Guildmaster

of the Jewellers' Guild, and the proprietor of Halazar's Fine Gems in Sea Ward. He speaks softly and is always watchful. Stromquil is no doubt involved in smuggling and probably an agent for the Shadow Thieves (the outlawed Thieves' Guild).

TATHLA "FLAMEHAIR" NIGHTSTAR (CG hf F4/T5; DEX 18, INT 18, CHA 16). Flamehair Nightstar is one of the shrewdest investors in Waterdeep today, and a friend to good-aligned adventurers (as a retired adventurer herself).

"MOTHER" TATHLORN (NG hf F0; DEX 17, INT 16, WIS 18, CHA 16). Mother Tathlorn is the proprietress of Mother Tathlorn's House of Pleasure and Healing in Castle Ward. She is old, stout, charming, skilled at massage, and perceptive of her customers' needs. She is a wise old lady who enjoys the company of folk and hearing about them—though she never passes on what she hears.

THOIM ZALAMM (LN spectator). Stranded in Faerun by long-ago magic, this calm individual entertains itself by observing life in Waterdeep, while taking care to avoid surprising adventurers and wizards who might attack it out of hand. The spectator likes to help adventurers, as their activities furnish it with much entertainment.

THUMIR AINGAHUTH (CE hm T4; DEX 17, INT 16). Thumir is the rat-faced proprietor of Nueth's Fine Nets shop in South Ward. (Nueth has been dead for a dozen years.) He is alert and has a sarcastic tongue.

THURVE THENTAVVA (LN hm F0; DEX 18, INT 17). Thurve, the balding,

bespectacled, and always calm proprietor of Thentavva's Boots in Trades Ward, is a contact for the mysterious Red Sashes (detailed on page 35 of FR1 *Waterdeep and the North*). He is armed with a set of *iron bands of Bilarro.*

TIIRLON WINDSTAR (NG half-elf m F5; ST 16, DEX 16, CHA 16). Tiirlon is a dancer, escort, bartender, and part-owner of the Copper Cup. A dignified fellow, Tiirlong is a skilled piper and harpist, and *very* tall for his race—almost seven feet.

TORST URLIVAN (LE hm T4; ST 17, DEX 17, CON 16). A tall, withdrawn, dignified man who dresses richly but smells of the stables, Torst is a lover of horses, who—unbeknownst to Volo—fences stolen horses and harness. He is the proprietor of the Gentle Rest inn in Trades Ward.

UGLUKH VORL (LE half-orc m F6). Treat Uglukh's double axe as a halberd. If hit by it, a character must successfully save vs. poison or fall

"Mother" Tathlorn

231

asleep in 1–4 rounds. This slumber lasts for 2–5 turns despite any physical stimuli applied.

ULSCALEER ANBERSYR (NE hm F9; ST 17, WIS 17). Ulscaleer is a retired sea captain and pirate who is now owner and keeper of the Fiery Flagon in Sea Ward. Fat, old, and weather-beaten, he seems to know every sailor who enters the place. He is the owner of a not-so-secret connection to subterranean Skullport and a busy sponsor of smugglers.

ULTHLO RELAJATYR (LN hm F7; ST 17, DEX 17, WIS 17). Ulthlo is the floor manager and deputy security chief · of the Gentle Mermaid in North Ward, and the second-in-command to Eiraklon Marimmatar. Ulthlo is dedicated to making the Mermaid a safe, relaxed, wonderful place to visit. He is a careful, courteous man who's always thinking several steps ahead in any situation of potential danger. He is quite skilled at anticipating the tactics and attacks of skilled thieves and adventurers who use magic, accomplices, or the like. He directs a staff of bouncers, some of whom look deceptively like charming waitresses or escorts not suited for or used to any sort of fight.

UNGER FARSHAL (NE hm F6; ST 17). Unger is the bald, close-mouthed, sinister proprietor of the Grinning Lion tavern in North Ward. He knows, tolerates, and says nothing of criminal activities in the ward (which keep him in profits). Unger has been known to conceal much-wanted goods and folk for a short time in exchange for exhorbitant fees, and to have smuggling connec-

tions "down below"—in other words, with Skullport.

VINDARA TZUNTZIN (NG half-elf f W8; DEX 17, INT 18, CHA 16). Vindara is the half-owner of the Misty Beard tavern in North Ward. She is slim, lithe, sarcastic, and quick to spurn would-be suitors. She plans to make herself a mage of great might and a power in Waterdeep, or failing that, to build and head a half-elven community, perhaps in nearby Ardeepforest. She owns and wields many wands (see the Misty Beard footnotes for a partial selection). She is firmly loyal to her sister, Allet.

VIVAELIA SUNDER (CN hf T6; DEX 17, CHA 15). Vivaelia is a dancer, escort, bartender, and part-owner of the Copper Cup. She is well known for her coldly planned revenges and investment acumen.

VOLOTHAMP GEDDARM (CG hm W5; INT 18, CON 17). Volothamp, or Volo, as he is more commonly called, is the author of this guide and of *Volo's Guide to All Things Magical*, a suppressed work. He was born in a bog somewhere in Faerun. He is widely traveled, learned in rare or strange spells of low to middling power (those he can cast), and is believed to have devised several minor but interesting spells concerned with the recording and snooping out of information. Volo is also a sage, with primary expertise in the spells and doings of human wizardkind and a secondary expertise (now occupying most of his energy and study) in the geography and lore of the known human realms of Faerun. Volo must conceal his identity from certain wizards

Volothamp Geddarm

whose spells he recently revealed—in the *FORGOTTEN REALMS® Adventures* sourcebook—or part company with his head (*after* he's spent "most of eternity as a dung beetle crushed under a rock at the bottom of a cesspool," to quote the (smiling) mage Snilloc).

VORN LASKADARR (NG hm F0). As the proprietor of the Dragon's Head tavern in Castle Ward, Vorn is a fast, efficient, and considerate host who also happens to be short, ugly, and stubble-faced. Vorn knows most of Waterdeep's officials, visiting diplomats, and their servants and agents by face and name.

WAENDEL UTHRUND (NE hm T3; DEX 16, INT 17). Waendel is the beady-eyed, always watchful proprietor of the Galloping Minotaur Inn in North Ward. A sardonic and grasping individual, he is a noted hard blade (merciless) moneylender who secretly backs smuggling, slaving, kidnapping, and thieving deals up and down the Sword Coast.

WELVREENE THALMIT (CN hf F2, ST 16, DEX 18, CHA 16). Welvreene, proprietress of the Crawling Spider tavern in Castle Ward, is a romantic who loves adventurers. She is petite, with a low, purring, raw voice and alluring dark eyes. Danger is the spice she seeks, and she has been known to seek out the company of known thieves, slavers, maniacs, lycanthropes, and killers.

WHISTLEWINK (CN hm W24?). Elminster does not know this mage's true name or powers, but believes him to be part human and part Arcane, and a veteran traveler of many planes and worlds. He is eccentric, giggling, and old, with a long, white beard. He wields many magic items and sells both major and minor magics. In Faerun, his shop has been known to appear atop the Earthspur mountain on the Dragonisle, in the Sea of Fallen Stars, and near Tashluta, as well as in Waterdeep. The shop is seldom seen, and Elminster believes Whistlewink's more concerned with events on other worlds.

WINESTAB (CE hm T6). Winestab is a thief who has at least two psionic wild talents: the psychometabolic devotions *catfall* and *displacement.*

XANATRAR HILLHORN (NG hm W11; INT 18, CHA 16). Xanatrar is the service-mage of the Castle Ward Aurora's chain outlet. A handsome man with an eye for ladies, he is known for his excellent singing. He is a regular at nobles' feasts.

XANDOS WAEVERYM (LN hm F1; INT 15, WIS 15). Xandos is manager of the Three Pearls Nightclub and is known as "the Dandy" around the city for his

pompous manner. He has a good sense of humor and feel for current public taste.

YAEREENE ILBAERETH (CG elven f W9; DEX 18, INT 18, WIS 16, CHA 16). Yaereene is the proprietress of the Elfstone Tavern in Castle Ward. She is tall, charming and regal, with silvery eyes. She is always armed with a *ring of shooting stars* and a *wand of magic missiles*, and always accompanied by a blue-green (old) faerie dragon named Pyrith (see Volume 3 of the *Monstrous Compendium*), who sits on her shoulder. It will use its spells to protect her and the tavern.

YULULEE LANTANNAR (NG hf T4; DEX 18, CHA 16). Yululee is a dancer, escort, bartender, and part-owner of the Copper Cup. She grew up as a Lantannan orphan child, stealing on the streets of Waterdeep. She stole the deed for the land on which the Cup now stands from the home of a merchant as he was being killed, downstairs, by another band of thieves. She acts simple and wide-eyed, but is not, having the eyes and reactions of a hawk and the memory of a grudge-holding goddess.

YUTH SAMMARDOUN (LN hm T7; DEX 16, INT 16). Yuth is middle-aged and retired from thieving, but with the hair on his head (only) turned prematurely snow white. He is the proprietor of Maerghoun's Inn in Sea Ward. A cynical, cunning man who prides himself on his extreme discretion, Yuth is involved in smuggling and in keeping many, many secrets, including hiding certain valuable items until they are reclaimed.

ZALANTHESS-DAUGHTER-OF-ZALANTHAR (NG hf B4; DEX 14, INT 14, CHA 16). Zalanthess is the house bard of the Three Pearls Nightclub. She is a skilled singer and harpist, and hails from Neverwinter.

ZARONDAR [or ZORONDAR, he uses both] "THE NIMBLE" RIAUTAR (LN hm F6 [now]; ST 16, DEX 18, CHA 16). Zarondar has a weapon specialization in light crossbow. He is proprietor of Riautar's Weaponry shop in Trades Ward, and a scowling, always wary man. He says little, but is nevertheless the public contact for the Fellowship of Bowyers and Fletchers.

ZOBIA SHRINSHA (pronounced *SHRIN-shaww*, CG hf W9; DEX 17, INT 18). Zobia is the quiet, but alert, proprietress of A Maiden's Tears tavern in North Ward. Her shy manner conceals a fearless nature and a curiosity about all her guests. She's been known to magically eavesdrop. She is a friend to the city watch and the Lords. She's always armed with at least two wands, and two rings as well, but what powers these have is not reliably known.

ZYGARTH "SLAYER" SAERN (LG hm F7; DEX 18, INT 18, WIS 16). Zygarth is the proprietor of Saern's Fine Swords shop in Trades Ward. He has acquired the ability to determine with 96% accuracy the age, quality, and condition of steel at a glance. He is 76% likely to realize that a blade carries a magical dweomer merely by looking at it. He is tall, gaunt, smiling, and unassuming. Few know he is a warrior, as his nickname was bestowed by a noble in jest.

Appendix II:
Index of Places

The abbreviations in parentheses following each entry represent the ward the location is found in.

Abbreviation	Ward
(CW)	Castle Ward
(SeaW)	Sea Ward
(NW)	North Ward
(TW)	Trades Ward
(SW)	South Ward
(DW)	Dock Ward

Alleys

Appendix III:
Color Map Key

Castle Ward

Mount Waterdeep: Harbor defense for Waterdeep, topped by lookout tower.

Castle Waterdeep: Four hundred feet high at the highest point, walls 60 feet thick, fully prepared to defend and sustain the population of the city.

Ahghairon's Tower: Landmark, magically protected, unenterable ever since its owner's death.

1. Mirt's Mansion (Home of Mirt "the Moneylender")
2. Crommor's Warehouse
3. The Sailors' Own (tavern)
4. The Yawning Portal (inn)
5. The Red-Eyed Owl (tavern)
6. The Sleepy Sylph (tavern)
7. Barracks of the Guard
8. Smithy of the Guard
9. Bell Tower
10. House of Naneatha Lhaurilstar, Lady of Waterdeep
11. The House of Gems (HQ: The Jeweller's Guild)
12. Mother Tathlorn's House of Pleasure (festhall and spa)
13. House of Loene the fighter
14. House of Shyrrhr, Lady of the Court
15. The Map House (HQ: The Surveyors', Map & Chart-Makers' Guild)
16. Fellowship Hall (HQ: The Fellowship of Innkeepers)
17. Palace Warehouse
18. Palace Stables
19. Palace Paddocks
20. The Dragon's Head Tavern
21. The Golden Key (locksmith)
22. The Master Bakers' Hall (HQ: The Bakers' Guild)
23. The Crawling Spider (tavern)
24. The Elfstone Tavern
25. House of Velstrode the Venturer
26. Halambar Lutes & Harps
27. Hilmer Warehouse
28. The Halls of Hilmer, Master Armorer
29. Balthorr's Rare and Wondrous Treasures
30. Tower of the Order (HQ: The Watchful Order of Magists & Protectors)
31. The Smiling Siren (nightclub)
32. Blackstaff Tower (home of Kelben "Blackstaff" Arunson)
33. Phalantar's Philtres & Components
34. Guildhall of the Order (HQ: The Solemn Order of Recognized Furriers & Woolmen)
35. The Jade Jug (inn)
36. The Blue Jack (tavern)
37. Pewterers' and Casters' Guildhall (guild HQ)
38. Olmhazan's Jewels
39. House of the Fine Carvers (HQ: The Guild of Fine Carvers)
40. The Pampered Traveler (inn)
41. The Singing Sword (tavern)
42. The Market Hall (HQ: The Council of Farmer-Grocers)
43. The Spires of the Morning (temple complex of Lathander)
44. Usual location of the Walking Statue of Waterdeep
45. Fair Winds (rental villa)
46. Marblehearth (rental villa)
47. Stormwatch (rental villa)
48. Heroes' Rest (rental villa)

Sea Ward

49. The House of Heroes (temple complex of Tempus)
50. Halazar's Fine Gems Shop
51. The Ship's Wheel (tavern)
52. Pilgrim's Rest (inn)
53. The Wandering Wemic (inn)
54. The House of Purple Silks (festhall)
55. Gounar's Tavern
56. The House of the Moon (temple complex of Selune)
57. Tchazzam family villa
58. Maerghoun's Inn
59. Dacer's Inn
60. The House of Inspired Hands (temple complex of Gond)
61. The Fiery Flagon (tavern)
62. Ruldegost family villa
63. The Dragon Tower of Maaril
64. Ilzimmer family villa
65. Urmbrusk family villa
66. Moonstar family villa
67. Assumbar family villa
68. Cassalanter family villa
69. Zulpair family villa
70. Husteem family villa
71. The Tower of Luck (temple complex of Tymora)
72. Wavesilver family villa
73. "Naingate" (tower of Nain the wizard)
74. Melshimber family villa
75. Iltul family villa
76. Shrine of Mielikki (The Lady's Hands)
77. Shrine of Silvanus
78. Emvoelstone family villa
79. Hiilgauntlet family villa
80. The Temple of Beauty (temple complex of Sune)
81. Gauntyl family villa
82. Eltorchul family villa
83. The House of Wonder (temple of Midnight—formerly Mystra)

84. Eirontalar family villa
85. Selchoun's Sundries Shop
86. Thongolir family villa
87. Eagleshield family villa
88. Dezlentyr family villa
89. Tesper family villa
90. Nesher family villa
91. Brokengulf family villa
92. Belabranta family villa
93. Irlingstar family villa
94. Gundwynd family villa
95. Tessalar's Tower
96. Raventree family villa
97. Bladesemmer family villa
98. Manthar family villa
99. Artemel family villa
100. Ammakyl family villa
101. Silmerhelve family villa
102. Rosznar family villa
103. Jhansczil family villa

North Ward

104. The House of Crystal (HQ: The Guild of Glassblowers, Glaziers, & Speculum-Makers)
105. House of Crystal Warehouse
106. Adarbrent family villa
107. Agundar family villa
108. Kothont family villa
109. Sultlue family villa
110. The Galloping Minotaur (inn)
111. Sulmest's Splendid Shoes & Boots
112. Meraedos Fine Furs (shop)
113. Phylund family villa
114. The Gentle Mermaid (tavern and festhall)
115. Maernos family villa
116. Cragsmere family villa
117. The House of Healing (HQ: The Guild of Apothecaries & Physicians)
118. Amcathra family villa
119. Lanngolyn family villa
120. Mascalan family villa
121. Talmost family villa
122. Piiradost family villa
123. Crommor family villa
124. Brossfeather family villa
125. Wands family villa
126. Hunabar family villa
127. Durindbold family villa
128. Hothemer family villa
129. Margaster family villa

130. Thorp family villa
131. Estelmer family villa
132. Maerklos family villa
133. Ulbrinter family villa
134. Hriiat Fine Pastries
135. The Grinning Lion (tavern)
136. Gost family villa
137. Lathkule family villa
138. Nandar family villa
139. Thann family villa
140. Thunderstaff family villa
141. Anteos family villa
142. Phull family villa
143. Snome family villa
144. Helmfast family villa
145. Roaringhorn family villa
146. Kormallis family villa
147. Majarra family villa
148. Tarm family villa
149. Stormweather family villa
150. Jardeth family villa
151. Hawkwinter family villa
152. Gralhund family villa
153. The Raging Lion (inn)
154. A Maiden's Tears (tavern)
155. The Misty Beard (tavern)
156. The Cliffwatch (inn)
157. Cliffwatch inn stables
158. Zun family villa
159. Ilvastarr family villa
160. House of Orlpar Husteem, noble

The City of the Dead

Unkeyed tombs are of individual noble or wealthy families. In several cases nobles families share a tomb, which usually leads to separate crypts beneath, and several floors above.

161. Mariner's Rest (those drowned at sea and ship captains)
162. The Hall of Heroes (warriors' tomb)
163. The Hall of Sages (sages)
164. Monument to the warriors of Waterdeep
165. Merchants' Rest ("The Coinscoffin" tomb, resting place of only those who prepay for the honor)

166. Ahghairon's Statue
167. The House of the Homeless (all who do not merit or cannot buy another tomb)

Trades Ward

Virgin's Square: Traditional hiring place for mercenaries and legendary sacrificial spot.

168. The Inn of the Dripping Dagger
169. The Riven Shield Shop
170. House of Myrmith Splendon (fighter)
171. Mhair's Tower
172. Dunblast Roofing Company
173. Gondalim's (inn)
174. The Citadel of the Arrow (HQ: The Fellowship of Bowyers & Fletchers)
175. Saern's Fine Swords
176. Costumers' Hall (HQ: The Order of Master Taylor, Glovers, & Mercers)
177. Thentevva's Boots
178. The Unicorn's Horn (inn)
179. Orsabba's Fine Imports
180. Riautar's Weaponry
181. The House of Song (HQ: The Council of Musicians, Instrument-Makers, and Choristers)
182. Patient Fingers Finework
183. Office of the League of Basketmakers & Wickerworkers (guild HQ)
184. Warehouse of the League of Basketmakers & Wickerworkers
185. The House of Cleanliness (HQ: The Launderers' Guild)
186. The Old Guildhall (HQ: The Cellarers and Plumbers Guild)
187. Thond Glass and Glazing
188. Belmonder's Meats
189. The Zoarstar
190. The House of Textiles (HQ: The Most Excellent Order of Weavers and Dyers)
191. The Gentle Rest (inn)

192. Gentle Rest Inn stables
193. Felzoun's Folly (tavern)
194. Surtlan's Metalwares
195. The Guild Paddock (HQ: The Stablemasters' and Farriers' Guild)
196. The Golden Horn Gambling House
197. Meiroth's Fine Silks
198. The Bowels of the Earth (tavern)
199. Cobblers' and Corvisers' House (guild HQ)
200. The House of Light (HQ: The Guild of Chandlers & Lamplighters)
201. Chandlers & Lamplighters' Guild warehouse
202. Stationers' Hall (HQ: The Stationers' Guild)
203. The Plinth (interdenominational temple)
204. The Grey Serpent (inn)
205. Wheel Hall (HQ: The Wheelwrights' Guild)

Southern Ward

206. The Stone House (HQ: The Carpenters', Roofers', and Plaisterer's Guild)
207. Brian the Swordmaster
208. The Jade Dancer (tavern and festhall)
209. Nueth's Fine Nets
210. The Spouting Fish (tavern)
211. The Red Gauntlet (tavern)
212. Pelauvir's Counter (goods store)
213. The Swords' Rest (tavern)
214. The House of Good Spirits (HQ: The Vintners', Distillers', and Brewers Guild and a working tavern and inn)
215. The Redbridle Stables
216. The Coach & Wagon Hall (HQ: The Wagonmakers' and Coach Builders' Guild)
217. Saddlers' & Harness-Makers' Hall (guild HQ)
218. House of Kappiyan Flurmaster (wizard)
219. Builders' Hall (HQ: The Guild of Stonecutters and Masons)
220. Nelkaush the Weaver
221. The Full Cup (tavern)

222. The Road House (HQ: The Fellowship of Carters and Coachmen)
223. Prestar's Furniture
224. Hlakken Stables
225. Metalmasters' Hall (HQ: The Most Careful Order of Skilled Smiths & Metalforgers)
226. Bellister's Hand (shop)
227. Bellister's House (warehouse)
228. Orm's Highbench (trading company)
229. Athlal's Stables

Dock Ward

Waterdeep Harbor: Patrolled by hired mermen against invaders, predators, and hazards to shipping.
230. Cookhouse Hall
231. Gelfuril the Trader
232. The Copper Cup (tavern, inn, festhall)
233. Thomm Warehouse
234. Melgard's Fine Leathers
235. The Butchers' Guildhall (HQ: The Guild of Butchers)
236. House of Jemuril (adventurer)
237. Fish Warehouse (belongs to the Fishmongers' Fellowship)
238. Smokehouse (belongs to the Fishmongers' Fellowship; also used by butchers for a fee)
239. Telethar Leatherworks
240. Torpus the Tanner
241. League Hall (HQ: The League of Skinners & Tanners)
242. Mariners' Hall (HQ: The Master Mariners' Guild)
243. Shipmasters' Hall
244. Watermen's Hall (HQ: The Guild of Watermen)
245. The Sleeping Snake (tavern)
246. Nestaur the Ropemaker
247. Khostal Hannass, Fine Nuts
248. Felhaur's Fine Fish
249. The Blushing Mermaid (inn, tavern, festhall)
250. Seaswealth Hall (HQ: The Fishmongers' Fellowship)
251. Full Sails (tavern; HQ:

The Most Diligent League of Sail-Makers and Cordwainers)
252. Arnagus the Shipwright
253. The House of Tarmagus (warehouse)
254. The Fellowship of Salters, Packers, and Joiners warehouse
255. Coopers' Rest (HQ: The Coopers Guild)
256. Shippers' Hall (HQ: The Fellowship of Salters, Packers, and Joiners)
257. The Blue Mermaid (tavern)
258. The Hanged Man (tavern)
259. The House of Pride (perfume shop)
260. The Purple Palace (festhall)
261. The Sleeping Wench (tavern)
262. The Hanging Lantern (escort service)
263. Muleskull Tavern (HQ: The Dungsweepers' Guild)
264. The Mermaid's Arms (inn, tavern, festhall)
265. Red Sails Warehouse
266. Shipwrights' House (HQ: The Order of Master Shipwrights)
267. Helmstar Warehouse
268. The Ship's Prow (inn)
269. The Thirsty Sailor (tavern)
270. Warm Beds (inn)
271. Lanternmaker Zorth Ulmaril
272. The Bloody Fist (tavern ["dive"])
273. Three Pearls Nightclub
274. The Thirsty Throat (tavern)
275. Serpentil Books & Folios
276. The Blackstar Inn
277. The Splintered Stair (inn)
278. The Rearing Hippocampus (inn)
279. The Metal House of Wonders (HQ: The Splendid Order of Armorers, Locksmiths, and Finesmiths)
280. Turnstone Plumbing and Pipefitting
281. Dhaermos Warehouse